Geographical Scale and Economic Development

Michael S. Yoder

Geographical Scale and Economic Development

Lessons Learned from Texas and Mexico

Springer

Michael S. Yoder
Department of Geography and the Environment
University of Texas
Austin, TX, USA

ISBN 978-3-031-36196-8 ISBN 978-3-031-36197-5 (eBook)
https://doi.org/10.1007/978-3-031-36197-5

This Springer imprint is published by the registered company Springer Nature Switzerland AG
The registered company address is: Gewerbestrasse 11, 6330 Cham, Switzerland

To the victims at Robb Elementary School in Uvalde, 24 May 2022; to their families and friends; and to the community.

Acknowledgments

First and foremost, I have to thank my wife, Joaquina. To write a book is not easy, and she has been so thoughtful and encouraging along the way. Had it not been for Joaquina's persistent encouragement, I may not have succeeded in completing this project. She has more faith in my ability to contribute a work to the body of literature on the geography of economic development than I have in myself.

I am grateful to Jean-Paul Rodrigue for offering suggestions on the format of the book, and John Tiefenbacher for recommending that I emphasize geographical scale in the organization of the case studies. I am grateful to Murray Rice for his suggestions about themes to include, and publishers to approach. Likewise, Mike Pisani offered invaluable recommendations for themes to include in the manuscript that I otherwise would not have thought of. Many thanks to my uncle, Frank Archibald, for his thoughtful comments on the original manuscript proposal.

I thank Daniel Covarrubias for his help in setting up two of the key interviews for the book that otherwise would not have been possible.

I am thankful for the comments on the first draft by the anonymous reviewers.

I am grateful to Stephen O'Connell and Noah Walker, two creative geographers of the Department of Geography at the University of Central Arkansas, for producing the maps.

I owe a huge debt of gratitude to several people who allowed me to bounce ideas off them, and who offered invaluable suggestions, including Christopher Di Piazza, Bill Doolittle, Richard Wright, Brooks Pearson, Matthew Connelly, Doug Voss, Shelby Fiegel, and Charles John-Arnold.

Finally, I thank my mentors in graduate school who provided me the foundations to become a geographer: Kent Mathewson, John Winberry, Chuck Kovacik, William Davidson, and Gregory Veeck.

Contents

About the Author

Michael S. Yoder (Ph.D.) is an academic geographer with 28 years of teaching experience in the discipline and 34 years of research experience in the geography of economic development, agricultural geography, urban geography, transportation, and community assessments. Michael holds doctoral and master's degrees in agricultural geography from Louisiana State University and the University of South Carolina, respectively, and a bachelor's degree in marketing from the University of Houston. His published academic articles and book chapters are primarily case studies involving field and archival research on suburbanization in the USA and Mexico, social housing and industrial development in Mexico, transportation corridors and interior ports in the USA and Mexico, and policy related to economic development. Michael's regional specializations include the American South, northern Mexico, South Texas, the US-Mexico border, and Central America. His teaching focuses on urban planning, political geography, the geography of Latin America, economic development, and world regional geography. He has served on several municipal and county advisory boards in Texas and Arkansas related to transportation infrastructure and urban planning.

Chapter 1
Background to Case Studies in Geographical Scale and Economic Development

Abstract This introduction chapter makes the case that studies of economic development benefit from a greater incorporation of the main themes of geography, including location, scale, region, connectivity, and distance. Case studies are valuable for discovering and understanding the differences in outcomes that economic development initiatives bring about from place to place. After a brief definition of economic development, the chapter explains two main themes of geography (scale and region) in some detail, and the functional economic region as the most appropriate type that applies to economic development. It highlights the nature of studying development at different scales, from the local to the global, and it states that the primary outcome of the book is to apply geographic themes to the study of economic development. The chapter concludes with three examples of global-scale economic development: China's Belt and Road Initiative, UNESCO's World Heritage Sites, and the World Trade Organization (WTO).

Keywords Economic development · Case study method · Geographical scale · Functional economic region · Belt and Road Initiative · UNESCO World Heritage Sites

The discipline of geography is often thought of primarily as the study of locations of cities, rivers, seas, mountain ranges, and the like. Thankfully, it is much more than that. Geographers carry out in-depth studies of spatial relationships of human activities, human–environment interactions, and natural landscape processes. The word "geography" literally translates to "earth description," and as such, many geographers study places to describe their unique and interconnected attributes, or the things that make each place distinct in terms of natural setting, economic activities, accessibility, political boundaries, and so on. Given this broad range of topics, academic geography conferences typically include an impressive array of diverse and even eclectic topics. In recent years, I have become increasingly appreciative of the spatial relationships within and between places that our discipline covers, and how they apply to other disciplines, such as economic development. To illustrate, in 2009, I attended a regional geography conference in North Little Rock, Arkansas,

M. S. Yoder, *Geographical Scale and Economic Development*,
https://doi.org/10.1007/978-3-031-36197-5_1

where an economic geographer from the University of North Texas, Don Lyons, presented a paper on spatial movements of scrap materials. What I thought would be a somewhat humdrum topic turned out to be fascinating. Don, with whom I had interacted for years at such conferences, laid out the latest trends at the time in the movements of scrap materials and the forces impacting that industry. In his Irish accent, he explained cross-Pacific movement of scrap metal, the market forces affecting it, and the implications for development of a closed, sustainable economy. A paper whose main focus was scrap metal was, in a word, amazing.

The use of scrap metal as a case study enables one to view economic activities at different scales: global, national, regional, and local. Economic geographers and economic developers regard the use of recycled materials, such as scrap metal, as the basis for a closed-loop economy, in which the need for newly mined materials is minimized, environmental sustainability is enhanced, and efficiencies are realized as a result. As Lyons et al. (2009, p. 287) state, "(w)hile the strategy of closed-loop industrial ecosystems via material recycling is intuitively attractive, at a more practical level it raises the question of the geographic scale(s) at which closed material cycling could occur." While policymakers, economic developers, and businesses might expect and advocate for material cycling at the local and regional scales, there is nothing inherent in it to keep the scale from being larger, even global. Transportation considerations are taken into account when decisions are made about the scale of the markets of materials like ferrous scrap metal, an increasingly important raw material for steel manufacturing. The relatively low cost of shipping scrap metal to China and other East Asian localities by container becomes a basis for avoiding the shipment of empty containers westbound across the Pacific. Thus, local-scale closed-loop industry is not always necessary, and the activities can be transcontinental or transoceanic (Lyons et al. 2009). In short, scrap is a window into the interconnectedness that underlies economic development.

Like those of many other industries that rely on transoceanic shipping, prices paid for scrap metal are sensitive to changes in supplies of containers, and to bottlenecks at maritime ports such as Los Angeles, Long Beach, and Shanghai, and intermodal facilities such as those in Chicago, Kansas City, and Dallas. The pricing for oceanic shipment by containers rose an average of 80% between November 2020 and January 2021, in part because of the shortage of containers, and in part because of scarce space on container ships (Taylor 2021a). The COVID-19 pandemic, and related boom in e-commerce, contributed strongly to shipping bottlenecks at the Los Angeles and Long Beach ports where containers awaited processing and were unavailable for use elsewhere (GSA Business Report 2021). This impacts profoundly not only scrap metal, but agricultural and other exports bound for East Asia (World Cargo News 2021).

Scrap metal serves as a suitable example of a category of commodities with relevance to economic development at multiple scales: global, regional, and local. The circular economy is global and links the different realms of the world: East Asia, South Asia, the Middle East, Europe, sub-Saharan Africa, Latin America, and Anglo America. Sub-national regions such as the American South rely on recycled steel for electric arc furnace (EAF) production of steel. Manufacturers in different regions of the world utilize the steel made from ferrous scrap for production of a nearly infinite number of steel products. From the steel mills to the manufacturing plants that utilize that steel, to retail stores that sell the products made from it, economic development arises at every stage. The Nucor Steel plant in Blytheville, Arkansas exemplifies local economic development through employment and production. China's changing scrap import policies impact scrap producers globally. The altered labor situation under COVID-19 meant alterations to the demand for ferrous scrap, to global steel markets, and so on. A change in one part of supply chains has ripple effects in other parts at multiple scales.

This book is not about scrap metal per se, but scrap metal serves as an excellent starting point for the use of case studies to examine the geography of economic development at multiple scales. Scrap metal does enter into the case studies outlined in the book: Gonzales, Texas, where recycling of surplus rail equipment occurs; shipment of scrap through the transload facilities of West Texas; US–Mexico trade in steel, in which US production is done mostly by EAF; the Port of Brownsville, where ships are recycled; the small East Texas city of Jewett whose largest employer is an EAF steel mill.

Using the example of ferrous scrap metal used in the production of steel, its market makes for a suitable, brief introductory case study to illustrate a fundamental point this book attempts to make: Connectivity is a key theme in economic geography and is fundamental to economic development. Steel manufactured in plants with EAFs utilizes scrap metal, and this type accounts for 70% of steel made in the United States, one of the highest rates in the world, though such steel is increasingly adding to the mix of steel production in Turkey, India, and East Asia, albeit to a smaller degree than in the US. Scrap markets, then, somewhat mirror overall steel markets. Both steel and scrap sales and shipments dipped during the early months of the Covid pandemic, owing to softened demand in manufacturing, and workplace lockdowns. However, both steel and scrap markets are again on the rise since early 2021 due to robust US pandemic-related stimulus, and future demand beyond 2022 is expected as the pandemic-related economic downturn diminishes (Taylor 2021b). These changes in demand and sales of scrap impact upon domestic and maritime (export) shipments of the material, and availability at any given time of shipping containers influences movements of scrap (Taylor 2021c). As Don Lyons illustrated more than a decade ago, scrap metal is indeed a good case study of economic transactions, connectivity, and shipments occurring at multiple scales, like so many other facets of economic development.

1.1 The Appeal and Logic of Case Studies

I was drawn to the case study method while finishing my bachelor's degree in marketing at the University of Houston in 1981. By happenstance, I took a section of the required capstone management course required of business students in their last semester that was taught by Professor Bernard Gross, a visiting professor from the

Harvard Business School. His approach to the course was to focus solely on the Harvard Case Method, which required that students read and reflect on case studies of businesses that had specific problems to tackle. Those that stood out to me, and that I remember, included a pen manufacturing company that had to make a decision about its mechanical pencil division, and another company that had a problem of personnel turnover. A third had a cash flow problem, and as a result, contemplated whether or not to borrow money or sell off part of its operation. In the class discussions, my fellow students and I had to draw on principles that we learned in our other business courses, and to consider them in the context of the details of the particular case-study companies. This process reminded me of fictionalized law school classes I had seen in television shows, especially "The Paper Chase," a program that was popular at that time, and whose star, John Houseman, who played the law professor and who was a spitting image of Bernard Gross. We carried out debate, and in them we incorporated the appropriate principles from our other business classes in finance, marketing, and management, much the way law students draw on impactful court cases in their class discussions and assignments.

As Zaniel (2007) argues, the case study research method is advantageous when quantitative-based research alone is incapable of producing the desired level of detail. Descriptive detail is often desired in a wide range of behavioral and social science research, including education, psychology, sociology, business management, and community development. A case study allows the researcher to examine a community, an entire industry, or an infrastructure project through qualitative inquiry, by considering a phenomenon in its "real world" context, while weighing quantitative patterns or trends. Although generalizations are impossible to make from one or a small number of case studies, researchers can in fact elaborate upon generalizations, to better understand them through the details derived from case studies (Zainal 2007), a key point this book attempts to make. Multiple case studies of a particular theme strengthen the ability to produce at least generalizations or recognizable patterns, even if the study is not intended to illuminate universal trends or policies. The case study almost always emphasizes how the topic under investigation is unique, because the descriptive approach allows for a portrayal of the context within which a phenomenon exists much better than quantitative studies, which require larger sample sizes (Mohd Poor 2008; Starman 2013).

Each case study of this book examines a challenge or a challenging situation: small cities that face hurdles of enhancing their competitiveness to attract employment; a small maritime port of a small metro area seeking growth despite its distance from the coast; a cargo corridor competing with others that are more established for funding and for the hearts and minds of policymakers; the relative remoteness of West Texas rail transload facilities; intermodal centers (dry ports) in a developing country; and steel production, a dramatic industry in the United States and in Mexico, its developing-world counterpart. (Figs. 1.1 and 1.2) The book does not tackle the well-known, well-documented examples of economic development such as Hollywood, Silicon Valley, Chicago's transport hub, Florida's tourism and status as a retirement haven; Houston's energy sector; London's and New York's financial districts; the Pacific Northwest's high-tech and aircraft hub; or Querétaro's

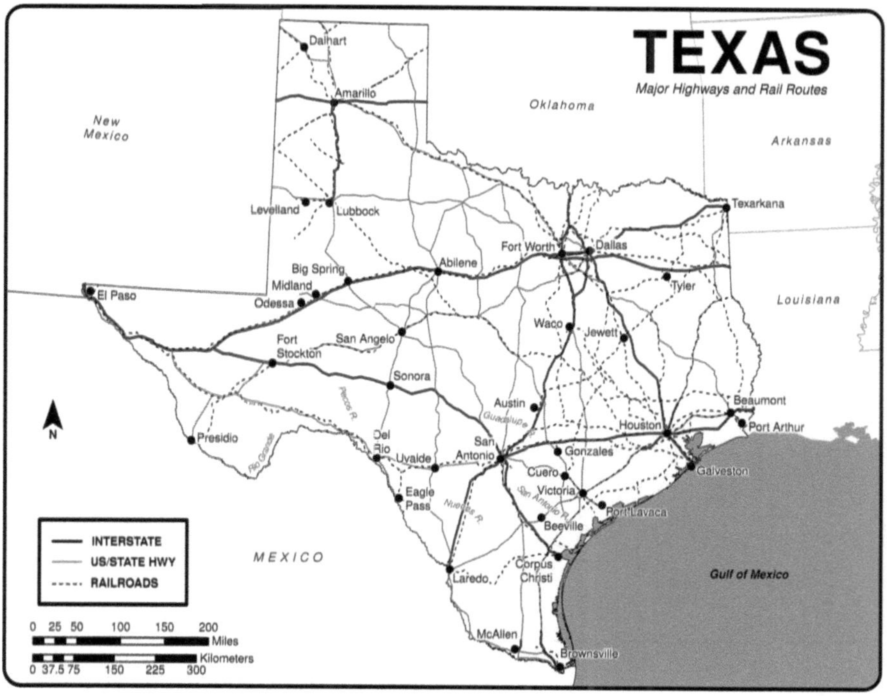

Fig. 1.1 Map of selected cities and transportation routes of Texas. (By Stephen O'Connell)

emerging aerospace complex. The latter have been written about sufficiently elsewhere, while the case studies of this book have not. The case studies in this book illustrate how the different scales work together: the Ports-to-Plains Corridor and the different localities along it; the US and Mexican steel industries and local economic development; Covid as a global pandemic with local impacts on retail shopping and dining in central business districts of small cities of South Texas.

1.2 Economic Development: A Brief Definition

The field of economic development involves the study of the outcomes of initiatives to attract, retain, or build sources of income for a given place, whether an individual community, a region, or a country. Additionally, it focuses on the processes by which actors of the public and private sectors carry out such economic pursuits. It takes the assets created by community development, such as development of work forces and more broadly, building on the natural, human, and locational assets of a place, to further the standard of living in the present and future. The study of economic development, therefore, involves consideration of policies originating and operating at multiple scales: federal, state, and local. The field also requires an

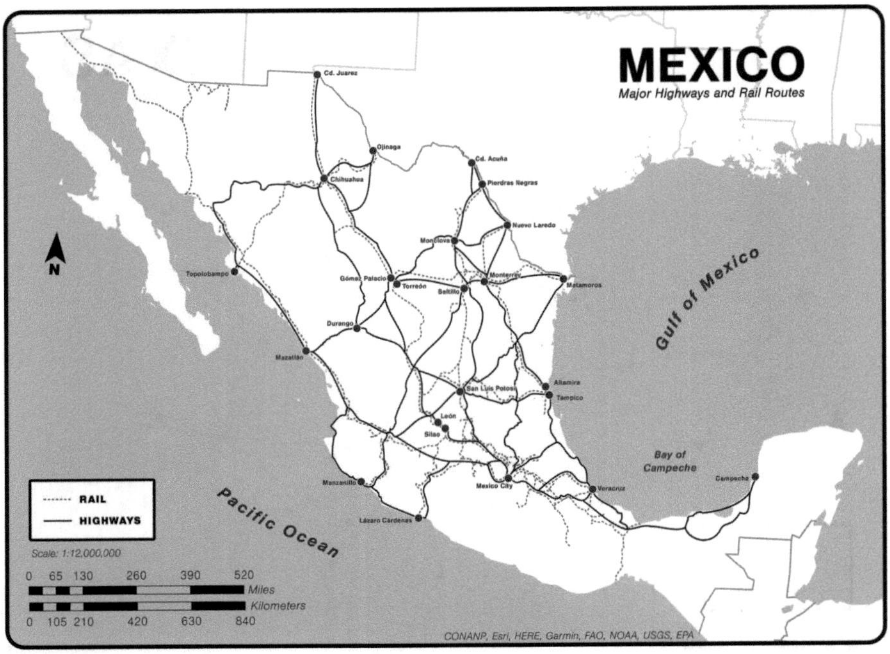

Fig. 1.2 Map of selected cities and transportation routes of Mexico. (By Noah Walker)

awareness of both the positive outcomes and processes involved in economic invigoration, but also the negative effects, such as those that might challenge the natural environment or create inequities (Phillips and Pittman 2015). In short, the processes and outcomes embodied in economic development vary from place to place, as does its spatial impacts, thereby making it a closely related field to human geography.

1.3 Tools for the Geography of Economic Development: Maps, Scale, Regions

The geography of economic development differs from standard economic geography in some subtle yet important ways. Geographical scale is important to both, as are such geographic themes as location, regions, and human–environment interaction; yet the former focuses its concerns more squarely on the processes underlying economic growth, including expanded transportation networks, information flows, employment, and incomes. As Fik (2000, p. 22) notes, "(d)evelopment implies making progress toward desirable goals and outcomes, the most important of which is improving the human condition. Economic development constitutes positive changes and progress in the human condition through economic means. It is a process that brings about 'positive' economic changes to a region." There are various ways that such processes unfold across space, such as investment patterns and the enhancement of connectivity and linkages.

Maps express different physical features of landscapes, spatial patterns related to human and natural phenomena, and connectivity. Depending upon the illustrated theme, each map will vary in terms of scale, or the extent of its coverage of a portion of the earth's surface. The scale of a map will determine how much detail can be covered. Scale applies not only to maps but also to the amount of area included in analyses of regions and localities discussed in this book. The region is for many geographers the starting point for the study of the surface of the earth. Regions involve space and territory, thus prompting many geographers to define the discipline's primary domain as the spatial science. There are different types of regions in the geographer's toolkit. These include the world's realms, or large cultural regions with historical interactions such as Latin America, Southeast Asia, or Europe. Each of these can be further subdivided (Western and Eastern Europe, for example) to provide more detail and nuance. The one thing that most definitions of regions have in common is that regional boundaries tend to be fluid, or at least include overlap. One exception is the political region, effectively a type of functional region whose boundaries are defined by laws or treaties: countries, states, counties, municipal boundaries, and so on, though these can be contested.

Some types of regions are defined in terms of the "functional interactions" that occur within and between them, and regions comprising cultural interactions, such as realms, are most basic to the discipline of human geography (Nijman et al. 2020, p. 11). Realms are large areas with "...a particular combination of environmental, cultural, and organizational properties." (Nijman et al. 2020, p. 7). Analyses of themes like economic development, demographics, culture, and climate can range from global in scale to smaller areas. Discussions of the scale at which geographers consider the surface of the earth more often than not lead them to refer to one or more regions, which themselves exist at different scales; that is, some fine-scaled regions are subsets of larger regions.

The "regions within realms" that geographers work with, such as a portion of North America, an area within Texas, or a unique section of the Mexican State of Guanajuato, are not scientific but nonetheless contain homogeneity throughout to some extent. The boundaries of regions within realms are often inexact, in which case they are delineated by transition zones (Nijman et al. 2020). Traditionally, geographers viewed each of these regions as an assemblage of different cultural and physical (natural) characteristics that define it, and, therefore, are distinct from others, in line with the twentieth-century notion of geography as the study of aerial differentiation (Kisala and Sifta 2017).

1.3.1 Functional Economic Regions and Economic Development

Functional regions are territories defined by a node, or focal point, where there is commercial interdependence throughout, and/or areas that are covered by particular administrative functions. Commuting regions, often referred to as laborsheds, represent an example of functional regions that impact companies (or communities) and their workforces. The node of a functional urban region is the "concentration of jobs, services, and other functions," surrounded by more scattered settlements that depend on those services and employment. Transportation corridors, including roads, highways, and public transit lines, are the backbones of functional regions (Medeiros 2017). Functional regions usually have well-defined boundaries, but rarely does a given urban functional area's system work in isolation from others. Rather, there is interconnection between urban functional regions. That interconnection can be global in scale, but they also can cover smaller territories (Nijman et al. 2020, p. 12).

One type of functional region, the functional economic region, is appropriate as a unit of analysis of the geographical scale(s) at which economic development occurs. Such regions are adjacent but not overlapping, and are defined in terms of "a number of economically interdependent nodes (centres) of varying sizes and with varying geographical extensions" (Karlsson and Olsson 2015, p. 2). The authors liken functional economic regions to Walter Christaller's Central Place arrangement, whereby each functional economic region consists of at least one principal node with a surrounding hinterland consisting of less prominent nodes in a hierarchy. The lesser nodes depend on the more prominent nodes, which leads to strong intraregional connectedness.

Furthermore, the extent to which each functional economic region (FER) specializes in particular tasks, such as raw material extraction or manufacturing, will drive inter-regional connectedness between adjoining FERs. That interconnectedness consists of flows of goods, labor, capital, services, and information. The availability and costs of transportation, therefore, are crucial, rendering transportation corridors and other transportation infrastructure essential to local and regional economic development. Such transportation has to be effective within the FER (node and hinterland) and between adjoining ones. Furthermore, density of activity and land use within a given FER impacts upon the success of transportation infrastructure. For goods subjected to the sensitivities of distance, the markets for goods and services within the FER are as important as between FERs, as is the quality and availability of transportation (Karlsson and Olsson 2015). To illustrate, the Permian Basin of West Texas and eastern New Mexico is a functional economic region with a common activity throughout (oil and natural gas extraction and production), linked throughout with highways and rail lines.

The advancement of transportation technology that makes personal mobility and the hauling of freight more rapid and longer in distance has changed the perception of the scale of functional economic regions. So too have changes in international law and trade agreements that make cross-border economic interaction more common, such that the cross-border regional scale is more difficult to define with precision. That is, the functioning of global-scale interactions in fact occurs at multiple scales: mega, meso, macro, regional, and micro, or the level of a locality straddling an international border (Jessop 2003). This cross-border phenomenon of regional rescaling is illustrated in Chaps. 3 and 4 on Mexican interior dry ports and the Ports-to-Plains Corridor, respectively, both of which have proliferated primarily because of NAFTA (The North American Free Trade Agreement of 1994) and the USA, Mexico, Canada Agreement, or USMCA (known as T-MEC in Mexico), that replaced NAFTA in 2020. In short, while South Texas and West Texas are subnational regions, as are the functional economic regions comprising the core cities of Guanajuato, Monterrey, and San Luís Potosí and their respective hinterlands, the functional economic regions interconnected by Ports-to-Plains are phenomena of three countries, and in some cases straddle borders.

1.3.2 Scale and the Case Studies

Except for global-scale economic development initiatives discussed in this chapter, the book includes cases of functional economic regions within North America, specifically in Texas and Mexico. The regions corresponding to the case studies of the geography of economic development included in this volume are as follows:

Global:

(a) China's Belt and Road Initiative (BRI).
(b) UNESCO World Heritage Sites.
(c) World Trade Organization (WTO).

Regional Type I: Functional Economic Regions of North America (NAFTA/USMCA):

(a) USA–Mexico trade in steel.
(b) Hinterlands and forelands of three Mexican interior dry ports.
(c) Ports-to-Plains Corridor (adjoining functional economic regions of Northern Mexico, Southwest Texas, West Texas, and the Great Plains).

Regional Type II: Subnational Functional Economic Regions:

(a) Four West Texas rail-served industrial and transload facilities: Lubbock, Levelland, Big Spring, San Angelo.
(b) Transportation Development in the Coastal Bend of Texas and the Victoria Metropolitan Area.

Localities:

Four small cities of South Texas: Beeville, Gonzales, Sonora, Uvalde.

With the exception of three brief examples of global-scale economic development in this introductory chapter, the book, through case studies in Texas and Mexico, focuses on regional and local economic development. In-depth studies of economic development initiatives and policies at the global scale would require an entire book to do the topic justice.

1.4 General Outcomes of the Book

While the regional- and local-scale case studies of economic development examined in this book emphasize Mexico and Texas, there are, nonetheless, differences in each that warrant inspection of their particular strengths, successes, and deficits. That said, there are some commonalities in the ways that planning and promotion for economic development are carried out, and in the ways that each case study exemplifies the most fundamental of geographic concepts, especially scale and connectivity. That is, the cases highlight ways that geographic thinking, concepts, and methods can be helpful to interested parties in other regions in evaluating economic development initiatives, as well as lessons hoped to be learned. Each case in economic development is unique, whether at the global scale, at regional scales (such as West Texas, South Texas, and the USA–Mexico border region), or at the level of localities such as small cities of South Texas or Southwest Texas. And yet, some common themes can be identified that weave through all of the case studies, especially themes related to geography, such as the merits of connectivity and regional spatial planning.

Common to all cases of economic development are geographic themes, including location (the amenities of a given site and how it is situated with respect to other places), region (the territorial functioning of economic development and related policies), scale (the size of such territorial workings of economic development), distance, connectivity (including transportation infrastructure), and modifications to the built environment. These geographic themes: location, region, scale, distance, connectivity, and the built environment, appear throughout the book and will be summarized in Chap. 9, which provides snapshots of those similarities and differences. Besides the viewpoints of geography, themes related to policy such as public–private partnerships apply to each case, though in unique ways. These, too, will be compared and contrasted in Chap. 9.

1.5 Global Scale Economic Development Initiatives

Economic development at the global scale is a topic meritorious of an entire book of its own, or even multiple books, and even then, authors would barely be able to scratch the surface of their nuances. I briefly discuss two examples, China's Belt and Road Initiative (BRI) and UNESCO's World Heritage Sites, to illustrate that development initiatives operating at the global scale necessarily involve activities in distinct localities and small-scale subnational regions. The World Trade Organization (WTO) is introduced, given its importance in providing legal frameworks for global trade, as an underlying driver of economic development. Therefore, an inclusion of some examples serves to illustrate the need to consider development at multiple scales. That is to say, an examination of a local-level economic development initiative, such as the effort by a given community to develop an industrial park, more often than not is articulated within the larger scale global economy. Likewise, global-level initiatives are carried out in localities. Development that occurs regionally involves forces and the functioning of markets, trade, and infrastructure at all scales: global, regional, and local. The global-level cases included in this chapter illustrate regional functioning of development at multiple scales, not unlike the global scrap metals industry discussed above. In addition to the BRI and UNESCO as global-scale phenomena, the WTO offers a global-scale framework for economic development, as described below.

1.5.1 China's Belt and Road Initiative (BRI)

The BRI is also known as "One Belt One Road," which refers to a twenty-first-century resurgence of the ancient Silk Road. The contemporary version is designed to link the People's Republic of China (PRC) by land with Central Asia, South Asia, the Middle East, and Europe, and by sea to Southeast Asia, Europe, sub-Saharan Africa, Latin America, and the Middle East (Fig. 1.3). The massive global economic development initiative involves the development of roads, rail, maritime ports, power plants, and the Internet infrastructure in the developing countries of these regions lacking in such infrastructure, especially sub-Saharan Africa and parts of South Asia (Sacks 2021a). Adjusted for inflation, the project is larger than the

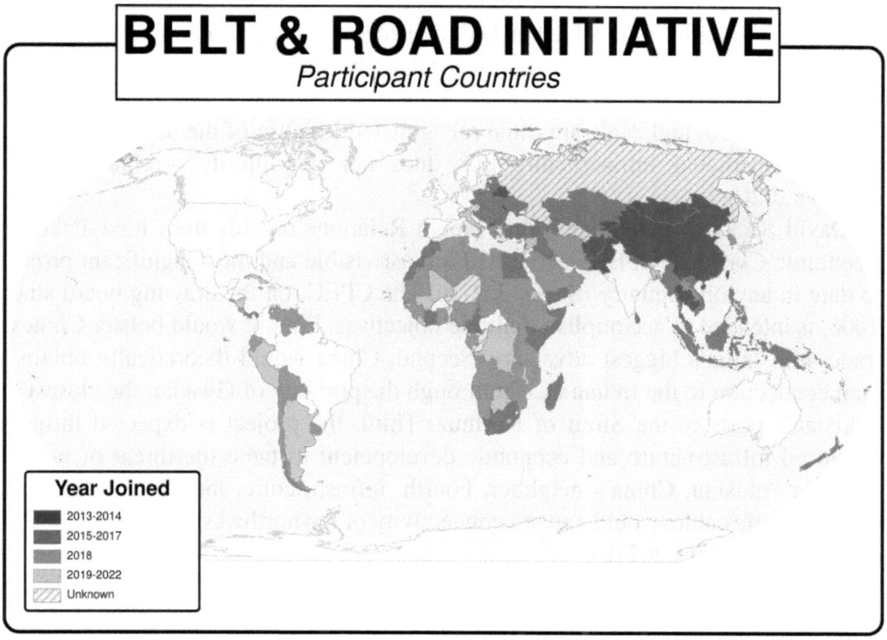

Fig. 1.3 Map of participant countries of the Belt and Road Initiative. (By Stephen O'Connell)

Marshall Plan economic development initiative that formed the basis for the rebuilding of Europe after World War II (Ziegler 2020). Xi Jinping launched the policy in 2013, a large development scheme, whereby China would finance the construction and installation of the features, and participating countries would pay back the loans. In 2017, Xi expanded BRI to Latin America, and that year Xi added the BRI into the constitution of the Communist Party of PRC. By 2019, a total of 139 countries had signed on in one way to another to the project, which collectively account for 63% of the world's population and 40% of global GDP (Sacks 2021a).

Most member countries (those that have signed memorandums of understanding, or MOUs) are in the lower and lower-middle income categories, though a few higher-middle and upper-income countries have also signed on. For example, Italy has signed an MOU, but there are no actual projects on the drawing board for that country. Nearly all sub-Saharan countries are members, and most have ports or roads on the drawing board (Sacks 2021a).

The BRI fulfills both economic and political ambitions of Xi Jinping. This high priority project in part is designed to bolster the legitimacy of the parts of the PRCs economic planning and execution that are the most centralized. After the 2007–2009 global financial crisis, Xi sought ways for PRC to regain its economic hegemony; as a major exporting country, he wanted to solidify markets for Chinese exports while securing steady supplies of needed imports. That means offering financing for freight infrastructure (roads, ports, pipelines) and broadband. Such developments around the globe directly benefit Chinese enterprises that manufacture hardware and equipment such as ship building and construction equipment, as well as construction itself. However, some weaknesses of the scheme have been identified, as some of the enterprises involved lacked the necessary experience of working internationally. Another criticism of BRI, especially by the USA, is that the lending is designed to benefit PRC, and for many countries, it is a debt trap; transparency is less than desired, and deals are often renegotiated because of the debt burden, and poorly constructed infrastructure that does not live up its original promise (Ziegler 2020).

David Sacks of the Council on Foreign Relations regards the China–Pakistan Economic Corridor (CPEC) as the BRI's most visible and most significant project to date in any one country (Sacks 2021b). The CPEC, on the drawing board since 2006, is intended to accomplish multiple objectives. First, it would bolster Chinese trade with India's biggest adversary. Second, China would theoretically obtain a land connection to the Indian Ocean through the port city of Gwadar, the closest of Pakistan's ports to the Strait of Hormuz. Third, the project is expected through enhanced infrastructure and economic development to tame the threat of radical Islam in Pakistan, China's neighbor. Fourth, infrastructure, including roads, rail, and fiberoptic cable, would expand connectivity of far-northwest China with southern Pakistan (Sacks 2021b).

To the disappointment of many in Pakistan and China, the $62 billion project is fraught with delays and underperformance. Much of the funding, in the form of loans, has in the end been earmarked not for transportation infrastructure, but for coal-fired power plants in light of the country's unreliable power generation.

Furthermore, the CPEC has experienced delays in construction and terrorist attacks. The delays in the completion of key components of the project have resulted in actions by Pakistan to delay repayment of the debt (Sacks 2021b). Furthermore, one of the most visible components of CPEC, modernization of the Port of Gwadar, has been quite a disappointment to both China and Pakistan. Container ships have barely begun to call on the port (Aamir 2021).

The case of Colombo, Sri Lanka illustrates the local-scale impacts of BRI. Adjacent to the booming business district of Sri Lanka's capital is a new project, Colombo Port City, a BRI-financed land reclamation project designed with Dubai, Singapore, and Hong Kong in mind, three prominent examples of cities built in part through land reclamation. A partnership with the China Harbour Engineering Company enabled the company to profit from the reclamation work, including dredging and related construction, while retaining 43% of the surface area in the form of a 99-year lease. That Chinese-leased portion of the land will be home to office buildings housing offshore banks and similar enterprise, and other land uses that are expected to benefit the Chinese construction company tremendously. The entire project is expected to be completed by 2040. Critics point to potentially unfavorable terms for Sri Lanka, including indebtedness to China, environmental degradation related to the massive movement of earth, and the prospects that the project could be, in effect, a colony of China's (Ethirajan 2022). The Colombo case raises questions about Xi Jinping's motives behind BRI in coastal South Asia, whether geopolitical in light of tensions with India, or the economic strategy of shoring up China's export market in Colombo and creating investment property on the city's shoreline.

Many countries of sub-Saharan Africa participate in Belt and Road, raising concerns that a new style of colonialism, what might be termed neocolonialism, is emerging throughout the realm. Roads, rail lines, pipelines, and ports are among the projects that create indebtedness to China for many countries of the realm. African ports on the Indian Ocean are viewed by Xi Jinping and Chinese national industries as opportunities to benefit economically from construction and trade through connections to Asian ports of the Indian Ocean and South China Sea, in line with Xi's vision of creating interdependent regions and localities spanning the globe. In sub-Saharan Africa, as in Pakistan and Sri Lanka, military agreements are tied to port developments; Djibouti is the clearest African example of the strategy. But the biggest priority of African countries is economic development, given the realm's generally underdeveloped port, road, and rail infrastructure. For China, this means overseas markets for its goods and construction services, and low-cost sources of raw materials (Nantulya 2019).

A criticism of BRI commonly made in the context of Africa, but applicable in all participating areas, is that Chinese labor and primary inputs are prioritized in the contracts over local labor and inputs. The assumption is that BRI in large part is designed to expand the global influence of Chinese state-owned firms. Some African projects involve the presence of Chinese security forces, many of them Chinese private companies, to protect them, which has drawn claims of the violation of local and national sovereignty. However, the biggest criticism of BRI in the realm of sovereignty is the problem of debt and financing of infrastructure and other construction projects. In the case of East Africa, there is some fear that the ports of Djibouti and Mombasa are presently collateral for loans for construction projects, which could lead to China owning them. The lack of transparency of arrangements made between China and many African countries remains a significant cause for concern (Nantulya 2019).

1.5.2 UNESCO World Heritage Sites: Campeche, Mexico and San Antonio, Texas

The list of World Heritage Sites was begun by the United Nations Educational, Scientific and Cultural Organization (UNESCO) in 1972 as a result of a treaty, the Convention Concerning the Protection of the World Cultural and Natural Heritage. In accordance with the treaty, the World Heritage Committee meets annually to determine the sites to be added to the list. All populated continents (and all of the major world realms) contain such sites, though they are proportionally greater in Western Europe and are less numerous in sub-Saharan Africa, where most but not all countries have at least one. The International Monetary Fund (IMF) has determined that the UNESCO brand enhances the attractiveness to tourists of the member tourist sites, and that as the economic strength of tourism increases, nearby areas grow economically as well, owing to the multiplier effects that tourism generates. Such beneficiaries generally include managerial skills and improved security and governmental transparency as part of national and local policies to boost tourism as a path to diversifying economic development (Arezki et al. 2009).

Of the 313 cities of the world on UNESCO's World Heritage List, Mexico has 28, which have formed an association, *La Asociación Nacional de Ciudades Mexicanas del Patrimonio Mundial* (National Association of Mexican Cities of World Heritage) to partner for funding for historic preservation. The port city of Campeche, located on the western side of the Yucatan Peninsula, benefits considerably from tourism in its central historic district. The Spaniards founded the city and began to construct its fortification in the sixteenth century, as it became an important connection point for Spain between Havana and Veracruz. The construction of the fortification of the central zone of the city, with walls in a hexagonal pattern, occurred between 1686 and 1704. The historic zone covers 181 ha (447 acres) and is filled with well-preserved buildings, including a highly regarded cathedral, in addition to the military fortification surrounding the zone. Although the Spaniards built numerous fortified cities in the Caribbean region that it dominated during its colonial heyday, Campeche is the only such city in Mexico that has been given UNESCO historical status. The baroque-style fortified city was important to colonial Spain for its port, commerce, and military protection against piracy, and Mexico takes pride in the preservation and restoration of it (UNESCO 2021a, b).

The city and the State of Campeche do not suffer from the same kinds of lingering dependence on low-income primary activities that many other parts of the developing world do, because petroleum (through the oil monopoly PEMEX) holds an important place in the state's economy since the mid-twentieth century. Thus, tourism in Campeche does not face the same "trap" as do island countries that rely so heavily on it. Offshore oil and the handling of petroleum bulk cargo at the port are major contributors to the community's economy, though tourism, especially that related to the historic district, accounts for around half the hotel business of the city. The historic district is the primary tourist attraction in the state. UNESCO placed the city center on the list of historic sites in 1999, and since then, the state's and city's economies have been bolstered, and the capacity for conventions to supplement regular tourism is enhanced (Campeche, State of 2015).

Even more so than Campeche, San Antonio, Texas's second largest city, enjoys a diverse economic base. And yet, its tourism industry, based in part on the five missions that are UNESCO sites, including the Alamo, remains important as key to local economic development. Five missions located in close proximity to each other in an expanse of 7.7 miles (12.4 km) within the basin of the San Antonio River were built in the eighteenth century under the direction of Franciscan missionaries, though their purpose was more than evangelizing the local Coahuiltecan peoples. They also served military defense purposes for Spain's viceroyalty of New Spain, and a means of colonizing through settlement the San Antonio River Basin of present-day South Texas. On display are multiple features of life on the northern Spanish frontier, including mills, churches, living quarters, and water distribution mechanisms, among others (Fig. 1.4). The missions and their artifacts display the ways that the Spaniards altered the culture of the hunter-gatherer Coahuiltecans by teaching them agriculture, as well as the reverse, the adoption by the Spaniards of the ways of adapting to and conquering the natural terrain of the region. Although urbanization of San Antonio has obscured much of the long-distance views of the five missions, planning restrictions nonetheless largely protect them from the excesses of urban sprawl or modernist crowdedness (UNESCO 2015).

Related to the field of economic development is community development, a perspective and a set of strategies that prioritize quality of life in a given town or city. Historic preservation is a key ingredient of community development. It involves partnerships between different stakeholders from the public, non-profit and private sectors. Both the Campeche and San Antonio UNESCO sites illustrate the collaboration and overlapping oversights of different government entities. The State of Campeche counts the city's historical district as key not only to economic development through attraction of tourists but also the preservation of heritage for the sake of residents as well. The five missions of San Antonio are managed by federal, state, and city entities that preserve and protect these historic assets. These include the National Register of Historic Places, the National Park Service, and the Texas Historical Commission. Historic ordinances of The City of San Antonio apply to the sites. The Archdiocese of San Antonio shares authority over the churches within the missions (UNESCO 2015).

Fig. 1.4 Mission Concepción UNESCO World Heritage site, San Antonio. (Photo by the author)

In short, the local success brought on by this global historic preservation and renovation initiative is an uplifting story in the geography of economic development. While the UNESCO World Heritage designation effectively serves as a "brand name" to boost attention toward such sites on the part of tourism stakeholders, local initiative in promoting the sites factors more in the multiplier effect ignited by each.

1.5.3 The World Trade Organization (WTO)

The WTO is a global structure of trade agreements providing a legal and policy framework for global trade that forms the basis of global economic development and global growth in GDP. "In brief, the World Trade Organization (WTO) is the only international organization dealing with the global rules of trade. Its main function is to ensure that trade flows as smoothly, predictably and freely as possible" (WTO n.d.). The WTO's main function is to provide certainty in trade rules, and such certainty makes trade negotiations, and therefore broad trade patterns, more predictable and makes planning for economic development based on trade more possible (WTO n.d.). However, despite nearly three decades of existence, the WTO is often dismissed as inept, given the failure of the Doha and Uruguay Rounds to be agreed upon, and frequent "cheating" by many of its 164 member countries. Given the fundamental role that imports and exports play in any country's economic development, the WTO is a global-scale framework that students and researchers of the geography of economic development should be mindful of.

1.6 Conclusion: Contemporary Issues in the Geography of Economic Development

In all case studies included in this book, COVID-19 has impacted economic development, sometimes in surprising ways, and in many cases negatively. Economic development has taken detours at all scales because of the pandemic, leading to a notably altered geography of business and state investments, transportation infrastructure, and related policies. Localities and regions have been forced to adapt their planning for lockdowns, changing workplaces, and alterations to consumption habits. Main Streets are impacted by closures of some retail storefronts, restaurants and taverns. So, too, are the layouts of manufacturing plants and offices. Questions loom about trends in the demand for office space once the pandemic has passed. The early stages of the obsolescence of shopping malls that began before the pandemic are more visible now, though economic developers are beginning to see the repurposing of such facilities to such uses as warehousing that supports e-commerce, which itself is a trend accelerated by the pandemic. The trucking, rail, and maritime shipping industries are witnessing enormous changes in the movements of cargo, owing to, among other things, bottlenecks related to growing e-commerce and shortages of shipping containers, disruptions, and other alterations to manufacturing in light of health-related lockdowns, and even rejections of some loads by freight carriers when equipment is tied up. In short, the pandemic impacts all of the case studies in this volume in some way, albeit differently from case to case. Impacts are expected to be felt for years to come, so at best, this volume can provide snapshots that hopefully offer some indications of the consequences of this part of twenty-first century history in the making.

By early 2023, the Russian invasion of Ukraine was upending global supplies and movements of energy commodities, which impacts each of the case studies in some way. Trade sanctions against Russia ignited rapid rises in prices of oil and natural gas, which are fueling more widespread inflation, and renewed interest in oil and gas production in the Permian Basin and Eagle Ford shale plays of Texas, as well as the prospects for exports of liquified natural gas (LNG). Geopolitical shifts regarding the global economy as a whole are leading to an interest on the part of companies to set aside just-in-time production and distribution strategies in favor of a "just-in-case" logistics strategy, meaning stockpiling of inputs to reduce the risks of interruptions in shipments. These trends collectively are impacting freight transportation, manufacturing, and retail shipping, as will be illustrated throughout the chapters of this book.

References

Aamir A (2021) Pakistan takes desperate measures to revive Belt and Road's port. Nikkai Asia. https://asia.nikkei.com/Spotlight/Belt-and-Road/Pakistan-takes-desperate-measures-to-revive-Belt-and-Road-s-port

Arezki R, Cherif R, Piotrowski J (2009) Tourism specialization and economic development: evidence from the UNESCO world heritage list. Working Paper WP/09/176, International Monetary Fund, 1 August

Campeche, State of (2015) Programa Sectorial de Desarrollo Económico 2016–2021. Secretariat of Planning, State of Campeche. Retrieved January 20, 2022, from http://www.seplan.campeche.gob.mx/copladecam/ps/ps-sedeco.pdf

Ethirajan A (2022) Colombo Port City: a new Dubai or a Chinese enclave? BBC News, Colombo. https://www.bbc.com/news//world-asia-59993386. Accessed 18 Jan 2022

Fik T (2000) The geography of economic development: regional changes, global challenges, 2nd edn. McGraw Hill

GSA Business Report (2021) Greer port moves record cargo volume as Pacific ports stall. GSA Business Report. https://gsabusiness.com/news/distribution-logistics/80166/

Jessop B (2003) The political economy of scale and the construction of cross-border micro-regions. In: Söderbaum F, Shaw TM (eds) Theories of new regionalism. Palgrave Macmillan, pp 179–196

Karlsson C, Olsson M (2015) Functional economic regions, accessibility and regional development. CESIS electronic working papers series, paper no. 415. Centre of Excellence for Science and Innovation Studies, The Royal Institute of Technology, Sweden. https://static.sys.kth.se/itm/wp/cesis/cesiswp415.pdf

Kasala K, Safta M (2017) The region as a concept: traditional and constructivist view. AUC Geographica 2017:208–218. https://doi.org/10.14712/23361980.2017.17

Lyons D, Rice M, Rachel R (2009) Circuits of scrap: closed loop industrial ecosystems and the geography of US international recyclable material flows 1995-2009. Geogr J *175*(4):286–300

Medeiros E (2017) What is an intermodal region? Universidade de Lisboa, Interrag Sverige-Norge. Retrieved September 5, 2021, from https://crossborder.ie/site2015/wp-content/uploads/2017/11/Dr-Eduardo-Medeiros.pdf

Mohd Noor M, Baharein K (2008) Case study: a strategic research methodology. Am J Appl Sci 5(11):1602–1604

Nantulya P (2019) Implications for Africa from China's one belt one road strategy. Spotlight: Africa Center of Strategic Studies, 22 March. Retrieved January 23, 2022, from https://afriocacenter.org/spotlight/implications-for-africa-china-one-belt-one-road-strategy/

Nijman J, Shin M, Muller P (2020) The world today: concepts and regions in geography, 8th edn. Wiley

Phillips R, Pittman R (2015) A framework for community and economic development. In: Phillips R, Pittman R (eds) Community and economic development handbook, 2nd edn. Routledge, pp 3–21

Sacks D (2021a) Countries in China's belt and road initiative: who's in and who's out. Blog Post, Council on Foreign Relations. March 24. https://www.cfr.org/blog/countries-chinas-belt-and-road-initiative-whos-and-whos-out?gclid=CjwKCAiArOqOBhBmEiwAsgeLmQJzc3nl7Wx86D5zDkW95Vgm-rAQOVyuffmg9y00ZG7YN_bzzQOb_RoCyGQQAvD_BwE

Sacks D (2021b) The China-Pakistan economic corridor: hard reality greets BRI's signature initiative. Council on Foreign Relations, Asia Unbound. https://www.cfr.org/blog/china-pakistan-economic-corridor-hard-reality-greets-bris-signature-initiative

Starman AB (2013) The case study as a type of qualitative research. J Contemp Educ Stud January:28–43

Taylor B (2021a) Shipping problems go well beyond recycling industry. Recycling News. https://www.recyclingtoday.com/article/container-shipping-problems-usa-asia-europe-recycling/. Accessed 2 Mar 2021

Taylor B (2021b) Worldsteel sounds optimistic note for steel sector. Recycling Today. https://recyclingtoday.com/article/worldsteel-steel-forecast-2021-2022-economy-rebound/

Taylor B (2021c) Ferrous high wire act to stay in place. Recycling Today. https://www.recyclingtoday.com/article/fastmarkets-panel-ferrous-scrap-recycling-2021-demand/

UNESCO (2015) San Antonio Missions. Retrieved January 24, 2022, from https://whc.unesco.org/en/list/1466/

UNESCO (2021a) El centro histórico de Campeche y las ciudades fortificadas de la región. UNESCO (Web Site). https://es.unesco.org/news/centro-historico-campeche-y-ciudades-fortificadas-region. Accessed 22 Jan 2022

UNESCO (2021b) San Antonio Missions. https://whc.unesco.org/en/list/1466/. Accessed 5 Oct 2021

World Cargo News (2021) US Agricultural exporters still seeking boxes. World Cargo News, 11 March. https://www.worldcargonews.com/news/news/us-agricultural-exporters-still-seeking-boxes-65874. Retrieved March 12, 2021

WTO (n.d.) WTO in Brief. World Trade Organization Web Site. https://www.wto.org/english/thewto_e/whatis_e/inbrief_e/inbr_e.htm#:~:text=In%20brief%2C%20the%20World%20Trade,predictably%20and%20freely%20as%20possible. Accessed 28 Sept 2021

Zainal Z (2007) Case study as a research method. J Kemanusiaan bil.9, June 2007: 1–6. Accessed 7 Mar 2021 http://psyking.net/htmlobj-3837/case_study_as_a_research_method.pdf

Ziegler D (2020) China wants to put itself back at the centre of the world. The Economist, 6 February. https://www.economist.com/special-report/2020/02/06/china-wants-to-put-itself-back-at-the-centre-of-the-world. Accessed 10 Jan 2022

Chapter 2
Binational Trade and Economic Development: USA–Mexico Steel Trade Since 1940

Abstract Studies of economic development addressing trade policy, including trade agreements and tariffs, are important as they shed light on the thinking of economic development stakeholders in localities directly affected by such policies. To provide one binational regional case study of a global industry, this chapter addresses USA–Mexico trade in steel, and the trade agreement framework under which it operates. The chapter provides a brief history of that two-way trade since World War II to illustrate how such policies can change over time. Through discussion of both countries' steel trade policy since the mid-twentieth century, it questions protectionism as appropriate economic development policy. To explore ways that trade in steel impacts economic development at the local scale, the chapter includes brief economic and geographic overviews of Monclova, a mid-sized Mexican city with a strong history in steel production, and Jewett, Texas, a Texas town also defined by steel. It concludes that tariffs and other protectionist measures are not particularly constructive, nor are they helpful for economic development prospects in Monclova or Jewett. Rather, USA–Mexico trade in steel is complementary and based on each country's strengths, and therefore benefits both localities, each of which specializes in particular steel products.

Keywords Steel · International trade · Tariffs · USMCA · NAFTA · Monclova, Coahuila · Jewett, Texas

2.1 Introduction

Worldwide trade in steel is a complex and genuinely global example of economic development. The manufacture of steel and other metals is regarded as a fundamental activity and desirable for any country that can carry it out efficiently such that they can avoid imported products at the very least, and profit from exports in the best case. Furthermore, as an important intermediate good used in the manufacture of many basic goods and in construction, its manufacture is regarded as a strategic activity that has historically been included in national industrial planning in so

M. S. Yoder, *Geographical Scale and Economic Development*,
https://doi.org/10.1007/978-3-031-36197-5_2

many countries, and, therefore, affected by tariffs. Because of the many types of steel, it is rare for a country to produce all of its needs domestically; even the biggest steel exporting countries import some. As a component of global-scale economic development, it nonetheless impacts localities that produce it, as well as those that buy it and fabricate it into more complex products that form supply chains.

The historical geography of steel production and its impact on regional economic development comprise complex stories surrounding the volatility of the industry since World War II. For example, the North American Manufacturing Belt of the Midwest portion of the USA and southeastern Canada, where steel production was once dominant, have largely transitioned away from that industry, leaving many communities with high rates of manufacturing unemployment and the need to redevelop their economic bases through alternative manufacturing activities. In large part, the pattern has been the result of a transition from coal-fired steel plants that smelted iron ore to newer electric arc furnace manufacturing, based on melting of ferrous scrap in plants that more often than not arose in lower-wage areas of the US Sunbelt. The exodus of steel production from the North American Manufacturing Belt has also resulted in part from increased imports of raw and semi-finished steel from overseas producers in Asia and Latin America. The pattern of coal-fired plant closures found in the USA applies also to Monterrey and Mexico City, as new plants emerged in such states as Michoacán and Coahuila. Given the strong economic multiplier effects of steel production, the industry is a basic one in the overall historical geography of economic development, which requires empirical case study examinations of it to shed light on its future trajectory. Case studies of international trade in steel likewise are valuable to an overall understanding of the role of this basic industry in regional economic development processes insofar as regions become more or less integrated in global trade.

This chapter examines binational trade in steel within the North American functional economic region; specifically between the USA and Mexico, as a case study within the body of the global steel trade. Global supply, demand, and price trends impact upon this binational trade, thus rendering the case study as a window into the global trade, the nature of trade relationships between the USA and Mexico, and localities whose economies are built on steel production. Furthermore, steel trade policy between the two countries reflects not only the global nature of the industry but also the political relations of the two countries. Such relations are a factor in the role of steel in economic development in each country, and in each community that produces the metal, whether in large part or modestly, for export. To illustrate the impact of the industry and its exportability on localities, the chapter includes a brief snapshot of steel production and its impact on local economic development in the mid-sized Mexican metropolitan area of Monclova, and the small East Texas town of Jewett.

A case study of trade in steel products is effective in portraying the different geographical scales at which economic development occurs. As an intermediate product, steel is associated with both backward linkages (raw materials) and forward linkages (finished goods made of steel). Agglomeration of both forward and backward linkages often, but not always, occurs in proximity to steel mills, especially those that utilize coal as a power source to smelt iron, whereas steel produced by electric arc furnace (EAF) technology exhibits a different geography that is more flexible and spread out, whereby scrap metal can profitably be sourced from longer distances than the heavier inputs used in traditional steel mills. Therefore, in this chapter, the impacts of steel production on the Monclova metropolitan area differ dramatically from those of the more flexible mini mill of Jewett, Texas. Furthermore, despite its reputation as an aging heavy industry associated with national security in all countries in which it has historically been produced, steel manufacturing nonetheless remains an important component of economic development at all scales: global, national, regional, and local.

Despite its increasingly lower labor requirements, steel production and trade remain important to cross-border connections and networks. Thus, the industry continues to exhibit interesting geographic patterns of production and exchange. Steel mills represent fixed capital in the landscape that require sizable portions of land and, usually, significant transportation infrastructure linkages for the hauling of raw material inputs and finished product outputs that contribute to steel mills' multiplier effects. In the Mexican case, steel serves as an example of a successful component of the country's import substitution development policy of the 1940s–1980s. As a heavily traded product, manufactured steel is commonly subjected to tariffs and other trade restrictions because of its importance nationally to both Mexican and American economic development, and a suitable example of the role of such tariffs in economic development.

Economic development studies addressing trade policy, including trade agreements and tariffs, are important as they shed light on the thinking of economic development stakeholders and company management in different localities if they are affected directly by such policy. In the case of intermediate goods such as steel and steel products, trends in trade and tariffs unavoidably impact not only global markets but the local economic results of such policy. Thus, such policy operates at multiple scales, from global to local. Local dependence on steel production and trade, such as that which exists in many steel-producing regions of the world, translates to vulnerabilities to global steel markets and related governmental policies. While Texas is not among the most important of American states in steel production, there nonetheless are several communities that depend heavily on that industry. Likewise, the Mexican cities of Monclova and Lázaro Cárdenas are important centers of that country's production. As such, the case study covered in this chapter is a subset of the global scale of trade in steel, a complex set of relationships given the array of steel products traded, and a decentralized geography of its production.

After the US presidential election of 2016, "uncertainty" was among the terms invoked in the finance and economics media in the USA, Mexico, and Canada to describe the future of trade policy between the three trade partners. Donald Trump made his criticisms of NAFTA a centerpiece of his campaign for the presidency as early as 2015, and continuing through the election season. Upon his inauguration, threats of cancelling NAFTA continued, though they were interspersed with his thoughts of renegotiation of the 24-year trade agreement, which in the end occurred in July 2020. Steel was among the products mentioned by the administration as a source of job loss due to globalization and free trade. After all, steel is a strategically important product around the globe, and one that can stir emotions, especially among labor organizations and other citizens of the advanced economies and emerging markets skeptical of globalization.

In light of the real possibility of a USA–Mexico trade war that loomed among skeptics of NAFTA and USMCA, and even the talk of elimination of any trade agreement altogether, this chapter examines policy underlying the binational trade relationship in steel products between the USA and Mexico. Steel is an appropriate industrial product to study in this context, as it is a strategic intermediate product of international trade, and as such, is the source of actual, past, and future protectionism around the globe. While individual news articles exist on planned or implemented steel-related policies involving its movement between the two countries, few studies provide concise overviews of the development of these policies through time, a paucity that this chapter seeks to address. Contemporary discussions of steel trade policy between the two countries are largely rooted in events in the World War II era; therefore, the chapter begins by tracing the respective conditions of steel manufacturing in the 1940s. It traces changes in the ownership status in 1991 of Mexico's largest steel plant, which by that time had become oriented more toward exports than it had been before, and it addresses attempts by the USA to utilize tariffs to protect the American steel industry that increasingly faced competition from lower-cost producers of some categories of steel. Finally, it places the most recent threats of protectionism in the context of this short but dramatic history and concludes that the USA would have more to lose than to gain from such policy ideas, especially given the growth potential for American manufacturers of rolled steel, and, therefore of increased demand for pipes in light of the opening of the Mexican petroleum industry to foreign investment.

Following an overview of USA–Mexico trade relations in steel products, and a snapshot of macro- and local-level conditions of the industry in both countries, the chapter traces salient features of Mexican steel manufacturing in the twentieth century, especially since 1940, as a basis for that country's contemporary policy in that sector. Following that is a brief overview of steel policy in the USA from World War II to the signing of NAFTA in 1993. The next two sections of the chapter briefly examine recent US and Mexican policy toward international trade in steel, especially between the two countries. I then identify future opportunities for US steel exports through new market opportunities for steel in light of Mexico's growing demands. The basic impacts of steel production on the economic development of one community in Mexico and one in Texas are touched on. The conclusion section broadly sums up the similarities and differences in steel trade policy between the two countries through time.

2.2 Steel and USA–Mexico Relations in 2018

One glaring example of the lack of understanding on the part of the Trump Administration and its supporters toward USA–Mexico trade that is quite revealing is the nature of binational trade in steel products, including those related to energy infrastructure, particularly pipes and tubes for natural gas and oil. In January 2017, the Houston Chronicle portrayed some Trump supporters' views on USA–Mexico trade in steel products. The article cites officials who apparently believe that Mexican steel imports pose a threat to the Nucor steel mill in Jewett, Texas, which produces steel bars primarily for construction (Handy 2017). Data on Mexican steel imports and exports in 2018 by the International Trade Administration (ITA) of the US Department of Commerce (2019a, b) show that Mexico imports more steel in tonnage from the USA than it exports in total steel to the USA (3.8 versus 3.52 million tons in 2018), and Mexico imports more of the type of steel used in petroleum pipeline than it exports. The latter category, "*rollo en caliente*" (hot rolled), or "*tubos sin costura*" (seamless tube), is one that benefits companies and employees in both countries, though slightly more in the USA in the case of hot rolled steel, and more in Mexico in seamless tube (CANACERO 2019). Likewise, other categories, especially flat laminated rolled products, or sheet metal and plates ("*productos planos laminados*"), are dominated by US producers. Mexico currently experiences a large trade deficit in that category. Meanwhile Mexico experienced in 2018 a small trade deficit in "*productos largos*," or steel wire, bars, cables, rods, and rails (CANACERO 2019). Mexico dominates in the manufacture and export of pipe, seamless tube, and semi-finished steel products (US Department of Commerce 2019b).

Given that the USA on balance exports more steel by value and weight to Mexico than it imports, the kinds of steel tariffs against Mexico that Donald Trump and his supporters have championed, and that the spokespersons from the Nucor plant in Jewett seemed to want, could have resulted in retaliatory tariffs that could very well harm all US steel exports to Mexico, especially flat laminated products, or *productos planos laminados*, more than the reverse. This assessment is based on historical precedent and on counter threats at the time by Economy Minister Ildefonso Guajardo and other Mexican trade officials. Clearly, total steel exports from the USA to Mexico would suffer from such tariffs. Furthermore, advocates for tariffs on Mexican steel fail to take into account the highly anticipated growth in opportunities to export to Mexico their hot rolled product for manufacture of gas and oil pipelines, given the opening of the country's state-owned petroleum sector (PEMEX) to foreign investment under President Enrique Peña Nieto (2012–2018). Such privatization is targeted toward drilling and exploration of oil, and to the supply of natural gas, both of which could utilize the kind of steel produced in numerous steel plants of the USA that specialize in the raw steel needed to manufacture pipes (Nucor 2018). From the perspective of the management of the Nucor plant and community leaders in Jewett, USA–Mexico trade in steel products would more appropriately be seen as an opportunity than a threat.

Mexico clearly does not represent a net negative to the US steel industry, but is a market more appropriately regarded as an opportunity. The USA ranks fourth in total global steel production and produces 4.8% of the global total, whereas Mexico ranks 13th and produces 1.1% of the global total (Table 2.1). And Mexico has, in recent years, imported an increasing amount of natural gas from the USA for generation of electricity, as its middle class and its manufacturing activity grow (Expansión 2017). Mexico's dramatic reliance on the USA for gas creates

Table 2.1 Top 15 steel-producing countries, 2021

Country	Production, millions of tons	Percentage of global total
1. China	1032.8	52.9
2. India	118.2	6.1
3. Japan	96.3	4.9
4. USA	85.8	4.4
5. Russia	75.6	3.9
6. South Korea	70.4	3.6
7. Turkey	40.4	2.1
8. Germany	40.1	2.1
9. Brazil	36.2	1.9
10. Iran	28.5	1.5
11. Italy	24.4	1.3
12. Taiwan	23.2	1.2
13. Vietnam	23.0	1.2
14. Ukraine	21.4	1.1
15. Mexico	18.5	0.9

Source: World Steel Organization. https://worldsteel.org/steel-topics/statistics/world-steel-in-figures-2022/

additional opportunities for steel companies in the USA who manufacture tubing and pipes. Singling out Mexico for tariffs on steel, and the resulting retaliations, could wound the US steel industry. So too would ignoring the increased market potentials for American steel and natural gas in Mexico.

Table 2.1 Global production of steel, top 15 countries, 2021.

2.3 Mexico's Steel Industry 1940–2001: A Brief Overview

Mexico had two major steel production facilities at the onset of World War II, including the large, private Fundidora Monterrey and La Consolidada, S.A., a private company established in Mexico City in 1913 with the help of Harry Wright, an American steel expert. Given that Mexico was heavily dependent on steel imports, and these prior companies were not capable of meeting the country's steel requirements, the Mexican government began to apply the principles of Import Substitution Industrialization (ISI) to that particular industrial sector. Wright tried to convince the Mexican government to impose tariffs on steel imported from the USA, given that steel was a basic industry to the Mexican economy and was a continued basis for Mexican dependence on imported manufactured goods. But, because of the need for affordable imports, the government bowed to pressures by metal fabricators and other steel consumers, and declined to pursue such a policy, despite an increase in such imports of 305% between 1910 and 1920 (Corrales 1996). Finally, the state turned La Consolidada into a "parastatal" enterprise, largely state-owned, and partly financed by private investors. The state held majority interest by the late 1930s and began to impose modest tariffs on US imports. Eventually the ruling PRI (Institutional Revolutionary Party) felt the Mexican state was competing against the Monterrey facility (Corrales 1996; Minello and Barranco 1995).

The desire to compete with the Monterrey mill was not the only condition motivating the Mexican government to establish a new steel production facility in the north. Wartime steel shortages threatened the Mexican economy and security by disrupting industrial production and infrastructure development in the country. As part of the ruling PRI's policy of ISI, the federal government oversaw the construction of a new steel mill that would be a parastatal enterprise to produce rolled products like tin plate and sheet metal (Corrales 1996; Yoder 1999; Minello and Barranco 1995). The federal government established a plant in Monclova, Coahuila, then a small city in the center of the State of Coahuila in north-central Mexico, some 240 kms (150 miles) from the USA–Mexico border. The location provided favorable rail linkages to Mexico City, to iron mines in the State of Chihuahua, and to the USA–Mexico border at Piedras Negras. Harold Pape, an engineer with ARMCO, the US steel giant, oversaw the establishment of the plant, the planning of which began in 1941, and its operation beginning in 1942. The funding for the parastatal enterprise came from a public funding entity, Nacional Financiero, S.A., that included several private investors as junior partners. Pape and ARMCO had two large-scale objectives: to ensure that Mexico offered a supply of rolled steel that could be imported into the USA in light of wartime steel shortages, and to have a customer to which the company could sell its surplus production equipment from its aging steel mill in St. Louis (Yoder 1999, 2009; Minello and Barranco 1995).

Steel production in Mexico in the mid-1940s was strongly linked to the country's rapid turn to *la industrialización sustitutiva de importaciones* (import substitution industrialization, or ISI), which enabled the industry to enjoy protectionism through tariffs and state subsidies. These policies, interestingly, occurred in tandem with global shortages of steel, given wartime disruptions of supply and increases in demand. Such conditions strongly favored the establishment of the AHMSA facility in Monclova, with the hopes that the plant would meet the country's domestic demand, and produce a surplus for export. The strategy worked until a glut occurred in global steel supplies in the 1970s, which prevented plants in the USA and Mexico, including AHMSA, from reaching full capacity (Rueda Peiro 1994). Just before the glut, AHMSA opened a second blast furnace in Monclova to boost production for the export market. To alleviate the growing problems of dependence on domestic- and export-oriented production of raw steel, the State of Coahuila and Monclova's economic development efforts turned toward pipes, fuel tanks, laminated products, and construction-worthy steel to create forward linkages to the AHMSA plants. This condition remained through the early twenty-first century, forming the basis for the continued efforts for AHMSA and other Mexican companies to export more raw and indirect steel products (Yoder 2009). In short, ISI coincided with an overcapacity of steel in Monclova and elsewhere in Mexico, which ultimately paved the way for privatization in 1991 (Rueda Peiro 1994; Minello and Barranco 1995).

The turn in the late 1980s toward a more neoliberal steel policy, including tariffs reduced to a maximum of 10% (well below the 40% allowed under GATT rules) in addition to the privatization of AHMSA, came in part as a result of pressures from the International Monetary Fund (IMF) on the Mexican federal government to restructure the country's debt, and to reorient the economy toward export-oriented industrialization. These policies, of course, continued to evolve once NAFTA was planned and approved (Cornejo 1994). The export-oriented policy resulted in some impressive gains in steel exports for Mexico, despite failing to overcome its trade deficit in steel.

2.4 The US Steel Industry and Related Policy, 1940–2002

Steel import tariffs were regularly imposed from 1870 to 1900 as the US steel industry, and presidents that supported it, prioritized a healthy domestic market with expanded production. Generally, though, steel import tariffs were minimal from 1900 to 1962. But in 1960, John F. Kennedy promised on the campaign trail to help industries harmed by too many imports in the latter 1950s, while maintaining the country's strong political and economic alliance with Europe. This balancing act was complicated by a tough tariff wall around the European Economic Community (EEC) that impacted US steel exports. To balance both objectives, his administration enacted the Trade Expansion Act (TEA) in 1962, a policy that impacted an array of imported goods, from textiles and apparel to poultry and steel. In 1959, for the first time in the twentieth century, steel imports exceeded exports, which drew Kennedy's attention. The resulting Section 232 of the TEA was based in part on national security concerns over supplies of steel, and in part to entice Europe to reduce tariffs (Irwin 2017). Section 232 of the TEA was later invoked by George W. Bush in 2002 and was the linchpin of Trump's steel policy in 2017–2018.

The Nixon Administration was the last to invoke Section 232 of the TEA before GATT became the WTO in 1995 (Schlesinger and Mauldin 2017). President Reagan generally opposed tariffs on imports, but during his first term (1981–1984), in response to an increase in steel imports due to dumping, his administration had pressured steel exporting countries to voluntarily cut their exports to the USA, a policy that Lyndon Johnson pursued in 1967 toward Japan and West Germany, and one that today would be illegal under WTO rules (Sanger 2002). This policy tool is referred to as a VRA, or Voluntary Restraint Agreement. Presidents Ford and Carter generally avoided tariffs and VRAs, to keep steel prices low for domestic metal fabricators, and to promote international goodwill during the Cold War; however, Reagan reacted to dumping, particularly by Europe, and enacted selected VRAs, including with Mexico (Irwin 2017). George H. W. Bush, bowing to pressures from large-scale consumers of steel, such as heavy machinery manufacturers, eventually rolled back all steel protections (Irwin 2017). In 1993, President Clinton, before he embraced neoliberalism, imposed duties on imported steel from 19 countries, including Mexico, which was illegal according to GATT rules. Clinton's rationale was to combat dumping, though it revealed once again the inevitable conflicting interests between steel makers on the one hand, and steel users and port workers on the other (Worthington 1993). Thus, US policy toward Mexico changed from one of supporting Mexican steel production and exports in the 1940s to one of protectionism against Mexican steel production in 1984 and 1993 (Irwin 2017; Rueda Peiro 1994).

2.5 Steel Policy and Trends in the USA Since 2000

In March of 2002, President George W. Bush enacted tariffs of up to 30% on imported steel from Asia, Europe, and South America (Martínez de Rituerto and Pozzi 2003). At the time, the USA imported a fourth of the steel it used. The administration invoked dumping as justification (Irwin 2017). The purpose was to enable US steel producers to enjoy some "breathing room" to become more competitive against foreign producers, and to reduce layoffs of steel workers. The tariffs signed into law were designed to expire in 3 years. The move set off an intense debate between ailing steel companies, like Bethlehem Steel, which had filed for bankruptcy on the one hand, and industries that purchased imported steel on the other. The latter claimed that the higher priced US-made steel might cause some companies that utilized the metal to shift operations to foreign countries. Indeed, many more metal-fabrication jobs in the USA were lost than those that would have been saved in steel plants, in large part because steel prices rose (Donnan 2018; Sanger 2002). The tariffs applied mostly to different forms of rolled steel and they did not apply to Mexico or Canada. The highest tariffs (30%) were applied to rolled steel, including tin plate, while slab steel, a raw material for smaller steel mills to smelt, was subject to a lower 10% tariff (Sanger 2002). Ultimately, the Bush Administration lifted the tariffs after 20 months, given that steel prices had risen by 70%, the WTO declared the tariffs illegal because Bush failed to prove dumping, and several trade partners threatened retaliatory tariffs on a host of US exports (Lee 2017). Furthermore, the fact that neither Mexico nor Canada were included in Bush's "selective tariff" scheme prompted the WTO to declare that the USA practiced a double standard (Martínez de Rituerto and Pozzi 2003).

Similar arguments against tariffs began swirling after President Trump announced in the summer of 2017 his intention to levy 30% tariffs on unspecified steel imported products from unspecified countries to combat dumping (De Haro 2017). As in 2002, the USA still imports about 25% of its steel, which remains a political issue in states such as Ohio that have lost steel manufacturing jobs. Critics of Trump's proposal point to the same problems anticipated (and that came to fruition) with the Bush tariffs, including higher prices to metal fabricators and other users of steel. Such industries, which tend to be small businesses, employ more than twenty times as many workers as do steel plants. Furthermore, the lack of precision of Trump's proposal in terms of the kinds of steel products involved left many users of imported steel products, which are not produced in sufficient quantities in the USA, feeling nervous.

What was different about Trump's proposal is that he invoked national security concerns as a way to skirt WTO rules against such tariffs. His administration argued that certain steel products were made by too few domestic producers, and tariffs were necessary to help more producers to compete with imports, by making more of such products as hot rolled steel and slab steel (Lee 2017; De Haro 2017). Trump's administration, including former Secretary of Commerce Wilbur Ross and former US Trade Representative Robert Lighthizer, argued correctly that global steel capacity is too high, leading many countries to dump product on the world market. However, the late 2010s surge in imports of steel by many users in the USA, including manufacturers of pipes and other metal fabricators, was driven more by market needs than by dumping or by stockpiling of imports in anticipation of tariffs (Economist 2018). Many economists speculated that Mexico would no longer be exempt from such tariffs, given Trump's promises on the campaign trail in 2016 to target the country. Furthermore, Trump's threatened cancellation of NAFTA early in his presidency caused Mexico and Canada to feel the threat of new tariffs (Donnan 2018).

The USA remains the world's largest steel importer, accounting for 19% of global steel imports in 2016, though the quantity imported had fallen somewhat that year, and fell dramatically to 9% in 2017 (WITA 2017; Morales 2016; US Department of Commerce 2019b). It has fairly consistently imported around 25–30% of its raw steel for at least the past decade, though the share of each source country from which steel is imported has shifted. For example, the share imported from China, against whom Trump railed quite regularly during the 2016 campaign, fell from 16% of the US market during the 2007–2008 recession, to 3% in 2016, while Canada became the top source. Mexico, the other target of Trump's rhetoric during his campaign and early in his presidency, went on to rank fourth among source countries in the late 2010s, after Canada, South Korea, and Brazil, and second by 2021 (Table 2.2). Speculation had heightened in early 2018 that Trump would attempt to levy tariffs against the North American trade partners (De Haro 2017; Economist 2018), though this ultimately did not occur.

Critics of Trump's plan to impose tariffs under Section 232 of the Trade Expansion Act of 1962 pointed to several problems with the proposed policy. First,

Table 2.2 The top five source countries of US steel imports, 2021

Country	Tonnage (millions)	Percent increase in 2021
Canada	6.970	34%
Mexico	4.760	44%
Brazil	4.365	8%
South Korea	2.748	36%
Russia	1.633	280%

Source: American Iron and Steel Institute (2022). Steel Imports up 43% in 2021. https://www.steel.org/2022/02/steel-imports-up-43-in-2021/

automotive manufacturers use many types of steel (in chassis, bodies, and other parts). To remain competitive in the global automobile market, the industry takes the position that steel tariffs would be harmful. Manufacturers of pipes, construction materials, machinery, and other users considered the uncertainty to be harmful, as reflected in higher steel prices. One small steel wire manufacturing company with 100 workers indicated that the total number of employees in steel fabrication manufacturing was nearly 100 times that of steel mills. Pipe and wire manufacturers concluded that they would have difficulties competing with German and other companies enjoying access to cheaper Chinese raw steel (Lee 2017). However, data from the Bureau of Labor Statistics indicates that the figure is closer to 20 times. A paradox of the Trump position is that many small steel manufacturers actually import steel slab to smelt down, yet it is unknown if steel slab would have been included in the proposed tariffs. Furthermore, port workers who handle steel imports warned of a downturn in port activities from Trump's proposals. Section 232 would surely have brought about either charges via the WTO, or retaliatory tariffs on various US goods in the name of national security. Critics point to the fact that Trump's proposal was designed to protect an industry that employed 140,000 workers, and that the 2002 Bush tariffs, which excluded the NAFTA partners, cost upwards of 200,000 job losses in steel and metal fabrication industries due to price increases of up to 70% (Lee 2017). It is reasonable to assume that if Mexico and Canada were actually targeted, job losses in the metal fabrication sector by 2020 would have been even greater than in 2002.

2.6 Recent (Post 2001) Steel Policy in Mexico

Despite Mexico's historic pattern of importing more steel overall than it exports, the country in recent years has been much less protectionist than it was immediately after World War II and until the privatization of AHMSA in Monclova. The latter occurred under the presidency of Carlos Salinas de Gortari (1988–1994), an ardent neoliberal policymaker who believed that Mexico could enter the global arena of the exportable steel trade. By 2016, Mexico, which ranked fourth among source countries of US steel imports, was the only country of the top ten exporters to the USA to not see declines in the penetration of the US market from 2015 to 2016 (Morales 2016).

Between 2007 and 2016, Mexican steel production increased from $240 to $369 billion Pesos. Production was highest in 2016 during the period, and lowest (at $224 billion) in 2009, the depth of recession. Employment in steel manufacturing, however, has steadily declined because of increased automation, from 130,205 in 2011 to 112,000 in 2016. In 2016, Mexico produced 18.8 million tons of total steel, an increase of 16% over 8 years. The State of Coahuila, where AHMSA is located, ranked first, and accounted for 29.5% of the country's production (CANACERO 2017). AHMSA and the State of Coahuila figure highly in federal steel trade policy, given the company's attempts to broaden its product offerings, and Coahuila's attempts to produce forward linkages locally and regionally, including in the USA. Citing employment data in the entire steel supply chain, from coal mining to steel mill outputs, officials and elected representatives of the State of Coahuila and executives of AHMSA have lobbied Mexico City to continue the minimal tariffs that exist on steel produced in countries like China, with which Mexico has no formal trade agreements (Zócalo Saltillo 2017).

Despite noteworthy increases in steel production and efficiency of production, Mexico saw in 2016 a continuation of its steel trade deficit with the USA. The trade balance in 2016 comprised exports of 4.5 million tons, imports of 13.9 million tons, and a resulting steel trade deficit of 9.4 million tons with its neighbor to the north (CANACERO 2017).

Mexico's then Secretary of Economy, Ildefonso Guajardo, highlighted 166 legal infractions (in accordance with WTO trade rules) in 2016 alone carried out by steel exporters to Mexico, most noteworthy China. For that reason, Mexico, in early 2017 imposed tariffs of up to 30% on imported steel produced by any country with which Mexico had no formal trade agreements (Rangel 2017). These tariffs, generally less than 10%, resulted largely from concerns on the part of leaders of AHMSA and officials of the State of Coahuila, including the governor's office and state- and federal-level legislators concerned about losses in steel manufacturing employment (Zócalo Saltillo 2017). Such activity demonstrates that, if it deems necessary, the Mexican federal government is well disposed to the use of tariffs on steel (and other) products, albeit minimally, since the neoliberal era of privatizations of the early 1990s.

2.7 Future Prospects for Binational Steel Trade

Despite the recent volatility of oil and natural gas prices, new rounds of investment are expected in Mexican hydrocarbon exploration and drilling, and, therefore, investment in the infrastructure needed for the growth and maintenance of these important energy resources. The multiplier effects produced by the oil and gas industry are considerable, especially in terms of supply chains for the necessary infrastructure and employment. This multiplier effect can be binational, especially considering Mexico's opening of its petroleum industry (natural gas and oil exploration) to foreign investment, which was expected to increase the demand for steel tubes and pipes produced on both sides of the border. One oft-cited narrative that (in this researcher's view) is misguided is the economic "threat" posed by continuing trade with Mexico, and the continued calls by admirers of the Trump Administration to levy tariffs on steel imports from Mexico. That view is indicative of a lack of understanding of the international nature of the production of steel in general, and in particular oil and gas infrastructure, such as tubing and pipes that utilize rolled steel. Likewise, in our neighboring country to the south, the term *incertidumbre* (uncertainty) is frequently used in the context of trade relationships with the USA overall, given the Trump Administration's lack of precision in trade policy other than frequent threats to scrap NAFTA and to impose such tariffs. Anti-neoliberal and pro-nationalization rhetoric on the part of current Mexican president López Obrador, with respect to energy production, adds to the uncertainty.

Given the increase in demand for gasoline and other petroleum products in Mexico, and its inability to meet its own domestic demand, the USA is well poised to see further increases in exports to Mexico of those products by rail and pipeline, notwithstanding López Obrador's call for more self-sufficiency in energy. A return to the 2018 energy policy could certainly translate to increased demand for US-made steel pipes for the growing gasoline, oil, and natural gas markets in Mexico (Martínez 2018). Because of the growth of its middle class, six of seven Mexican households use natural gas as its primary source of energy, and given that 65% of Mexico's gas is imported, the situation is favorable for the manufacture of steel pipes (Torres 2018). US steel plants remain at below capacity, but only in part because of imported raw steel, which, in 2017, accounted for 26% of demand by steel fabrication companies such as manufacturers of pipes of various diameters for the petroleum industry. To illustrate, Welspun, a Little Rock manufacturer of large diameter (24″–60″) pipe for oil transportation, including for the controversial Keystone XL Pipeline, could reasonably expect to sell products to a more open Mexican petroleum industry. Interestingly, the vast majority of the raw steel used by India-based Welspun is imported from India (Munson and Swanson 2017).

On his first day in office in January 2021, President Biden canceled the Keystone XL pipeline that lacked some 500 miles of completion. The company associated with the development of the pipeline, Alberta-based TC Energy, had attempted to lobby the Canadian government to convince Biden to reverse his decision, but in June 2021, TC Energy announced it would abandon the effort in light of PM Trudeau's reluctance to apply pressure on Biden. In 2020, under Trump, who revived the pipeline, Welspun Tubular LLC of Little Rock (located at the Port of Little Rock and using imported steel from India) obtained the contract to manufacture 190 miles of 36-inch diameter pipe; that manufacturing came to a halt upon the cancellation of the remainder of the pipeline from the Canadian border to Steele City, Nebraska (Southeast Nebraska) via Montana. Strong opposition to the pipeline had brewed since 2008 because tar sands require more greenhouse gases to process, and because the planned route passed through lands regarded as sensitive by indigenous groups (Brown 2021).

Table 2.3 Illustrates basic USA–Mexico steel trade data broken down by product category in 2017, soon before Trump proposed tariffs. The USA enjoys advantages in flat (rolled) raw steel and stainless steel. Mexico enjoys a slight trade advantage in the pipes and tubes category, long products (cable, rod, rail), and semi-finished products (US Commerce Department 2017a, b).

The USA produces 38% of the steel Mexico imports, while Mexico produces 9% of the steel the USA imports. Although Mexico has a steel trade deficit with the USA, it sends 69% of its exports to its neighbor to the north. Thus, tariffs enacted against Mexico would surely have resulted in retaliatory tariffs that would have damaged the US steel industry, as well as US companies supplying raw materials like scrap metal, iron, coke, coal, and recycled steel, and companies exporting pipes,

Table 2.3 USA–Mexico steel trade data, January–September 2017, millions of metric tons

Product category	Mexican exports to the USA	US exports to Mexico
Flat (Rolled) Products	0.65	1.33
Long Products	0.4	0.28
Pipe/Tube	0.65	0.1
Semi-Finished	0.7	0.02
Stainless Steel	0.1	0.22

Source: US Department of Commerce (2017a, b)

Table 2.4 Mexico steel imports, 2018

Product category	Imports, millions of tons	US portion of total imports
Flat (rolled) products	6.8	35%
Long products	1.5	35%
Semi-finished (slab)	1.5	5%
Stainless steel	0.665	58%
Pipe/tube	0.583	28%

Source: US Department of Commerce (2019b)

tubes, cable, and construction materials. Mexico made it quite clear during the NAFTA renegotiations that its steel industry would be protected if necessary, and the proof that this was not a bluff was the precedent for imposing tariffs on steel imported from non-NAFTA countries (Lara 2017a, b). President Trump had until April 11, 2018 to decide whether domestic steel production was in such bad shape as to constitute a national security problem, and therefore, whether to invoke Article 232 (Cassella 2018). Steel manufacturers were delighted that the likelihood was high of such a finding, while metal fabrication companies and advocates for consumers were not. The Mexican government and steel industry, US metal fabricators, and economic development stakeholders on both sides of the border were, needless to say, quite relieved when the tariff threat receded, and the tariffs ultimately were not imposed.

Table 2.4 illustrates Mexican steel imports in 2018 by product category, and the portion of the totals originating in the USA.

2.8 Two Locality-Scale Snapshots of the Steel Industry: Jewett, Texas and Monclova, Coahuila

Two brief case studies of communities that rely on steel manufacturing for local economic development shed light on ways that the steel industry functions at multiple scales. One case is a rural community in East Texas whose dominant employer is a small steel plant. The second case is a mid-sized northern Mexican city that is home of that country's largest steel mill.

2.8.1 Steel Production in a Rural Community of East Texas

Jewett is a town of some 1220 people (2019) in East-Central Texas 70 miles east of Waco, 130 miles north-northwest of Houston, and 115 miles south-southeast of Dallas. The town is at the junction of a north-south BNSF rail line, and a west-east UP line. Nucor's Jewett Plant is located on the west side of town on US Highway 79, adjacent to the UP-BNSF junction, in rural Leon County. One of four Nucor plants in Texas, the Jewett plant utilizes electric arc furnace technology for melting scrap metal. For the rural area of which the town is part, the plant, which employs 425, is important to the local economy, which spills over into adjoining counties that are part of its laborshed. Indeed, it is the largest employer in the county (K. Vandegriff, personal communication, April 20, 2022). The plant commenced operation in 1975. Today it produces steel bars, especially rebar used in construction, at a rate of about 900,000 tons annually (Global Energy Monitor Wiki 2020). The plant's annual production capacity after its upgrade in 2002 is a million tons. The plant receives scrap (shredded steel) from metal recyclers, particularly in the Waco and Dallas-Fort Worth regions (Recycling Today 2002). Union Pacific Railroad (UP) transports much of the scrap and other recyclable steel to the plant's property, which has three spurs connected to the main rail line. Rebar and other steel bar is shipped from the plant by truck (K. Vandegriff, personal communication, April 20, 2022). Ironically, considering that some stakeholders in the local economy favored the Trump-era tariffs on Mexican steel, 100% of foreign sales of steel produced in Jewett are for the Mexican market (Panjiva 2022).

2.8.2 Steel Production and Forward Linkages in Monclova, Coahuila, Mexico

The Mexican federal government established AHMSA in 1942 as a result of wartime global shortages of steel, and the decision to produce more steel domestically than was the case at the time. Harold Pape, an official with the giant American steel company ARMCO (American Rolling Mills Company), oversaw the establishment of the plant in Monclova, the facilities of which were a dismantled shuttered ARMCO plant in St. Louis. The USA favored the establishment of a steel plant within close proximity to the border in light of the shortages of rolled steel products. AHMSA represented a major economic development initiative in Monclova, not only for the creation of its large workforce, but also the worker housing the company built. The combined population of Monclova and Ciudad Frontera nearly doubled from 16,864 in 1940 to 32,614 in 1950 (Yoder 1999). Pape not only oversaw construction and initial operation of the plant but he envisioned the establishment of additional companies that could buy output from the mill for further processing, and therefore, the establishment of forward economic linkages in the community. To accomplish that, he formed a consortium of small enterprises under the umbrella of Grupo Industrial de Monclova, S.A. (GIMSA). In 1991, the government adopted a more neoliberal posture, and began to privatize many state-owned enterprises, including AHMSA. The layoffs from privatization freed up a workforce for the companies affiliated with GIMSA, which sought to export as much of the metal-related products the companies under its umbrella produced (Yoder 2000). The move by the government to privatize was designed primarily to unleash efficiencies as well as to boost export-oriented industrialization (Yoder 2009).

Today the company's two blast furnaces produce rolled steel products in several configurations, including hot rolled steel, cold rolled steel, steel plate, chrome laminated steel, and tin plate. The company boasts of being the only producer in Mexico of steel plate (AHMSA 2022). In addition to these finished products, the plant also produces liquid steel, much of which is of use to local metal processors. The company accounts for 12% of Mexico's finished steel exports, 24% of total national production of rolled steel products, and 13% of total Mexican steel production (Argus 2019). Prior to the Trump-era tariffs, AHMSA's exports, all of which were sent to USMCA partner countries, represented 12% of total sales; the tariffs reduced exports by 25%, or 100,000 tons during that period. By late 2018, exports from AHMSA had rebounded to a total of 454,000 tons that year, close to the pre-tariff level (Argus 2019).

Local economic development stakeholders, including those of the governments of the State of Coahuila, and the municipalities of Monclova and Ciudad Frontera, continue to build on a strategy that began in the 1990s upon privatization of AHMSA. Since then, there has been a robust effort to promote the forward linkages of steel in the immediate area. By 2005, a fifth of the plant's output was processed locally in metal fabrication companies (Yoder 2009). For more than two decades, GIMSA has developed a manufacturing base to utilize AHMSA steel for such products as railroad tank and hopper cars for export, and custom die casting and steel parts for metal smelting plants (GIMSA 2022). PROMSA operates a metal processing plant that utilizes steel from the AHMSA plant, as does IMMSA, a manufacturer of trash collection trucks and dumpsters (PROMSA 2022). Thus, Harold Pape's vision of creating a metallurgical cluster in Monclova has largely been realized. The municipal government of Monclova continues to work with the economic promotion arm of the Coahuila state government, and has created the Economic Development Council (Consejo de Desarrollo Municipal) to promote the Central Coahuila Region for domestic and foreign investment in manufacturing through marketing and the offering of incentives, primarily tax abatements and provision of infrastructure and worker training (Mexicano 2022; Yoder 2009).

2.9 Conclusions: Sizing Up USA–Mexico Steel Trade Policy

Clearly, the USA and Mexico have pursued similar steel trade policies, though at different times. While in its earliest stages, US policy protected the steel industry through heavy tariffs even though the vast majority of the industry was oriented to the domestic market. By contrast, Mexican policy in the beginning favored a secure supply of the least expensive steel possible, and de-prioritized tariffs. The post-World War II period saw something of a reversal of policy, because the US dominated global markets, and Mexico was entering the import substitution phase of economic development. After the privatization of AHMSA, Mexico again pursued less protectionist policies, while the USA continued to place occasional tariffs on imports, as domestic production increasingly slipped in comparison to national capacity. Mexico has largely been spared the tariffs enacted by the USA toward non-NAFTA countries until the thinking aloud in 2016–2018 by the recent populist US president, who eventually suspended tariffs on Mexican and Canadian steel and aluminum as leverage in the USMCA negotiations. In trade policy during the Trump era, uncertainty reigned supreme. Since then, trade has been robust, albeit with a temporary Covid-related downturn. Communities dependent on steel, such as Monclova and Jewett, continue to experience thriving manufacturing that underlies their economic development. The two communities' steel manufacturing illustrates the complementarity between the USA and Mexico in steel production, and the lack of need for protective tariffs that would hamper economic development at the binational and local scales.

References

AHMSA (2022) Altos Hornos de Mexico, S.A. Nuestros Productos Retrieved February 10, 2022, from https://www.ahmsa.com/nuestros-productos/

Argus (2019) Mexico's Ahmsa to boost output after US tariffs lifted. Argus Media, May 21. https://www.argusmedia.com/en/news/1906966-mexicos-ahmsa-to-boost-output-after-us-tariffs-lifted

Brown M (2021) Plan dead to build Keystone pipeline, Arkansas Democrat Gazette, June 10. https://www.arkansasonline.com/news/2021/jun/10/plan-dead-to-build-keystone-pipeline/

CANACERO (2017) Infografía de la Industria de Acero en México 2017. Cámara Nacional de la Industria del Hierro y del Acero de México. Retrieved December 23, 2017, from http://www.canacero.org.mx/En/assets/infografia_de_la_industria_del_acero_en_mexico_2017.pdf

CANACERO (2019) México Panorama Siderúrgico 2018. Cámara Nacional de la Industria del Hierro y del Acero de México. Retrieved May 18, 2022, from https://www.canacero.org.mx/aceroenmexico/descargas/infografia_canacero_2019.pdf

Cassella M (2018) Commerce sends Section 232 steel report to Trump. Politico, January 12. https://www.politico.com/newsletters/morning-trade/2008/01/12/commerce-sends-section-232-steel-report-to-trump-072717

Cornejo OS (1994) La industria siderúrgica mexicana y AHMSA ante el TLC. In: Rueda Peiro I (ed) Tras las huellas de la privatización: El caso de Altos Hornos de México. Siglo Venitiuno Editores and Instituto de Investiaciones Económicos, UNAM, pp 233–266

Corrales S (1996) Notas sobre la historia económica de La Consolidada, S.A.(1936-1991). Estud Front 37-38:157–178

De Haro JL (2017) Los aranceles de Trump al acero extranjero desatarán la próxima guerra commercial. Economia Hoy, July 17. http://www.economiahoy.mx/economia-eAm-mexico/noticias/8502185/07/17/Los-aranceles-de-Trump-al-acero-extranjero-desataran-la-proxima-guerra-comercial.html

Donnan S (2018) La historia puede darle un revés a Trump con los aranceles. Financial Times, January 21. http://www.elfinanciero.com.mx/financial-times/la-historia-puede-darle-un-reves-a-trump-con-los-aranceles.html

Economist (2018) America's trade policies: steel wars. Economist, January 13, p 63

Expansión (2017) El gas natural, negocio que le deja a EU 3,600 MDD desde México, Expansión, April 6. http://expansion.mx/empresas/2017/04/06/el-gas-natural-un-negocio-de-3-600-mdd-entre-mexico-y-eu

GIMSA (2022) Grupo Industrial de Monclova S.A. de C,V. Retrieved March 2, 2022, from http://www.cegimsa.com.mx/division-industrial.php

Global Energy Monitor Wiki (2020) Nucor Steel Jewett Plant. Retrieved March 8, 2022, from https://www.gem.wiki/Nucor_Steel_Jewett_plant

Handy RM (2017) Trump spurs hope in Texas town that relies on oil, coal and steel. Houston Chronicle, January 19. http://www.houstonchronicle.com/business/article/Trump-spurs-hope-in-town-that-relies-on-oil-coal-10867258.php

Irwin DA (2017) Clashing Over Commerce: A History of US Trade Policy. University of Chicago Press

Lara R (2017a) EU endurecerá sus importaciones de acero. Manufactura, January 24. http://www.manufactura.mx/industria/2017/01/24/eu-puede-endurecer-sus-importaciones-de-acero

Lara R (2017b) Después del azúcar, el acero está en la mira de una guerra comercial. Expansión, June 28. https://expansion.mx.empresas/2017/06/28/despues-del-azucar-el-acero-esta-en-la-mira-de-una-guerra-comercial

Lee D (2017) Trump's plan to slap tariffs on steel imports carries big economic and political risks. Los Angeles Times, June 28. http://www.latimes.com/business/la-fi-steel-tariffs-20170628-story.html

Martínez E (2018) Más autos y más gasoline impulsan el negocio de…¿los ferrocarriles? El Financiero, February 8. http://www.elfinanciero.com.mx/empresas/mas-autos-y-mas-gasolina-impulsan-el-negocio-de-los-ferrocarriles

Martínez de Rituerto R, Pozzi S (2003) La OMC oblige a Estados Unidos a eliminar los aranceles a las importaciones de acero. El Pais, November 11. https://elpais.com/diario/2003/11/11/economia/1068505216_850215.html

Mexicano L (2022) Crean Ayuntamiento de Monclova el Consejo de Desarrollo Económico con apoyo de empresarios, Vanguardia MX, February 11. https://vanguardia.com.mx/coahila/crean-ayuntamiento-de-monclova-el-consejo-de-desarrollo-economico-con-apoyo-de-empresarios-XF172237

Minello N, Barranco L (1995) El Desarrollo de una Industria Básica: Altos Hornos de México 1942–1988. Arte y Cultura Monclova, S.A

Morales R (2016) México, único proveedor de acero de EU con avance. El Economista, December 22. https://www.eleconomista.com.mx/empresas/Mexico-unico-proveedor-de-acero-de-EU-con-avance-20161222-0016.html

Munson S, Swanson A (2017) If Trump wants the pipes built in America, what does that mean? Washington Post, February 24. https://www.washingtonpost.com/business/economy/if-trump-wants-the-pipes-built-in-america-what-does-that-mean/2017/02/24/2dae1176-faaf-11e6-bf01-d47f8cf9b643_story.html?utm_term=.3eab1e4b1057

Nucor (2018) Products. Nucor Corporation. Retrieved January 3, 2018, from http://www.nucor.com/products/locations/us/

Panjiva (2022) Panjiva S&P global market intelligence. Retrieved March 5, 2022, from https://panjiva.com/Nucor-Steel_Jewett-Texas/31800034

PROMSA (2022) PROMSA, Procesadora de Metales Santa Ana. Retrieved March 2, 2022, from http://www.promsa-mva.com/empresa.php

Rangel M (2017) Los aranceles que aplica México. Milenio.com, February 28. Retrieved January 31, 2018, from http://www.milenio.com/firmas/j-_jesus_rangel_m/aranceles-aplica-mexico-impuestos-cuotas-empresas_exportadoras-dumping-milenio_18_911488843.html

Recycling Today (2002) Nucor increases investment in Texas mill. Recycling Today, June 27. https://www.recyclingtoday.com/article/nucor-increases-investment-in-texas-mill/

Rueda Peiro I (1994) El contexto. In: Rueda Peiro I (ed) Tras las huellas de la privatización: El caso de Altos Hornos de México. Siglo Veintiuno Editores & Instituto de Investigaciones, Universidad Nacional Autónoma de México, pp 21–59

Sanger DE (2002) Bush puts tariffs of as much as 30% on steel imports. The New York Times, March 6. http://www.nytimes.com/2002/03/06/us/bush-puts-tariffs-of-as-much-as-30-on-steel-imports.html

Schlesinger J, Mauldin W (2017) Trump to revive 1962 law to explore new barriers on steel imports. Wall Street Journal: Market Watch, April 20. https://www.wsj.com/articles/trump-to-revive-1962-law-to-explore-new-barriers-on-steel-imports-1492661339

Torres A (2018) Heladas en UE, la antesala de un 'gaselepazo' en México. El Financiero, September 1. http://www.elfinanciero.com.mx/economia/heladas-en-eu-la-antesala-de-un-gaselepazo-en-mexico.html?utm_source=El+Financiero&utm_campaign=6

US Department of Commerce (2017a) International Trade Administration. Mexico Country Commercial Guide, Mexico-Trade Barriers, September 17. Retrieved January 18, 2018, from https://www.export.gov/article?id=Mexico-Trade-Barriers

US Department of Commerce (2017b) International Trade Administration. Steel Imports Report: Mexico. Global Steel Trade Monitor, September. Retrieved January 18, 2018, from https://www.trade.gov/steel/countries/pdfs/2017/q2/imports-mexico.pdf

US Department of Commerce (2019a) International Trade Association. Steel Imports Report: United States. Global Steel Trade Monitor, March. https://legacy.trade.gov/steel/countries/pdfs/2018/annual/imports-us.pdf

US Department of Commerce (2019b) International Trade Administration. Steel Imports Report: Mexico. Global Steel Trade Monitor, May. https://legacy.trade.gov/steel/countries/pdfs/2018/annual/imports-mexico.pdf

WITA (Washington International Trade Association) (2017) Steel imports report. Retrieved January 18, 2018, from http://americastradepolicy.com/steel-imports-report-united-states/#.WmeEfa6nFdi

Worthington R (1993) Good, bad from U.S. Steel Tariffs. Chicago Tribune, May 24. Retrieved March 27, 2018, from http://articles.chicagotribune.com/1993-05-24/business/9305240172_1_steel-tariffs-steel-companies-american-steel

Yoder M (1999) Monclova, Coahuila: The Social Geography of a Medium-Sized Industrial City in Northern Mexico. SECOLAS Annals 11(1):122–132

Yoder M (2000) Northeast Mexico in the global economy: the contemporary urban geographies of three mid-sized cities. Aldo Tatangelo Annual Lecture in the College of Arts and Humanities, Texas A&M International University, April 18

Yoder M (2009) Landscapes of Industry and Transport: Monclova and Torreón, Mexico. Journal of Big Bend Studies 21:179–200

Zócalo Saltillo (2017) Tranquilidad a AHMSA; aranceles aprobados. Zócalo Saltillo, October 18. Retrieved February 5, 2018, from http://www.zocalo.com.mx/seccion/articulo/tranquilidad-a-ahmsa-aranceles-aprobados

Chapter 3
Inland Ports of Mexico and the Geography of Intermodal Shipping

Abstract The movement of freight and the associated logistics are essential components of the fields of economic geography and economic development. Studies of supply chains, connections between (and within) firms, and the infrastructure to bring them about are important toward building deeper understandings of the geography of economic development. Research on maritime ports goes a long way toward illuminating changes in globalization and regionalization, but largely absent are studies of interior ports, or "dry ports," that link to maritime ports and allow the transfer of cargo between rail and truck away from the shoreline. This chapter examines three inland ports of Mexico as important features of the country's cargo transportation and logistics. The three are not only intermodal transfer facilities but are likewise industrial parks that make land available to manufacturers in need of direct rail and highway access. They include Guanajuato Puerto Interior, Interpuerto San Luís Potosí, and Interpuerto Monterrey. The chapter includes overviews of the private–public partnership in their planning and their provision of industrial sites. The chapter concludes that the three dry ports enhance Mexico's ability to attract nearshoring of manufacturing activities from East Asia, and to build on the country's development of a freight transportation land bridge linking ports on both coasts with the USA.

Keywords Inland ports · Transportation geography · Nearshoring · USMCA · USA · Mexico trade · Guanajuato · San Luís Potosí · Monterrey

3.1 Introduction

The movement of cargo is an important part of the historical geography of capitalism. It reflects shifting patterns of investment, of connectivity between places, and of the creation of infrastructure and other features of the built environment. Studies of supply chains, inter- and intra-firm connections, and related infrastructure are needed to enhance a deeper understanding of regional development in the context of globalization (Coe et al. 2004). However, the geographies of cargo transport and

M. S. Yoder, *Geographical Scale and Economic Development*,
https://doi.org/10.1007/978-3-031-36197-5_3

logistics are underrepresented in the economic geography and economic development literature in comparison to their weight in the global economy. In particular, the growing trend of the creation of inland ports, which redefine and often broaden the hinterlands of maritime "blue" ports, is worthy of additional study, given the role of such facilities in shaping the changing spatial patterns of the global economy (Rodrigue et al. 2010; Hesse and Rodrigue 2004).

This chapter examines inland ports of Mexico as important features of the country's cargo transportation and logistics. Using qualitative research, the study draws geographic inferences of inland ports from published content in the Mexican business press and on web sites of logistics and transport companies. It relies on a small number of open-ended interviews of logistics service providers, economic development leaders, and trucking company management. While aggregate data exist on the numbers of rail cars and truck trailers that move throughout the country, very little exists outside of corporate offices on the actual origins and destinations of cargo. Through three case studies of inland ports of Mexico, the chapter provides insights applicable to such interrelated themes as the roles of inland ports to Mexico's export-oriented manufacturing, the increasing sophistication of the movement of goods for both domestic and foreign markets, and implications of such infrastructure investment for the development of supply chains. The three case studies include facilities in Silao (Guanajuato), San Luís Potosí, and Monterrey (see Fig. 1.2). The chapter includes discussion of inter-urban connectivity, and the continued development of dominant cargo transportation (highway and rail) corridors in Mexico. It briefly addresses the marketing of the inland ports and the provision of incentives to attract mostly foreign investment to those sites, through the construction of manufacturing plants.

While not yet as developed as their counterparts in the USA and Western Europe, inland ports of Mexico are nonetheless growing in importance as the country experiences globalization to a greater extent, and economic growth in general. To illustrate, while the North American trade region remains strong globally compared with such core areas as the European Union, the value of truck and rail cargo shipments between the three countries has fluctuated; however, shipments between the USA and Mexico continue to see increases in value overall, notwithstanding a temporary Coronavirus-related downturn in 2022. Bidirectional trade in goods between Mexico and the USA amounted to $661.2 billion in 2021, and cross-border trade between the three North American countries represents 16% of global trade (US Department of Commerce 2021). Thus, the potential for growth in the importance of inland ports is obvious, which justifies further studies of that and related infrastructure.

Cargo transport systems and the logistics industry are deeply intertwined functionally and in terms of their geographies. Changes in the location and scale of manufacturing are directly related to those of logistics, which, broadly defined, is the collection of activities involved in the physical distribution of finished goods, and the management (storage and inventorying) of raw materials and other inputs (Murphy and Knemeyer 2015; Hesse and Rodrigue 2004). Logistics includes a wide array of activities, from supply chain management, to the physical movement of cargo, and warehousing. Such activities have increasingly become outsourced to experts in tandem with similar trends in manufacturing. The logistics industry continues to evolve in order to enhance uninterrupted production and flows of goods and production information across borders, as global capitalism requires (Aoyama et al. 2006). Thus, logistics is inherently geographic. For example, in Mexico, logistics company advertisements in trade publications and their web sites promote not only the services they provide in the linking of disparate locations, but also the merits of the locations where they operate. As the case studies in this chapter reveal, Mexican logistics service providers, particularly those who affiliate with intermodal inland ports, tend to favor specific cargo transport corridors.

Logistics as a percentage of gross domestic product (GDP) varies considerably by country. For example, in the USA the weight of logistics was 8.5% and in Vietnam it was 22.0% in 2014. The figure was 9.9% in Mexico in 2012 (Bonney 2012). Even in the countries where the weight of logistics in national economies is lower than the global average, it nonetheless comprises a high percentage of GDP; therefore, that sector of the economy warrants further study, including its geographical expressions in the form of interior ports, industrial parks, and other such landscape features that can be quite prominent.

While inland ports share many similarities with their maritime counterparts, they likewise demonstrate unique characteristics. As special nodes, they have two main geographic components in need of study: connections to other cities and regions from which cargo originates and to which cargo flows, and the logistics and manufacturing activities occurring within the immediate area. Thus, the concepts of "hinterlands" and "forelands" ascribed to maritime ports are more difficult to define in the case of inland ports. Furthermore, maritime ports almost always have larger cranes for containers, given that container ships handle much higher stacks than rail cars or trucks. Inland ports' crane equipment must be nimble, to accomplish those facilities' goals of speeding up the handling of cargo into interior areas as part of overall more efficient logistics (Soto Correa 2009).

Given that they function as nodes, inland ports are appropriate topics of study to assist in telling the story of the geography of manufacturing and logistics, especially through case studies. All interior "dry" ports involve intermodal shipping, and they continue to emerge and grow in tandem with increased global shipments of containers. To become successful, they require direct, high-capacity connections to maritime ports, and are crucial to enhancing maritime ports' economies of scale by relocating to remote locations those port activities that use up scarce land. Thus, they are an important component of global supply chains, and are among the more important features of cargo transportation infrastructure that impact upon the efficiency of maritime ports (Rodrigue et al. 2010; Notteboom and Rodrigue 2007).

Containerization not only has enabled more rapid and efficient movement of goods across the globe, but likewise has ushered a more dynamic and expanded set of connections between maritime ports and their resulting enlarged onshore hinterlands (Rodrigue and Notteboom 2010; Roso et al. 2009). Furthermore, when additional value-added activities, such as manufacturing, are located near inland ports, supply chains and logistics not only become more efficient but greater engines of economic development (Leitner and Harrison 2001).

3.2 Inland Ports: The Three Main Types

There are three basic categories of inland ports, based on a simplification of the rather elaborate typologies provided in the transport geography literature. They include river (barge) ports, binational ports along borders, and interior, or "dry" ports. The latter are either the onshore spillover of maritime ports, or intermodal facilities at strategic locations near manufacturing or airfield-oriented distribution centers, such as Chicago, Kansas City, Memphis, and Leipzig. Dry ports are specifically connected to maritime ports by rail and move the land-hungry activities of intermodal containerization away from the crowded coastal area, though the other two categories of inland ports are also linked to maritime ports (Fleming and Hayuth 1994; Ng and Gujar 2009). Rail is a key component of inland ports because of its greater economies of scale compared to trucking. Logistics services provided at inland ports that add value to the supply chain include customs activities (paperwork and inspections, especially at border inland ports), scheduling of shipments and deliveries, warehousing, and even packaging (Roso et al. 2009). Because of their increasing importance to the development of supply chains and their contribution to value added, both the private and public sectors have a vested interest in them, and their financing often involves private–public partnerships (Rodrigue et al. 2010). The proximity of dry ports and border ports to manufacturing activity provides enhanced just-in-time or just-in-sequence deliveries (Roso et al. 2009). As such, public–private partnership in financing the planning and construction of cargo transport infrastructure is evident in the case study areas.

3.3 Inland Ports of Mexico: An Overview

Most of Mexico's inland ports are located in the northern half of the country, where the manufacturing and logistics activities associated initially with NAFTA, and now USMCA, are most heavily located. These nodes of cargo interchange between truck and rail have been promoted by the Secretariat of Communication and Transport (SCT) of the Mexican government, by rail companies, and by other actors of the logistics industry as a means of transferring cargo more efficiently between the country's maritime ports, the larger metropolitan areas of the interior, and the ports located along the USA–Mexico border (Soto Correa 2009). In 1992, the SCT opened up inland ports to private investment, both for development and operation of intermodal ports, as well as associated industrial parks. The latter change in law allowed for private companies to acquire existing state-run intermodal facilities in dry and maritime ports of Mexico (Salazar et al. 2014).

The value of truck and rail shipments combined between the USA and Mexico continues to increase in both directions, led by produce, parts and components (inputs for manufacturing), and machinery (USDOT 2016). Overall, freight shipments by rail increased 14.6% between 2010 and 2015, from 104.6 to 119.6 million tons. The top two rail companies in Mexico are Ferromex (formerly a state-owned enterprise that is now private) and Kansas City Southern de México (KCSM). They dominate rail shipment in the center and north of the country. Ferromex experienced an increase in total shipments (domestic, export, and import) of 59% between 2004 and 2015, and KCSM experienced a corresponding 23% increase (Martínez 2016c). In particular, the increased usage of rail shipments within Mexico is led by the automotive industry, which has relevance for the three case-study interior ports of this study (Martínez 2016a). Exports shipped by rail increased 41.4% by weight between 2014 and 2015 to 18 million tons, led by assembled automobiles, shipping containers, and beer (Martínez 2016d). While rail cargo shipments measured by weight and value remain one-fifth those by truck, the rail sector, and rail-truck interchange nonetheless are regarded as having greater growth potential than trucking alone (Martínez 2016b; Soto Correa 2009).

The three ports are important sites of *maquiladoras*, or in-bond assembly plants that dominate Mexico's export-oriented manufacturing. The Mexican government established this category of assembly plants in the mid-1960s to alleviate unemployment in the far north of the country while attracting foreign direct investment. Furthermore, the plants were intended to provide reduced duties and tariffs on imports of components and exports of finished products to the USA. Although maquiladoras originally were set up to receive US investment, companies from regions such as East Asia and Europe could invest as well. With the implementation of NAFTA in 1994, companies could establish maquiladoras deeper into Mexico, beyond the immediate border zone adjoining the USA; therefore, the program's streamlined customs functions and reduced tariffs were no longer limited to Mexican border cities, but to all regions of the country. That said, the northern states remain important for locating maquiladoras because of their proximity to the US market. Furthermore, policies in Mexico related to maquiladoras have been liberalized to the point that foreign investors can partner with Mexican-owned businesses and have the option to set up a "virtual" company through a "corporate shelter service," whereby one of a number of companies based in the USA and Mexico operate the Mexican plant for the foreign investor (Tecma Group 2023).

The fortunes of all three of the case-study inland ports are tied to the automotive industry, in terms of both finished vehicles and components. They rely increasingly on manufacturing of aerospace (aviation) components, though to a lesser extent than on automobile parts and components. In both cases, however, local supply chains remain underdeveloped. Specialty operations, such as powder coating, anodizing, polishing, and chemical (liquid) filling, often need to be done in the USA, which then requires that components be shipped across the border for these specialty services, and later shipped back to Mexico for additional supply-chain activity (Trimble 2016). This decentralization of production within North America has implications for Mexico's inland ports as the shipment of components is increased in light of less-than desired supply chain development in Mexico, and as industrial parks adjacent to the transport hubs become desirable localities for companies providing specialty services for the larger manufacturers. That is, supply chain development in Mexico would depend in large part on inland ports.

One key component of the marketing of inland ports of Mexico, especially those in which rail companies were instrumental in their development, relates to the advantages of that mode of cargo transport. Trucks are flexible in terms of arrivals and departures, and continue to dominate in Mexico's cargo shipments, including shipments to and from the USA. However, trucking is subject to slowdowns at the border. One reason is that, by law, Mexican customs brokers assume responsibility for the goods shipped, and the reliability of paperwork, whereas in most countries, the importer takes on those responsibilities. Because of the arrangement, Mexican customs brokers must conduct thorough and time-consuming inspections to avoid irregularities that might jeopardize their licenses (Ornelas 2016).

An additional time-consuming characteristic of shipping by truck in Mexico relates to the crossing of trailers from the USA into Mexico, and the requirement that a Mexican truck driver hauls the trailer across the border. In some cases, an additional "handoff" occurs, whereby the driver moving the trailer across the border, via a process called "drayage," delivers it ("hands it off") to the chosen Mexican customs broker, who hands it off to a Mexican trucking company, which then hauls it to its destination (Ornelas 2016). This additional drayage step is mandatory in Laredo-Nuevo Laredo. At other crossings, the Mexican trucker hauling merchandise to and from the interior of Mexico can cross to the immediate border zone on the US side to pick up or deliver trailers (F. Gonzalez, personal communication, May 27, 2016). The fact that all goods in a given trailer must be processed by a sole Mexican customs broker, tends to create the need for full load shipments. The latter, then, require that warehousing be set up in US border cities, especially El Paso and Laredo. Shipments are therefore delayed until a full truck load bound for a given customs broker can be assembled via the process of warehousing consolidation (Ornelas 2016). Rail, according to its promoters, can avoid all of this complication by moving cargo from the border directly to its destination, such as an inland port. The latter is particularly streamlined if the destination is a free trade zone, or *recinto fiscalizado estratégico* (RFE) (WTC SLP 2016).

It is common for Mexico's maritime ports, the largest of which are private–public partnerships, and the private railroad companies to form agreements for creation of corridors and both dry (interior) and maritime intermodal ports. Mexican Customs (*Aduana*) is likewise an actor in establishing such corridors and interior ports (É Logística 2010; Soto Correa 2009). For example, municipal, state-level, and federal public participation, especially the SCT (Secretaría de Comunicaciones y Transportes), in the planning process of inland ports is designed to leverage private investment in the intermodal facilities as well as manufacturing and warehousing facilities in the adjacent industrial parks, which theoretically would feed on itself to attract yet more such investment. The master plan typically is driven by the public sector at all three levels, with participation from private developers of industrial parks and stakeholders of logistics and rail companies (Mendoza Ruiz 2011).

State governments strive to attract investment in manufacturing plants (*maquiladoras*) within or near the industrial parks that accompany the dry ports. This is a trend that has accelerated since the decentralization of Mexico's economic policymaking away from Mexico City and to the different state capitals. Thus, the states are as keen as the federal government to see foreign direct investment (FDI) in the country. One such initiative is the provision of fiscal and other types of incentives to companies, whether foreign or domestic, to supplement other site advantages of a given location, such as the local workforce, the availability of energy, and transport connectivity. Each state is different in its provision of incentives, and each recognizes that incentives are not the primary asset that attracts companies. Some states offer land, some pay for workforce development, and many provide tax abatements, mostly in proportion to the promised addition to local employment numbers (Lara and Durán 2013).

3.4 The Three Case Studies

I selected the three inland port case studies based in part on geographic criteria (they are in different areas of the country where the automotive industry is important), and on the fact that the involvement of the country's two largest rail companies differs in each. Guanajuato Puerto Interior is affiliated with Ferromex, and more recently with BNSF through its partnership with Ferromex. It is in the middle of a large automotive cluster, toward the west end of the Bajío region. Interpuerto San Luis Potosí is a project in which KCS de México, the country's second largest rail carrier, has been heavily involved. That city, a growing automotive center and the site of the country's first RFE immediately adjacent to the interior port, is at the northern end of El Bajío. Interpuerto Monterrey involves both Ferromex and KCS de México. The inland port is located in the country's second largest industrial region, and one that is experiencing growth in automotive-related manufacturing, especially parts and components. Thus, each locality is unique, and each is important in the shipping and logistics industry of Mexico. All three are suitable examples of the decentralization of industry away from Mexico City after the devastating 1985 earthquake, and the resulting boost in infrastructure development in and between many urban areas outside Mexico City to accommodate this spatial shift in economic development (J. Acevedo, personal communication, December 7, 2021).

3.4.1 Guanajuato Puerto Interior (GPI)

Conceived in 2006, GPI is presently the largest logistics center in the country and, by some measures, the fourth largest interior dry port in the world (Oropeza 2014, 2015a; J. Acevedo, personal communication, December 7, 2021). It employed over 10,000 people by 2015, and had received over three billion Pesos in investment since its creation (Madrazo 2015). It consists of four separate industrial parks, clustered close to the state's major airport, El Bajio International, in the municipality of Silao (Fig. 3.1). As of late 2014, three of the parks were filled and the fourth was 67% occupied. In 2015, the port had 93 present and future resident companies,

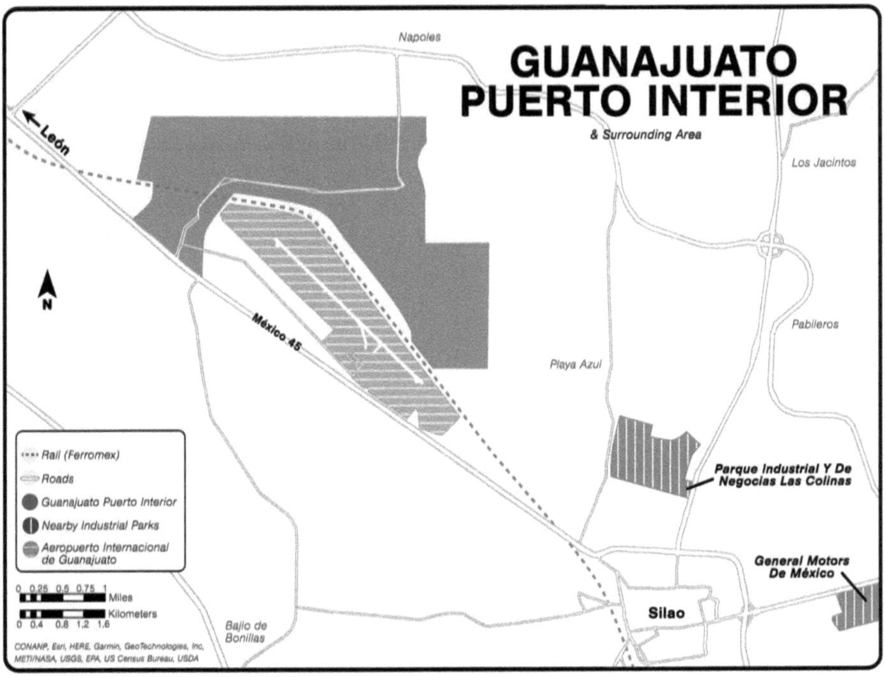

Fig. 3.1 Map of Guanajuato Puerto Interior. (By Noah Walker)

representing investments from 15 countries (led by Japan, and secondly by Mexico), but by 2021 the number had increased to 127 companies based in 18 countries (GPI 2021). Among the dozen economic sectors represented at the port are automotive plants, logistics companies, pharmaceutical companies, and apparel/footwear manufacturers (Rodríguez Canales 2014; Madrazo 2015; Cluster Industrial 2015). Within a radius of 160 km are eight automotive assembly plants and an engine plant (Oropeza 2015a). The facility boasts three "business class" hotels and is promoting a unique activity, industrial tourism (GPI 2021).

Key to the connectivity of GPI is the service provided by Mexico's largest railroad, Ferromex. Ferromex (FXE) has partnered with Burlington Northern Santa Fe (BNSF) to create the large intermodal facility to serve a multistate area. Its primary corridor to the USA runs through Ciudad Juárez and El Paso, where BNSF's line from Chicago to the USA–Mexico border terminates. Thus, BNSF views the partnership with Ferromex and the latter's connection between Ciudad Juárez and Silao as a way to thrive from the growing automotive industry of the Bajío Region of Mexico (Progressive Railroading 2014). Ferromex, likewise, views the facility as a positive investment, and has partnered financially with commercial property developers to bring about the port facility from GPI's inception in 2006 (É Logística 2010). In mid-2014, BNSF indicated that the service between GPI and Chicago through El Paso would occur 5 days a week (Williams 2014). In October 2015, Union Pacific expressed an intention to provide service six times a week between the facility and Chicago, though the company did not specify whether the rail service would use a Ferromex route through El Paso or Eagle Pass, or KCSM's route through Laredo (UP 2015). The primary marketing feature of the intermodal facility at GPI is that trucks can deliver containers to the location for transfer to trains that ultimately will serve the Midwest, and US Customs functions can be done at the facility for such northbound shipments.

The promoters of GPI, including Ferromex, emphasize the east-west connections, including the corridors linking the intermodal port to the two maritime ports of Manzanillo, Mexico's leading port, and Veracruz, the leading Gulf of Mexico port (É Logística 2010). Likewise, they point out the existence of a Mexican customs facility and customs brokers at GPI, which theoretically streamline the process of moving freight southbound by rail from the USA–Mexico border to Silao, where containers can be lifted onto trucks (Bowen 2014). The existence of a customs facility and free trade zone at the site enhances the port's ability to attract freight moving to and from several states of the Bajio region (Oropeza 2015a). For example, in-bond shipments of automotive parts from the USA can avoid the timely processing of documentation at the border, because such documents can be handled at the final destination, the automotive plants (Williams 2014). The intermodal ramp operated by Ferromex is open 16 h a day Monday through Saturday, and the customs facility is open 16 h a day on weekdays (BNSF 2014).

Though primarily a private venture, GPI nonetheless depends on public–private partnerships. It has relied on annual public investment by the State of Guanajuato of 30 million Pesos until the facility is completely occupied, and companies are requesting that the State of Guanajuato continue providing incentives such as reduced property taxes (Cluster Industrial 2015; Oropeza 2014). Guanajuato's Office of Exterior Commerce (COFOCE) has a presence at GPI and is actively promoting the port's infrastructure and industrial facilities. The federal government operates a customs (*aduana*) facility at the port (GPI 2016). Furthermore, the National Council of Science and Technology (CONACYT) is assisting financially (300 million Pesos in 2015) with the creation of a seven-hectare (seventeen-acre) laboratory center for the development of technology and innovation in automotive manufacturing, agro-processing, petrochemicals, and other leading economic sectors for which the state has a competitive advantage. A public education institution offers coursework in manufacturing engineering (Campus Guanajuato del Institutio Politécnico Nacional) and another provides training in various manufacturing skills (CONALEP); both are based in Mexico City (GPI 2016). In addition to public education, GPI and CONACYT are partnering with la Universidad Iberoamericana León, a private university providing additional training and education to enhance development at the port (Oropeza 2015b). Besides training, incentives provided by the state government include installation of roads to entrances to manufacturing plants. Depending on the promised number of new jobs created, the state government provides some companies with land (Lara and Durán 2013).

Critics of GPI focus primarily on irregularities in the legal arrangements of the acquisition of some of the land that the facility occupies. Much of the facility includes former *ejido* agricultural land. *Ejidos* are the key feature of Mexico's agrarian reform and are important to the country's post-revolutionary history; they are regarded by many historians as key to social justice in rural Mexico, and a safety valve to prevent additional rebellions since the 1910s. During various times between the 1930s and 1970s, un- and underutilized private farmland was appropriated by the federal government and redistributed to landless and land-poor *campesinos* in various forms: collective parcels, individual parcels, or a combination. During the early 1990s, the privatization of ejido lands accelerated under the auspices of liberalization of the country's economy, to attract private investment on the state-owned farmland suffering low levels of agricultural productivity. This new phase, or reversal, of the agrarian reform occurred most prominently in areas closest to cities, to accommodate commercial and residential land uses. The "regularization" of land is supposed to be fair, meaning that the certified users of the land be reimbursed adequately (Yoder 2009).

In the case of GPI, however, the processes for some of the transferred land was not carried out properly by the State of Guanajuato. *Ejidatarios*, or original recipients of the usufruct rights, were promised employment opportunities at the port, which have largely failed to materialize. Furthermore, *ejidatarios* were unjustly obligated to pay property taxes for land that had been appropriated for the establishment of the port. The latter problem was rectified by the Peña Nieto Administration by 2016, but the quality of remaining farmland is poor; much of it became dump sites for discarded construction materials. Furthermore, *ejedatrios* and their legal representatives claim that the reimbursements paid by Guanajuato were only about 40% of the amount promised, while the state argues that the *ejidatarios* inflated the price above market value, thus prompting the eminent domain action. The state granted concessions to *ejidatarios* to operate taxis between the port and the nearby large city of León and installed lighting and drainage infrastructure in *ejido* settlements adjacent to the port (Espinosa 2016; J. Acevedo, personal communication, December 7, 2021).

3.4.2 Interpuerto San Luís Potosí

Interpuerto San Luis Potosí is a maturing intermodal port that enjoys a more centralized location within the country than the other two case study inland ports. The facility is located some 29 km south-southeast of downtown San Luis Potosí and adjacent to Federal Highway 57, a primary corridor of Mexico (Fig. 3.2). It is also connected to KCSM's main line that links Mexico City, Monterrey, and Laredo. The intermodal port facility, originally developed by Grupo Valoran, but owned and operated since 2011 by KCSM, capitalizes on its proximity to Monterrey, other points in northeast Mexico, the Port of Veracruz, and, more importantly, the Pacific Port of Lázaro Cárdenas (El Financiero 2016; Monreal 2012; Cruz 2012b; Plano Informativo 2011).

The port facility is part of a large industrial park, the World Trade Center San Luis Potosí, owned and operated by Grupo Valoran (El Financiero 2016; WTC SLP

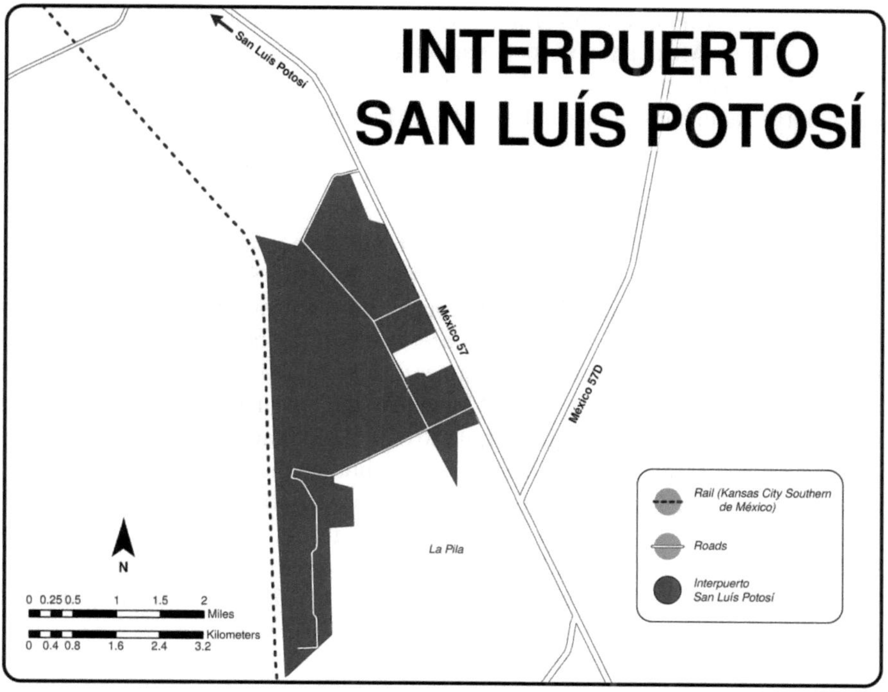

Fig. 3.2 Map of Interpuerto San Luís Potosí. (By Stephen O'Connell)

2016). The Borderless Consulting Group (BCG), a logistics service provider with a facility there, estimates that 75% of Mexico's GDP is located within 500 miles of the port (BCG 2016). Currently, it operates 16 h a day and 7 days a week, though customs service is available 24 h a day. It was the first inland port of Mexico to allow for in-bond movement of goods and the carrying out of customs services (BCG 2016; WTC SLP 2016). The quantity of annual intermodal lifts at the facility increased from 125,143 in 2013 to 133,780 in 2017, to 150,026 in 2019, versus a capacity during the time period of 194,400 lifts (KCSM 2015, 2022). In addition to KCSM, other important transport companies with a strong presence at the facility are JB Hunt and Schneider, two US-based trucking companies (Cruz 2012b).

The facility has two parts, including the industrial park, WTC Industrial (formerly Parque Logístico Interpuerto), which covers approximately 500 ha (1236 acres), and Interpuerto SLP, the intermodal port, owned by KCS (through a concession by Grupo Valoran), that is approximately 100 ha (247 acres) in area (Monreal 2012; J. Curts, personal communication, October 5, 2016; Trade and Logistics Innovation Center 2016). WTC Industrial is in the process of creating its Rail Services Terminal that will provide warehousing, cargo transfers, and shipping of diverse materials, including fuels (J. Curts, personal communication, October 5, 2016). The primary users of both the KCSM intermodal facility and the industrial park are members of the automotive sector (Cruz 2012b). However, the automotive sector is not the only one that benefits from the rail facility at the port.

Interpuerto SLP is an important project for Kansas City Southern Railroad (KCS), and its Mexican division, Kansas City Southern de México (KCSM). Though the smallest of class I railroads of the USA, KCS is the only one to be oriented north-south, and its ownership of KCSM is crucial to the company's strategy. The company boasts of its ability to connect Chicago and Minneapolis to the Mexican Pacific coast (KCS 2016). KCS/KCSM is the only rail operation that can provide virtually uninterrupted service north- and southbound across the USA–Mexico border. Whereas UP and BNSF must interchange with either Mexican rail company (Ferromex and KCSM) at the border, KCS/KCSM can avoid that extra step (KCS 2016; Solomon 2012). Of course, the company is not immune from border-related traffic congestion and speed limits in the border cities. The inland port is among three infrastructure investments in Mexico by KCS/KCSM, as are its intermodal facilities at Interpuerto Monterrey and the maritime port of Lázaro Cárdenas, which is connected to Interpuerto SLP (Solomon 2012). Currently, 8% of cargo shipments through Lázaro Cárdenas pass through the state of San Luis Potosí, and this percentage is expected to grow, given the importance of the inland port's location along two of KCSM's rail lines, and Highway 57. The 2007 agreement between the maritime port and the inland port that outlined their cooperation in developing intermodal service was reaffirmed in 2015, based on the projected growth in freight movement (API Lázaro Cárdenas 2015).

The marketing of Interpuerto SLP by KCS in the USA and KCSM in Mexico hinges on convincing shippers of the price savings that could be realized by using rail. To change shippers' behavior is a difficult task, given the dominance of truck shipments between Mexico and the USA. KCS claims that intermodal shipments of 800 miles or more is more cost-effective than shipping solely by truck, and as a result, some 40% of current shipments done solely by truck could benefit from the use of rail. Fuel costs, highway congestion, and shortages of truck drivers are among the advantages of shipping cargo across the border by rail (Solomon 2012). Furthermore, KCS is highlighting the advantages of nearshoring, and the role that its facilities at Lázaro Cárdenas and Interpuerto SLP will play in that. They claim that in 2011, it cost $2.91 per cubic foot of cargo and took 25 days to go from Shanghai to Chicago via the traditional route through the Ports of Los Angeles and Long Beach. This phenomenon has only gotten stronger in tandem with Covid-related bottlenecks of California ports. By moving plants to Mexico and using rail and truck through intermodal facilities like Interpuerto SLP, manufacturing companies could potentially enjoy considerable time and cost savings. The rate of increase of rail shipments by the automotive industry is a first step toward boosting the appeal of intermodal ports, such as that at San Luis Potosí (Martínez 2016a).

The relatively extensive logistics services available at the port, such as labeling, packaging, customs clearance, warehousing, billing, consolidation (combining) and deconsolidation (separation) of goods, and the availability of third-party logistics (3PL) services are features of the facility that are included in its marketing. Furthermore, the facility lists "soft-landings support," meaning assistance to foreign companies of going through the various hurdles of locating in Mexico, as well as project management services (WTC SLP 2016). The abundance of available land for development of manufacturing plants and distribution centers is key to the marketing of Interpuerto SLP. Likewise, the intermodal facility itself is crucial to the marketing of the *Parque Logístico* as a viable location for manufacturing (Logistics Plus 2016; TLIC 2016). The industrial park's marketing highlights WTC's fluids and general cargo terminal, in addition to the strategic location for global shipments of containers as well as the intermodal ramp (J. Curts, personal communication, October 5, 2016).

The marketing of the port to potential investors in manufacturing plants includes customized incentive packages based on expected employment, plant size, potential for value added through forward and backward economic linkages, and the extent to which research and development is carried out in the state. For example, up to 80% of licensing fees can be forgiven, along with similar reductions of property taxes for up to 10 years, negotiable reductions in payroll taxes, and a reduction of the real estate sales tax, or the *Impuesto de Adquisición de Bienes Inmuebles* for up to 10 years (Lara and Durán 2013).

Like Guanajuato Puerto Interior, Interpuerto San Luís Potosí has faced criticism for having unjustly absorbed *ejido* land as part of the development, beginning in the 1990s. An estimated 15,000 *ejidatarios* statewide, primarily close to the urban zone of the city of San Luís Potosí, were impacted by the state's acquisition by eminent domain of some 20,000 ha (49,400 acres), resulting in litigation that has not resolved claims of an unfair process. Interpuerto SLP occupies one of the contested *ejidos*, as do the easements for highways and rail lines leading to the industrial park (Azuara 2018).

3.4.3 Interpuerto Monterrey

Interpuerto Monterrey is a project that emerged in 2008, and its promoters remain highly confident in its potential for growth (T21 2014). Hernández (2013) claimed it has the potential to become the largest inland port in all of Latin America, though the more rapid growth of Guanajuato's interior port raises questions about this claim. It is located in the Municipality of Salinas Victoria, 35 km north of Monterrey. Its annual lift capacity in 2022 is 195,600, and it handled 160,780 total lifts in 2013; 156,329 in 2014; 164,610 in 2017; and 169,167 in 2021. The facility, which operates 24/7, enjoys access to Federal Highway 1, which connects to Nuevo Laredo (KCSM 2015, 2022). The facility is unique in that it involves not only the provision of rail service, but also investment and marketing by both of the country's major rail companies, Ferromex and KCSM, which broadens its rail connectivity to two border crossing points, respectively, Piedras Negras and Nuevo Laredo. It is the only such facility in the interior of Mexico where both of these rail companies converge (Flores 2014). Because of service by two rail companies, Monterrey is connected to both of Mexico's important Pacific maritime ports: Lázaro Cárdenas (KCSM) and Manzanillo (Ferromex). KCSM operates the container terminal adjacent to the port's eastern boundary; Ferromex does not enjoy direct access to the intermodal

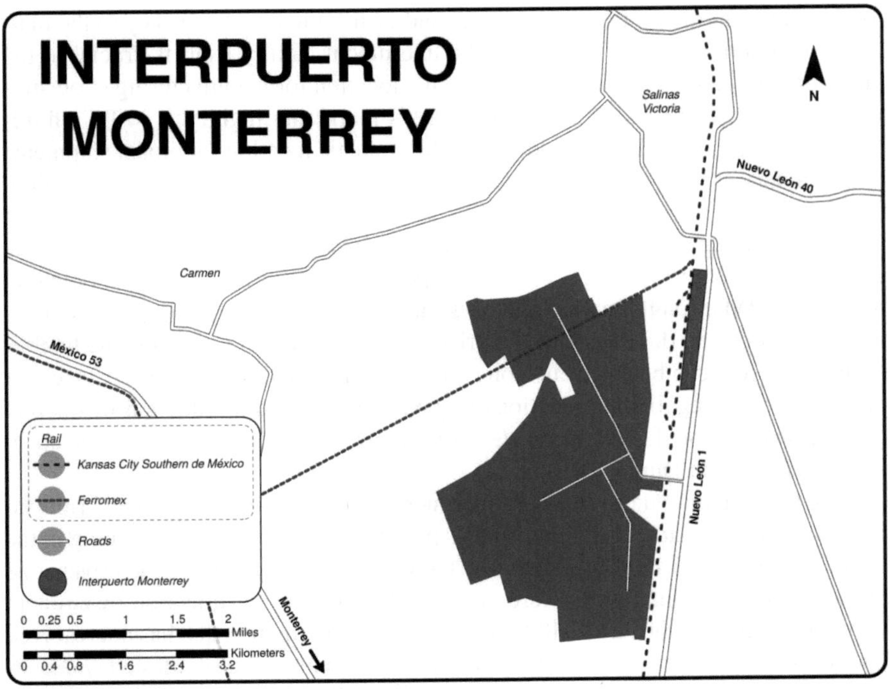

Fig. 3.3 Map of Interpuerto Monterrey. (By Stephen O'Connell)

ramp (Fig. 3.3). Within the park itself, companies use either of the two rail companies, but not both (M. Garza, personal communication, December 15, 2021).

Among its present tenants is the world's largest Oreo cookie plant, and Tubacero, a Mexican company that produces steel tubes (Flores 2016). In addition, the Monterrey terminal is expected to participate heavily in the growing automotive sector in Mexico, given the importance to the latter of its access to the US border, both for imports and exports. Two substantial automotive-related companies established plants at Interpuerto Monterrey by 2016, including Mobis Hyundai, a distribution center of parts for Kia and Hyundai plants in Mexico and the USA, and Tokai Rika, a Japanese manufacturer of seatbelts and electrical parts to supply Ford, GM, Mazda, Nissan, and Toyota plants in Mexico. Both companies have verbally agreed to employ as much of the local workforce as possible (T21, 2015). Since 2016, Interpuerto Monterrey attracted three additional manufacturers, one of which is automotive (M. Garza, personal communication, December 15, 2021).

KCS is marketing the Monterrey facility with greater vigor and is basing its marketing campaign on the advantages of shipping partly by rail over shipping by trucks alone. The company claims in its promotion of the port that a rail shipment from Monterrey to Chicago costs 40 cents per cubic foot and took 6 or 7 days in 2011, versus more than 80 cents by truck, which involved 5 days (Solomon 2012). Given that long distances are required for rail shipments to enjoy economies of scale, the port and its two rail companies are eyeing connections such as the major intermodal port complex of Chicago (M. Garza, personal communication, December 15, 2021).

According to its master plan, Interpuerto Monterrey is expected to have four lifts for intermodal shipments (containers), as well as terminals for steel shipments, primary products such as timber and minerals, completed automobiles, and grains. Clearly those marketing and using the facility are capitalizing on Monterrey's close proximity to the US border ports of Laredo and Eagle Pass, both via rail and highway (Inmobiliare 2012). As of mid-2016, the director of the facility indicated that Interpuerto Monterrey was on track to establish a *recinto fiscalizado estratégico* (RFE), or free-trade zone, which was expected to enhance the port's and the industrial park's efforts to market the combined facilities to manufacturing and logistics companies, especially those seeking access to the USA–Mexico border (Duarte 2016). The RFE is expected to be established in the early 2020s (M. Garza, personal communication, December 15, 2021). The State of Nuevo León is actively participating in the promotion of the facility, because it is seen as an important asset, or tool that the state can point to in order to attract additional manufacturing and logistics activities. State officials and private investors in the industrial park alike highlight the facility's connectivity with the maritime ports of Tampico, Alta Mira, and Veracruz; industrial centers of northern Mexico that include Saltillo and Monclova; and multiple border crossing points that include Laredo, Eagle Pass, Brownsville, and Reynosa (Flores 2014). Furthermore, the State Foreign Investment Law, or *Ley de Inversión Extranjera Estatal*, offers greatly discounted land at the port (Lara and Durán 2013).

Municipal incentives include a reduction in the land acquisition (sales) tax, discounts in the cost of permits for constructing manufacturing plant facilities, and annual property tax. The State of Nuevo León provides discounted payroll taxes and offers worker training, though not directly on site. Generally, Nuevo León's incentive structure is not as aggressive as most other states, because the state relies on its natural site advantages, including its trained workforce, as well as its situation, or its proximity to the USA, to attract investment in manufacturing plants. An increase in nearshoring is highly anticipated in light of bottlenecks related to supply chains involving East Asia. The proximity to Laredo and Eagle Pass is believed to give Monterrey an edge over other Mexican cities with rail ports trying to grow from nearshoring. During 2021, 140 ha (346 acres) of the port's industrial land had been sold for development in the near future (M. Garza, personal communication, December 15, 2021).

3.5 A Brief Analysis of Three Mexican Inland Ports

This section summarizes dominant characteristics of Mexico's inland ports, based on the three case studies. It provides a discussion of the significance of inland ports to local and national economic development and Mexico's logistics, manufacturing, and transport activities. It discusses the partnerships between manufacturers, logistics companies, commercial property (industrial park) developers, and governments.

Mexico's inland intermodal ports are useful to study because as nodes, they can become the starting point of the stories to be told about manufacturing and logistics. They are nodes because they are located in major industrial parks and are defining features of such industrial parks. Furthermore, they enhance the connectivity of manufacturing and distribution centers with maritime ports and border inland ports. This is especially the case when inland intermodal ports contain the customs functions (RFEs) that enable shippers to bypass these operations at crowded border and maritime ports, so long as rail is used. For example, rail cars carrying containers can cross the USA–Mexico border relatively seamlessly, and customs paperwork for parts and components can be processed, and payment made, at or close to the point of manufacture (Cruz 2012a). Thus, the differences in the ways that cargo terminals operate are increasingly as important as differences in transportation modes themselves in determining time efficiencies and costs in both manufacturing and distribution (Hesse and Rodrigue 2004).

The largest of the inland ports of Mexico (in terms of traffic and numbers of container lifts), generally is owned by either of the two major rail companies. The latter put a lot of effort into the marketing of their facilities (Cruz 2012a). Furthermore, they serve as examples of the country's trend toward decentralization of economic and governmental activities away from Mexico City since the late twentieth century. San Luis Potosí, Monterrey, and the region of El Bajío in Central Mexico are all growing in importance as manufacturing and transport/logistics centers outside the country's traditional core for these activities. Nearshoring is making such ports increasingly attractive to private-sector investors, and, therefore, policymakers. It is reasonable to assume that lingering Trump-era tariffs on Chinese goods will make nearshoring increasingly attractive, though uncertainties related to the López Obrador Administration's energy policies may somewhat offset such enthusiasm.

Clearly, the marketing of the private inland ports of Mexico rests on three primary things: (1) intermodal facilities (and the cost savings associated with shipment by a combination of rail and truck rather than by truck alone); (2) the streamlining of customs and the processing of paperwork and goods; and (3) the synergy between each intermodal facility and its adjoining industrial park (TLIC 2016). Key to the latter feature of inland ports is the array of incentives provided by, primarily, state governments. The three case study ports capitalize on their ability to handle in-bond shipments of parts and components, which translates to the streamlining of the paperwork for imported goods, and the paying of duties on them. Upon arrival to any of the interior ports with RFEs, shippers can clear the cargo through their customs broker of choice, so long as the broker is registered at the given port. Shippers can also pre-clear northbound shipments by their US customs broker of choice. Thus, streamlined customs is a key selling point. The rail companies take a leading role in the marketing of each port, given that the ports' fortunes rest on shippers increasingly utilizing rail. Ferromex and KCSM both emphasize the avoidance of highway congestion on Mexican and US highways, congestion at the border crossings that afflict trucks, and the lower costs per ton of shipping goods over medium-to-long distances that rail provides. The railroad companies, in marketing the respective ports, emphasize the proximity of these nodes to nearby manufacturing cities as well as the local industrial park to which the ports are attached.

The role of the governmental sector in the promotion and development of interior ports is not limited to the RFEs and their customs clearance procedure. The Secretariat of Commerce and Transport (SCT) identified in 2004 that Mexico's overall strategies of promoting manufacturing for export, and developing into a middle-income consumer-oriented country, would necessarily rely heavily on streamlined logistics. The agency oversaw the signing of an agreement by various governmental and private entities to make cargo transport more competitive through the development of ten primary intermodal corridors to link interior distribution points to maritime ports on the one hand and to USA–Mexico border ports on the other. The case study ports fare prominently in the SCT-led initiative (Maldonado Carrasco 2008).

3.6 Conclusions

Economic development based on export-oriented manufacturing in *maquiladoras* commenced before the implementation of NAFTA in 1994, and began to be distributed throughout the country, beyond the USA–Mexico border zone and the traditional manufacturing regions of Mexico City and Monterrey, a decade earlier. Thus, the country's political geography of increased federalism and decentralization in the 1990s of political decision-making to the states was quickly accompanied by a territorial expansion of economic development and associated freight transportation infrastructure to enhance manufacturing. In line with this rather rapidly changing economic geography, future development of inland ports in Mexico will depend upon the country's ability to sustain its present export-oriented manufacturing trajectory. Foremost among the country's export-oriented activities is the automobile industry, including both finished vehicles and parts. According to the Federal Reserve Bank of Dallas, Mexico is now the leading supplier of auto parts flowing into the USA, while some 40% of the components making up total imports from Mexico actually originate in the USA (Coronado 2016). In 2015, auto parts firms invested $3.34 billion (US) in new manufacturing capacity in Mexico, ignited by the country's automotive "boom," and making Mexico and its 2400 plants the world's sixth largest producer of auto parts. The auto parts sector is increasingly clustering close to automobile assembly plants in the country (Sánchez 2016). Thus, the USA and Mexico enjoy a geographic synergy, whereby manufactured goods flow north- and southbound across the border, as part of automotive supply chains.

Logic dictates, and recent trends in global supply chain development indicate that Mexico's inland ports will capture an increasing share of global trade as North American regional automotive supply chains evolve, especially among those facilities that contain the RFEs that streamline customs brokerage functions. Additionally, domestic appliance manufacturing is a heavy user of containers, and is regarded as an increasingly important driver of intermodal shipping (Salazar et al. 2014). Given that each of Mexico's inland ports are affiliated with industrial park development, but with the extra feature of intermodal infrastructure to enhance the ability to switch containers between rail lines and highways, partnerships between developers of such facilities and the tenants are important. So too are relationships between these actors and the public sector, as the latter ultimately controls land use planning and the provision of incentives and infrastructure to attract foreign investment.

Northbound crossings of containers from Mexico into the USA have grown fairly steadily since 2010, which indicates that Mexican intermodal ports continue to show promise for nearshoring (Table 3.1). The ports of Laredo and Eagle Pass are the leading container crossing points for goods imported to the USA from Mexico. The increase in numbers is not exactly consistent among rail crossing points. For example, beginning in 2016, Brownsville surpassed El Paso as the third ranking container crossing point, and in 2020, Brownsville likewise surpassed El Paso (Bureau of Transportation Statistics 2022).

Inland ports of Mexico can shed light on the different transportation corridors to which they are connected and for which they serve as nodes. As such, additional research on the topic could provide useful insights, if not serve as starting points, for analyses of Mexican cargo transport corridors. Corridors are in competition with one another as appropriate routes for cargo shipments throughout the country and to the other member countries of the USMCA. Logistics specialists, including freight forwarders, must make appropriate decisions about which corridor is preferable for a particular client (shipper), and the presence or absence of interior ports could increasingly factor in such decisions. Additional topics recommended for further study include greater details of the land-use planning process related to inland ports in Mexico, and other aspects of the role of the public sector, at the federal, state, and municipal levels. This latter theme ought to include the social and agricultural

Table 3.1 Incoming containers by rail, Mexico to the USA, Texas Rail Crossings

Year	Total US	Laredo	Eagle pass	El Paso	Brownsville
2010	706,067	327,453	182,665	327,453	41,860
2011	770.965	371,553	194,731	92,182	39,450
2012	827,763	399,839	287,895	94,089	54,023
2013	837,326	413,401	201,939	84,519	44,407
2014	909,993	405,076	254,327	99,295	65,293
2015	938,540	392,416	274,232	109,120	73,559
2016	995,381	401,567	318,730	107,279	85,518
2017	N.D.	421,263	351,057	109,115	88,971
2018	N.D.	441,475	359,088	108,265	93,355
2019	N.D.	464,371	336,540	120,699	99,311
2020	1,014,873	474,766	334,512	68,388	69,781
2021	N.D.	508,192	331,386	108,824	84,974

Source: United States Bureau of Transportation Statistics, January 2022 ramifications of the planning of ports as features of the ongoing suburbanization process. Finally, comparative analyses of Mexico's inland ports with those of other emerging markets, such as India and Argentina, are warranted.

References

Aoyama Y, Ratick S, Schwarz G (2006) Organizational Dynamics of the U.S. Logistics Industry: An Economic Geography Perspective. Prof Geogr 58(3):327–340

API Lázaro Cárdenas (2015) Puerto Lázaro Cárdenas y WTC Industrial de San Luis Potosí Reafirman Lazos de Colaboración Comercial. Administración Portuario Integral, Lázaro Cárdenas. Retrieved June 27, 2016, from http://www.puertolazarocardenas.com.mx/plc25/mptocoas/637-wtc-san-luis-potosi-reafirman-lazos-de-colaboracion-comercial

Azuara P (2018, December 19) 5 municipios han sido afectados por conflictos agrarios, El Sol de San Luís. https://www.elsoldesanluis.com.mx/local/5-municipios-han-sido-afectados-por-conflictos-agrarios-2818403.htms. Accessed 2 Feb 2020

BCG (2016) Borderless consulting group. Company web site. Retrieved June 27, 2016, from https://www.borderless.com.mx/index.php/en/borderless-intermodal-en

BNSF (2014) Silao Transborder Intermodal Service via El Paso. http://www.bnsf.com/mexico/pdf/silao-service-bnsf-fxe-service-guidelines-es.pdf. Accessed 9 Aug 2016

Bonney J (2012, October 17) Report: Logistics Costs Make Up 9.9 Percent of Mexico's GDP. J Commer. Retrieved July 5, 2016, from http://www.joc.com/economy-watch/world-economy-news/report-logistics-costs-make-99-percent-mexico%E2%80%99s-gdp_20121017.html

Bowen DJ (2014, May20) BNSF, Ferromex set Chicago-Mexico intermodal service. Railway Age. http://www.railwayage.com/index.php/intermodal/bnsf-ferromex-launch-chicago-mexico-intermodal-service.html

Bureau of Transportation Statistics (2022) U.S.-Mexican Border Land-Freight Gateways: Number of Incoming Truck or Rail Container Crossings. https://www.bts.gov/content/us-mexican-border-land-freight-gateways-number-incoming-truck-or-rail-container-crossings

Cluster Industrial (2015, March 30) Cumple 9 años Puerto Interior. Cluster Industrial. http://clusterindustrial.com.mx/cumple-9-anos-puerto-interior/

Coe NM et al (2004) 'Globalizing' regional development: a global production networks perspective. Trans Inst Br Geogr 29(4):468–484

Coronado R (2016, May 24) Coronado: Mexico's Bright Auto Future. Rio Grande Guardian. http://riograndeguardian.com/coronado-mexicos-bright-auto-future/

Cruz O (2012a, November 5) Puertos interiores, en blanco y negro T21 http://t21.com.mx/opinion/bitacora/2012/11/05/puertos-interiores-blanco-negro

Cruz O (2012b, September 6) San Luis Pototsí, nodo del intermodal *T21*, 6 September. http://t21.com.mx/opinion/bitacora/2012/09/06/san-luis-potosi-noda-intermodal. Accessed 27 June 2016

Duarte E (2016, May 25) Interpuerto Monterrey busca el despacho aduanero conjunto T21. http://t21.com.mx/logistica/2016/05/25/interpuerto-monterrey-busca-despacho-aduanero-conjunto

É Logística (2010, July 20) Inaugura Guanajuato Puerto Interior Terminal Intermodal Ferromex. É Logística. http://www.logisticamx.enfasis.com/notas/17092-inaugura-guanajuato-puerto-interior-terminal-intermodal-ferromex

El Financiero (2016, April 21) Watco y WTC Industrial almacenarán y proveerán hidrocarburos en SLP. El Financiero. http://elfinanciero.com.mx/bajio/watco-y-wtc-industrial-almacenaran-y-proveeran-hidrocarburos-en-slp.html

Espinosa V (2016, June 17) Expropiaciones ejidales en Guanajuato: negocio de antaño, Revista Proceso. https://www.proceso.com.mx/reportajes/2016/6/17/expropiaciones-ejidales-en-guanajuato-negocio-de-antano-165959.html

Fleming DK, Hayuth Y (1994) Spatial dimensions of transportation hubs: centrality and intermediacy. J Transp Geogr 2(1):3–18

Flores L (2014) El Interpuerto Monterrey, ¿el detonante de la logística? Obrasweb. Retrieved June 27, 2016, from http://www.obrasweb.mx/construccion/2014/07/29/el-interpuerto-monterrey-el-detonante-de-la-logistica

Flores L (2016, April 28) Durante 2016, llegarán dos empresas más a Interpuerto. El Economista. http://eleconomista.com.mx/estados/2016/04/28/durante-2016-llegaran-dos-empresas-mas-interpuerto

GPI (2016) Guanajuato Puerto Interior. Retrieved August 29, 2016, from http://www.puertointerior.com.mx

GPI (2021) En Guanajuato Puerto Interior se "Viven Grandes Historias," Guanajuato Puerto Interior. Retrieved October 8, 2021, from https://boletines.guanajhuato.gob.mx/2021/03/19/en-guanajuato-puerto-interior-se-viven-grandes-historias/

Hernández A (2013, July 3) Interpuerto Monterrey, el mayor puerto seco de AL. Altonivel. http://www.altonivel.com.mx/36550-interpuerto-monterrey-logistica-de-alto-nivel.html

Hesse M, Rodrigue JP (2004) The transport geography of logistics and freight distribution. J Transp Geogr 12:171–184

Inmobiliare (2012, June 22) Interpuerto Monterrey. Inmobiliare. http://inmobiliare.com/interpuerto-monterrey/

KCS (2016) Kansas City Southern railway. Retrieved July 15, 2016, from http://www.kcsouthern.com/en-us/why-choose-kcs

KCSM (2015) Intermodal ramps. Kansas City Southern de México. Retrieved July 5, 2016, from http://www.kcsouthern.com/en-us/pdf/kcsm-intermodal-ramps/kcsm-mexico-intermodal-ramps.pdf

KCSM (2022) Intermodal ramps, February 2022. Kansas City Southern de México. Retrieved May 20, 2022, from https://www.kcsouthern.com/pdf/kcsm-intermodal-ramps/kcsm-mexico-intermodal-ramps.pdf

Lara I, Durán C (2013, March) Incentivos: Imán para las nuevas inversiones, Somos Industria. Retrieved April 12, 2022, from https://www.somosindustria.com/articulo/incentivos-iman-para-las-nuevas-inversiones/

Leitner SJ, Harrison R (2001) The Identification and Classification of Inland Ports. University of Texas Center for Transportation Research, Austin.

Logistics Plus (2016) Logistics Plus web site. Retrieved June 27, 2016, from http://www.logisticsplus.net

Madrazo P (2015, March 27) Cumple 9 años Puerto Interior. AM León Guanajuato. http://173.236.14.43/leon/local/cumple-9-a%C3%B1os-puerto-interior-190422.html

Maldonado Carrasco AG (2008) La multimodalidad en México. Comercio Exterior 58(10):720–730

Martínez E (2016a, August 2) 'Acelera' transporte de autos por tren; triplica crecimiento de carga ferroviaria general, El Financiero http://www.elfinanciero.com.mx/empresas/acelera-transporte-de-autos-por-tren-triplica-crecimiento-de-carga-ferroviaria-general.html

Martínez E (2016b, September 7) Grandes autotransportistas duplican flota en una década. El Financiero. http://www.elfinanciero.com.mx/empresas/grandes-autotransportistas-duplican-flota-en-una-decada.html

Martínez E (2016c, September 28) Empresas se 'bajan' del tren Chiapas-Mayab. El Financiero 28. http://www.elfinanciero.com.mx/empresas/se-bajan-del-tren-chiapas-mayab.html

Martínez E (2016d, September 27) Exportaciones por ferrocarril crecerán 56% ante dólar fuerte. El Financiero. http://www.elfinanciero.com.mx/empresas/exportaciones-por-ferrocarril-creceran-56-ante-dolar-fuerte.html

Mendoza Ruiz J (2011) La coordinación intergubernamental en la planeación y el desarrollo regional del Estado de Hidalgo, un análisis desde el federalismo subsidiario. Unpublished Manuscript, Universidad Autónoma del Estado de Hidalgo

Monreal E (2012, April 6) Parque Logístico de SLP solo es utilizado al 20%. Plano Informativo. http://planoinformativo.com/nota/id/189269/noticia/parque-logistico-de-slp-solo-es-utilizado-al-20.html
Murphy PR, Knemeyer AM (2015) Contemporary Logistics, 11th edn. Pearson Publishing, New York
Ng KYA, Gujar GC (2009) The spatial characteristics of inland transport hubs: evidences from Southern India. J Transp Geogr 17:346–356
Nootteboom T, Rodrigue JP (2007) Re-Assessing Port-Hinterland relationships in the context of global commodity chains. In: Wang J et al (eds) Inserting Port-Cities in global supply chains. Ashgate, Farnham, pp 51–66
Ornelas S (2016) Editor's Interview: Here is why there are long truck-lines at the border. Border Now 2(17):8–12
Oropeza P (2014, February 10) Guanajuato Puerto Interior, rumbo a la autosuficiencia. El Financiero. http://www.elfinanciero.com.mx/empresas/guanajuato-puerto-interior-rumbo-a-la-autosuficiencia.html
Oropeza P (2015a, June 29) Puerto Interior de Guanajuato, la logística como clave del desarrollo. El Financiero. http://www.elfinanciero.com.mx/bajio/puerto-interior-de-guanajuato-la-logistica-como-clave-del-desarrollo.html
Oropeza P (2015b, March 5) Crearán polígono de laboratorios tecnológicos en Guanajuato Puerto Interior. El Financiero. http://www.elfinanciero.com.mx/crearan-poligono-de-laboratorios-tecnologicos-en-guanajuato-puerto-interior.html
Plano Informativo (2011, October 24) Kansas City compra Interpuerto de SLP. Plano Informativo. http://planoinformativo.com/nota/id/162006/noticia/kansas-city-compra-interpuerto-de-slp.html
Progressive Railroading (2014, May 21) BNSF, Ferromex to offer intermodal service between Chicago and Silao, Mexico. Progressive Railroading. http://www.progressiverailroading.com/class_is/news/BNSF-Ferromex-to-offer-intermodal-service-between-Chicago-and-Silao-Mexico%2D%2D40493
Rodrigue JP, Notteboom T (2010) Foreland-based regionalization: Integrating intermediate hubs with port hinterlands. Res Transp Econ 27:19–29
Rodrigue JP et al (2010) Functions and Actors of Inland Ports: European and North American Dynamics. J Transp Geogr 18(4):519–529
Rodríguez Canales A (2014, December 14) Prevé Guanajuato Puerto Interior atraer 500 mdd de inversión en 2015. El Financiero. http://www.elfinanciero.com.mx/bajio/preve-guanajuato-puerto-interior-atraer-500-mdd-de-inversion-en-2015.html
Roso V, Woxenius J, Lumsden K (2009) The dry port concept: connecting container seaports with the hinterland. J Transp Geogr 17:338–345
Salazar AL, Vargas JH, Medina Armienta J (2014) Intermodalismo: La operación del transporte intermodal. In: Presentation at the 7th LogisticSummit & Expo. Asociación Mexicana del Transporte Intermodal A.C., Mexico
Sánchez A (2016, May 23) Compañias de autopartes 'aceleran' inversion a nivel histórico por boom automotriz. El Financiero. http://www.elfinanciero.com.mx/empresas/companias-de-autopartes-aceleran-inversion-a-nivel-historico-por-boom-automotriz.html
Solomon MB (2012, April 18) KCS to make aggressive push into U.S.-Mexico intermodal market, DC Velocity. https://www.dcvelocity.com/articles/25904-kcs-to-make-aggressive-push-into-u-s-mexican-intermodal-market
Soto Correa U (2009) Estrategia para evaluar la capacidad técnica y la rentabilidad de puertos secos en la República Mexicana. Masters Thesis, Facultad de Ingeniería, Universidad Nacional Autonoma de México, Mexico City
T21 (2014, July 1) Grupo Denso invertirá 35.8 mdd en nueva planta en Interpuerto Monterrey. T21. https://t21.com.mx/logistica/2014/07/01/grupo-denso-invertira-358-mdd-nueva-planta-interpuerto-monterrey

T21 (2015, December 1) Tokai Rika se instala en Interpuerto Monterrey. T21. https://t21.com.mx/logistica/2015/12/01/tokai-rika-se-instala-interpuerto-monterrey

Tecma Group (2023) What is a Maquiladora in Mexico? https://manufacturingmexico.org/maquiladora-in-mexico/

TLIC (2016) Trade and Logistics Innovation Center 2016. Retrieved June 27, 2016, from http://www.ciltec.com.mx/es/infraestructura-logistica/parques-logisticos/principales-parques-logisticos-en-mexico-parque

Trimble S (2016) Manufacturers in Mexico are still looking for a local supply chain. Border Now 2(21):18–22

UP (2015) Expanded eagle premium service to/from Silao, Guanajuato, Mexico. Announcement, Union Pacific Railroad Web Site, 6 October. Retrieved June 29, 2016, from https://www.up.com/customers/announcements/intermodal/allintermodal/IM2015-396.html

US Department of Commerce (2021) US Trade with Mexico 2021. https://www.bis.doc.gov/index.php/documents/technology-evaluation/ote-data-portal/country-analysis/3028-2021-statistical-analysis-of-u-s-trade-with-mexico/file#:~:text=In%202021%2C%20U.S.%20exports%20to,%25%20(%245.5%20billion)%20decrease

USDOT (2016, May) United States Department of Transportation, Bureau of Transportation Statistics. BTS Statistics Release. North American Freight Numbers. Retrieved July 29, 2016, from http://www.rita.dot.gov/bts/press_releases/bts040_16

Yoder M (2009) Landscapes of Industry and Transport: Monclova and Torreón, Mexico. Journal of Big Bend Studies 21:179–200

Williams M (2014, June 4) Rail providers boost services for automotive between US and Mexico. Automotive Logistics. http://automotivelogistics.media/news/rail-providers-boost-services-for-automotive-between-us-and-mexico

WTC SLP (2016) World Trade Center, San Luis Potosí. Retrieved July 28, 2016, from http://www.wtcindustrial.mx/index_es.php

Chapter 4
Ports-to-Plains: A Case Study in Cargo Transport Infrastructure Policy and Planning

Abstract The USA, Mexico, and Canada form a highly competitive and globally connected regional production platform. The implementation of the USMCA in 2020 emphasizes nearshoring of production from East Asia. As such, policymakers, manufacturing companies, and logistics companies are among the stakeholders advocating improved cargo transportation linkages between the three countries. The proposed Ports-to-Plains Corridor, linking Laredo to West Texas, Denver and the Western Canadian Prairie Provinces, is an idea dating to the 1990s and designed to expand cargo transport capabilities west of the dominant I-35 and I-69 NAFTA corridors. Legislation filed in the US House of Representatives in 2020 and signed into law in 2021 and 2022 is thought to pave the way for I-27 to expand beyond its present route in West Texas, to enhance trucking infrastructure, and ultimately to form the backbone of highway connection between Mazatlán and Canada's western Prairie Provinces. This chapter is a case study that explores the underlying policy implications of the corridor and the emerging political partnerships to bring it about. The chapter provides a brief identification of the economic geographic regions along the corridor (especially in Texas), a discussion of the history of the plan, and commentary on the ways that the corridor is promoted to potential users in the manufacturing, agriculture, and energy sectors. The chapter concludes that the case study method and open-ended interviews are useful in the sub-discipline of geography concerned with cargo transportation policy and economic development.

Keywords Transportation infrastructure · Ports-to-Plains corridor · USA · Mexico trade · USMCA · West Texas · South Texas · Functional economic regions

4.1 Introduction

Transportation corridors and the planning that brings them about are essential to the geographic study of economic development, because they are among the most obvious features of development that play out at multiple scales. Such corridors are relied upon to link localities near and far to each other, and to the maritime and

M. S. Yoder, *Geographical Scale and Economic Development*,
https://doi.org/10.1007/978-3-031-36197-5_4

inland dry ports that connect places along such corridors to the global economy. And yet, some localities along highway corridors do not experience enhanced economic development automatically. Thus, such infrastructure is generally a necessary but not sufficient condition for enhancing activities such as manufacturing and distribution. They force localities along them to think in terms of regional development, beyond the scope of merely their own municipalities, to avoid isolated development.

The study of highways in North America, whether existing or proposed, that are macro in scale is necessary to broaden an understanding of the policy-making and political maneuvering to bring about economic connectivity. In light of the importance of trade between Canada, Mexico, and the USA, and the formation since the mid-1990s of the region as a globally-competitive production platform, this chapter addresses the emerging Ports-to-Plains highway corridor whose primary objective is to link the USA–Mexico border inland ports of Laredo/Nuevo Laredo, Eagle Pass/Piedras Negras, and Del Rio/Ciudad Acuña to the US and Canadian Great Plains stretching from Southwest Texas, West Texas, the Texas and Oklahoma Panhandles, Eastern New Mexico (via a connector route) and Colorado to Wyoming, Montana, North Dakota, and the US border with Canada's Prairie Provinces of Alberta and Manitoba. This chapter will emphasize primarily the Texas portion of the corridor, given the state's leadership in fomenting the project, and secondarily on the Mexican portion as a tool in the linkage of that country to Texas, in line with the primary geographical scope of this book.

Ports-to-Plains as a concept began in the mid-1990s as a way to enhance cargo handling capabilities of existing highways, most of which were then (and many of which still are) two-lane US Highways (Fig. 4.1). As the idea evolved, its promoters began to think of the existing collection of highways as a foundation for the creation of an interstate highway. In effect, that means the lengthening of Interstate I-27, an existing four-lane divided limited access highway between Amarillo and Lubbock. South of Lubbock, US Highways 87 and 277 are divided and four-lanes to San Angelo, and US 277 is two-lane between San Angelo and the point where it merges with Interstate I-35 some 18 miles north of downtown Laredo. It is marketed as a way to better enhance such localities' opportunities for North American trade. It also is marketed as a western alternative to the often-chaotic, crowded I-35 corridor linking Laredo to Duluth by way of San Antonio, Austin, Dallas-Fort Worth, Kansas City, Des Moines, and Minnesota's Twin Cities. The chapter discusses briefly the planned establishment and marketing of Ports-to-Plains within Mexico (between the Texas–Mexico border and the port city of Mazatlán) and the US Great Plains north of the Texas Panhandle, but the bulk of attention is placed on the portion that is presently gaining momentum to the greatest extent, between Lubbock and the Texas–Mexico border.

This chapter explores the underlying policy implications of the corridor and the emerging political partnerships to bring it about. It provides a brief identification of the functional economic regions along the corridor, a discussion of the history of the plan, and commentary on the ways that the corridor is promoted to potential users in the manufacturing, agriculture, and energy sectors. It concludes that a case study

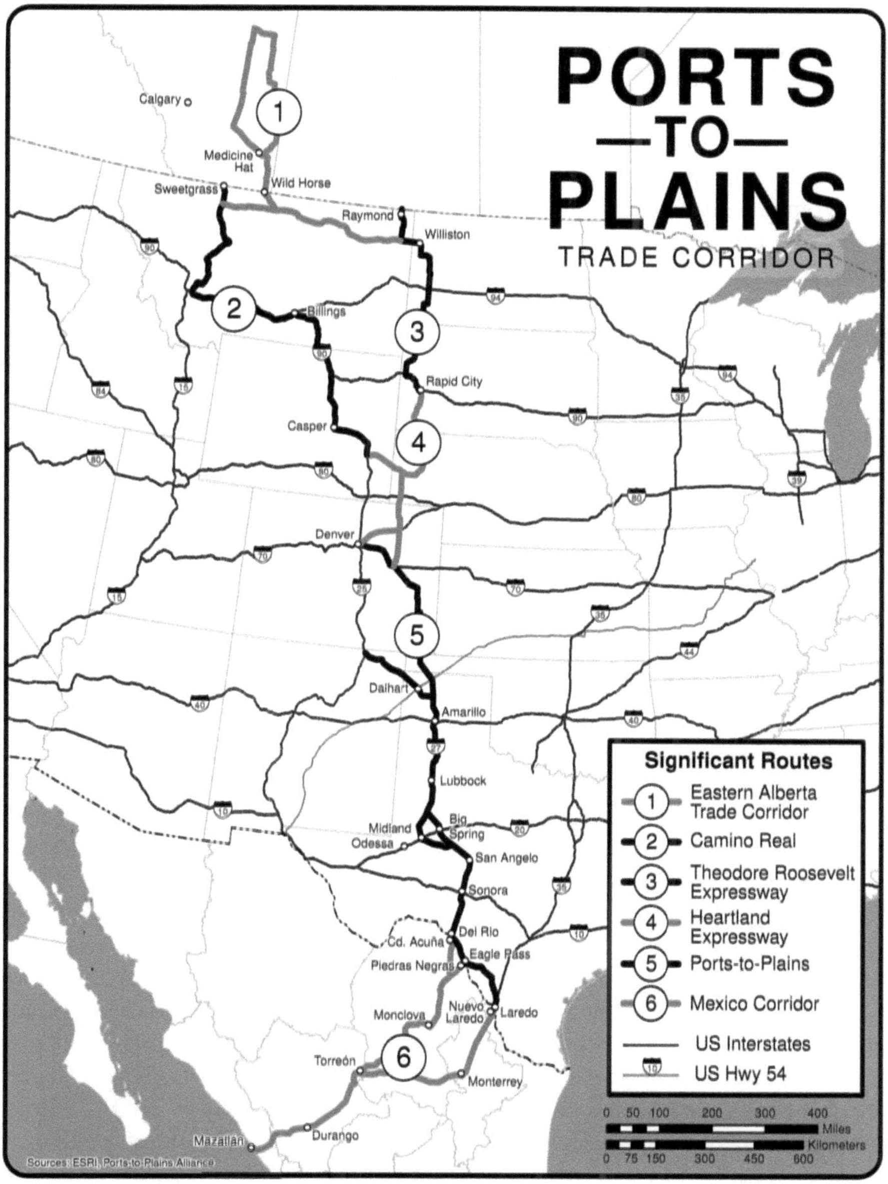

Fig. 4.1 Map of Ports-to-Plains Corridor. (By Stephen O'Connell)

of this type illustrates how useful such research is to the sub-discipline of geography concerned with cargo transportation policy and economic development. Likewise, the Ports-to-Plains case exemplifies one of the primary objectives of studies in economic development, namely, tying together the impacts on communities marked by a broad array of local and regional assets.

The research for this case study of a large regional-scale economic development initiative involved primarily qualitative research methods, and different forms of data gathering, including observational, descriptive, and numerical data published online. In addition to data produced by the Texas Department of Transportation and by different economic development corporations along the corridor, the research relied on a small number of open-ended interviews of stakeholders in its planning and promotion, in economic development, including directors of chambers of commerce and economic development corporations, local-level elected officials, and members of the Ports-to-Plains Alliance Board. Webinars on trends in trucking and USA–Mexico trade proved quite beneficial in providing context in the era of COVID-related logistics and supply chain complications. Articles in the business media on cargo handling, the energy sector, and USA–Mexico trade became the basis for many of the questions I posed during interviews. Websites of economic development entities along the corridor, and of rail-served facilities along the corridor (see Chap. 5), provided essential information of the priorities of the project's stakeholders. Finally, I gathered observational data in two cities of the corridor: the busy border city of Laredo, and the community of Sonora, Texas, specifically the junction of Ports-to-Plains (US Highway 277) and Interstate I-10.

4.2 Geography and Politics of the Ports-to-Plains Corridor

The plan for the corridor commenced in the mid-1990s following the passage of the North American Free Trade Agreement in 1992 and its implementation in early 1994. During the trade agreement's first decade, it increasingly became clear to members of the public and private sectors interested in the trade agreement that trade between the USA, Canada, and Mexico would require new routes linking the Canadian Prairie Provinces to Northern Mexico. To illustrate, the US Great Plains Region was insufficiently served by interstate highways oriented north-south. Furthermore, two cargo crossing points of El Paso/Ciudad Juárez and Laredo/Nuevo Laredo had already become bottlenecks, and stakeholders in USA–Mexico trade argued that more crossing points would be helpful to streamlining cross-border trade. The two crossing points under consideration were Eagle Pass/Piedras Negras and Del Rio/Ciudad Acuña. Thus, Ports-to-Plains was born (Yoder 2009). In 1998, the US Congress, under the Transportation Equity Act (TEA-21), designated Ports-to-Plains from Laredo to Denver as a "High Priority Corridor" with importance to the national highway system (Ports-to-Plains Alliance 2020c). It is worth noting that an early feasibility study conducted by the Texas Department of Transportation (TxDOT) in the late 1990s concluded that the costs of the corridor would outweigh the benefits (Clark 2020). But a quarter century later, the plan for the corridor has been revived in light of more recent cost-benefit estimates. It has evolved in greater detail to include the widening of current two-lane highways and modifying existing four-lane highways into limited access divided routes; that is to say, interstate-quality highway infrastructure. In short, the plan is to expand I-27, a short interstate highway connecting Amarillo and Lubbock, to the Mexican and Canadian borders. The estimated cost of construction is $23.5 billion, and its cost-benefit ratio is estimated at 2.4-to-1, given the dominance of the lucrative agriculture and energy industries in the region of West Texas through which the corridor passes (Rapaport 2020; Ports-to-Plains Alliance 2020a).

Prior to the issuance of federal monies for highway projects such as Ports-to-Plains, states are required by the Federal Highway Administration (FHA) to identify "Critical Freight Corridors," a designation that depends upon coordination between states when such highways will traverse two or more of them. Thus, one state cannot take the initiative alone to create corridors that involve multiple states. Such coordination requires the involvement of the respective states' transportation departments. Likewise, stakeholders at the local level, such as mayors and county administrators, get involved in such activities, especially when rural areas are advocating for improved connectivity, and this includes working across state lines as well as within each state that would be served by such a corridor. The Ports-to-Plains Alliance facilitates such coordination, and the entity lobbies members of Congress, especially members of the House of Representatives in districts touched by the corridors in the states involved: Texas, New Mexico, Colorado, Oklahoma, Nebraska, North Dakota, South Dakota, Montana, and Wyoming (Ports-to-Plains Alliance 2016). Such efforts will need to be maintained, to build upon the momentum achieved to date (Ports-to-Plains Alliance 2020a, b).

In June 2020, two Texas members of the US House of Representatives, Jodey Arrington (R-Lubbock) and Henry Cuellar (D-Laredo) filed a bill to create the Ports-to-Plains Highway Act of 2020, designed to boost the extension and expansion of I-27, and designate it as a federal interstate highway. The bill, H.R. 5171, followed approval by the Texas State Legislature in 2019 to fund a feasibility study for the project (Rapaport 2020). Senator Cory Gardner (R-CO) filed a companion bill, also titled Ports-to-Plains Highway Act of 2020, in the Senate. His bill focused specifically on the portion of the corridor from Texas to Colorado that was cosponsored by Senators Ted Cruz and John Cornyn, who filed a Senate bill in the fall of 2020. Gardner advocated for the expanded I-27 corridor, to connect West Texas and Eastern Colorado, on the basis of traffic congestion on both I-25 in the most populated part of Colorado, and I-35 (Minor 2020).

In early March 2021, given that neither of the 2020 bills passed, Representatives Arrington and Cuellar filed a bill similar to the 2020 bill, the Ports-to-Plains Highway Act of 2021 (H.R. 1608). Senators Cruz (R-TX) and Cornyn (R-TX), along with cosponsor Senator Kevin Cramer (R-ND) filed a companion bill, S. 705, in the US Senate (Ports-to-Plains Alliance 2021). A congressional designation is a necessary step toward obtaining funding to expand I-27 to Laredo, and northward to the Canadian border via Colorado. Of the four House cosponsors, three represent Texas districts through which the corridor is routed, and one is Kelly Armstrong, North Dakota's at-large representative (Dotray 2021); the two Senate sponsors are Texans, and the co-sponsors represent New Mexico (Ben Ray Luján), and North Dakota, respectively. It is interesting to note that of all sponsors and cosponsors of both houses, only Congressman Cuellar and one Senator, Luján (D-NM), voted for the Bipartisan Infrastructure Bill (the Infrastructure Investment and Jobs Act), promoted heavily by President Biden, in the Fall of 2021, an indication of the sometimes divisive nature of American politics. The Consolidated Appropriations Act of 2022, passed by Congress on March 11, 2022 and signed by President Biden March 15, 2022, includes an official designation of the Ports-to-Plains Corridor as an interstate highway, opening the door to more streamlined and certain federal funding (G. Andrews, personal communication, March 14, 2022).

The complexity of bringing about the necessary legislation, including the two House bills of 2020, the House bill of 2021, and the Senate bills of 2020 and 2021, can reflect disagreements in prioritizing the project. For example, Colorado stakeholders appear to be less enthusiastic as those of Texas about an expanded I-27. One reason is that the federal government would cover a maximum of 80% of the planning and construction costs, resulting in the State of Colorado bearing up to 20% of the costs to the state. While stakeholders in the eastern part of that state agree that the current highways there result in trucks passing through downtown areas of towns and small cities, the promised relief from that congestion is not enough to justify the state's spending of a hefty amount of its own transportation infrastructure budget, even while they acknowledge that interstate highways cannot be successfully created if they stop at state lines (Minor 2020). Clearly there are challenges associated with interstate highway planning under the federal system that requires partnership and consensus across state lines.

In Texas, skeptics of the corridor point to uncertainties related to an interstate highway that bypasses downtown areas of towns and small cities. Downtown businesses that rely on highway traffic are concerned that vehicular traffic will circumvent central business districts and impact negatively upon their sales figures. On balance, opposition to expanding the current highway system to interstate grade is limited (Hyde 2021; J. Osborne, personal communication, January 27, 2022).

4.3 Recent Economic Trends Relevant to Ports-to-Plains

A primary focus of marketing of the corridor by the Ports-to-Plains Alliance is the enhanced transportation requirements of North American trade codified by the passage of the USMCA, an updated version of NAFTA. The Alliance summarizes a study by the Texas Department of Transportation (DOT) that estimates a return on investment of 76% within 20 years of the completion of I-27, including $55.6 billion (US) added to the GDP of Texas, and $3.4 billion per year in cost savings for both personal and business (freight) travel, including less wear and tear on truck operating costs. Additionally, the Alliance and TxDOT emphasize the safety benefits of the corridor, given that so much of it today is not divided highway (LEDA 2020).

Like the board members of the Ports-to-Plain Alliance and other stakeholders from Laredo to the Montana–Alberta border, professionals interested in economic development in northern Mexico see the corridor as a natural companion to USMCA. Especially vocal about the merits of the corridor are public officials and business stakeholders of the Mexican state of Coahuila and of some municipal governments in that state. The latter participated in direct talks not only with counterparts in the USA but also in Canada. Such talks are predicated on the belief that Coahuila is ripe for Canadian investment in manufacturing to supplement investment from US. companies. The most noticeable effort toward such outreach has focused on Ciudad Acuña and Del Rio, sister cities with a lengthy history of "twin plants" (*maquiladoras* in Mexico and warehousing plus logistics activities in the USA) with a hunger for expanding the scale of manufacturing operations and logistics support (Castro 2021). Economic stakeholders, especially in northern Mexico, emphasize the need for better highway infrastructure in light of the nearshoring of manufacturing from East Asia to Mexico, a process described in Chap. 3.

The Texas portion of Ports-to-Plains is divided into three segments for administrative purposes, including the production of feasibility studies (Fig. 4.2). Those necessary studies, carried out by Texas Department of Transportation (TxDOT) and mandated by the State Legislature (House Bill 1079 in 2019, signed by Governor Abbott in June of 2019), include estimated vehicular traffic (cars and commercial trucks), safety (reductions in vehicular crashes), traffic congestion relief, and economic development, including job creation (Ports-to-Plains Alliance 2020a, b). Segment 1 extends from the Texas–Oklahoma state line southbound to the boundary between Hale and Lubbock Counties. Segment 2 stretches from the Hale/Lubbock County line southbound to the Sutton and Val Verde Counties line, and Segment 3 extends from Valverde County southbound to Laredo and the USA–Mexico border (Ports-to-Plains Alliance 2020a).

4.4 Marketing of Ports-to-Plains

The marketing of the corridor is based largely on three themes: accessibility, traffic bottlenecks, and highway safety. The lack of limited access divided highways traversing north and south in the country's midsection is a key argument in favor of expanding existing highways into I-27. Little in the way of north-south interstate highways exist between I-25, which links Las Cruces and Denver, and I-35, linking Laredo and Duluth. Intense traffic Bottlenecks along I-35 is another point underlying the efforts by supporters of Ports-to-Plains to lobby for legislation in favor of funding the project; for many shippers and carriers, I-27 would act as an alternative to I-35. The existing two- and four-lane highways of Ports-to-Plains are less safe in terms of vehicle collisions than a typical interstate highway. The Ports-to-Plains Alliance and TxDOT estimate a reduction in vehicular crashes of 21% when I-27 is completed, given that much of the corridor today is two- or three-lane undivided highway (LEDA 2020). A fourth marketing theme, related to accessibility, is the corridor's potential to intersect with rail service, thereby enhancing economic development.

A freight trucking corridor's ability to bring about economic development can be greater if facilities exist along or adjacent to it that allow transfer of loads between

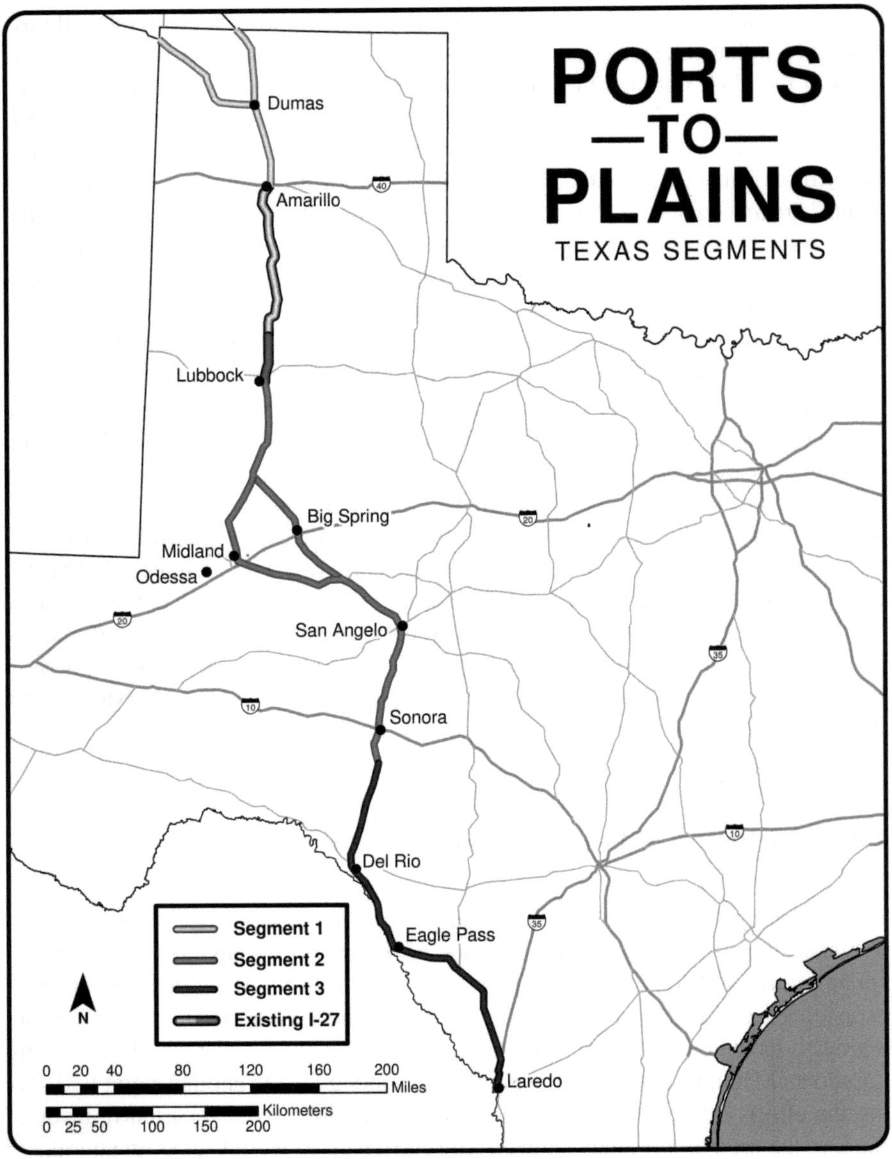

Fig. 4.2 Map of Texas segments of Ports-to-Plains. (By Stephen O'Connell)

rail and truck. These can be transload facilities or intermodal facilities. The difference Between "Intermodal" and "transload" must be made clear to economic developers and transportation planners. Although the promotional content from the Ports-to-Plains Alliance's website makes mention of the "intermodal potential" of several West Texas localities along the corridor, there is likely little chance of true intermodal infrastructure development, at least in the short- and medium-terms.

Only Laredo has a true intermodal facility. "Intermodal" implies the transfer of shipping containers between truck and rail, and the appropriate infrastructure would include an "intermodal ramp," or a surface with crane service to lift the containers and transfer them between truck "chassis" (trailer pulled by truck that carries a container) and flat cars or well cars. Such infrastructure is expensive and requires a minimum amount of container movement per month or per year to make it work economically (Yoder 2021). However, several transload facilities for transferring bulk loads between rail and truck are located along or in close proximity to the corridor in West Texas, as is one rail-served industrial facility not specifically for transloading of bulk materials. The lines of five rail companies connect with (or are adjacent to) the corridor in Texas: BNSF in Lubbock; West Texas and Lubbock Railroad (WATCO) in Levelland; Union Pacific in Big Spring and Laredo; Texas Pacifico in San Angelo; and Kansas City Southern in Laredo.

Chapter 5 discusses in detail four rail transload and rail-served industrial facilities in West Texas, including San Angelo, Big Spring, Lubbock, and Levelland. These facilities are oriented toward unloading bulk materials, such as sand for hydraulic fracturing, gravel and other aggregates used in construction, agricultural goods (grain and cotton), and scrap metal, for placement on trucks, many of which use Ports-to-Plains for delivery to end users. Thus, rail companies are among the stakeholders that have an interest in the highway corridor (R. Horton, personal communication, November 13, 2020). In addition to such transload activities, some stakeholders in cities along the corridor predict that true intermodal activity, namely, the transfer of shipping containers between trucks and rail, will eventually come about in West Texas. That would require an even more elaborate public–private partnership arrangement than has developed thus far in West Texas.

4.5 Economic Development in Selected Communities Along the Corridor

4.5.1 Amarillo

Amarillo, located squarely within a major agricultural region of the USA, enjoys I-40 access. Interstate I-27, whose northern end terminates at Amarillo, therefore provides the city with two interstate highways. North of Amarillo, Ports-to-Plains follows US 87 north to Dumas where it branches northwestward into New Mexico and to Denver, where it adjoins I-25, some 1390 miles from Laredo. At Dumas, a second branch, US 287, goes more directly northward into Oklahoma. Thus, economic promoters in Amarillo are eager for the city to have more direct interstate access to both Denver and to the Mexican border (Clark 2020). Furthermore, favorable rail service by BNSF boosts the city as a freight transportation crossroads at the confluence of the rail line and Interstates I-40 and I-27. The company's rail yard in

Amarillo is well connected to its Alliance Texas intermodal rail facility on the north side of Fort Worth.

4.5.2 *Lubbock*

Lubbock is located in the heart of the West Texas agricultural region that represents a major activity for the corridor and a justification for its importance. To illustrate, in counties along the Ports-to-Plains corridor in the greater Lubbock area, annual agricultural production by the latter 2010s had reached $11 billion. Lubbock, the tenth largest city of Texas, can benefit from the extension of I-27 south of the city for reduction of traffic congestion and highway safety. Furthermore, a more rapid and efficient roadway to the south will enable Lubbock to be even better connected to Mexico for binational trade (Ports-to-Plains Alliance 2020a).

Twenty miles west of downtown Lubbock is Levelland, the core city of the Levelland Micropolitan Area, located in a highly agricultural area of West Texas, especially cotton, and well within the Permian Basin petroleum region. The Levelland Industrial Rail Park on the small city's east side is a rail-served facility with land available to companies in need of industrial land, including those requiring direct rail access, discussed in Chap. 5. Its connectivity to large farms, farm product distribution centers, and facilities of the oil and gas industry depends in part on its access to Ports-to-Plains, 30 miles east by way of Texas Highway 114. The highway parallels the track of West Texas & Lubbock Railway, a short line owned by WATCO, a major freight and logistics company, that links to BNSF. Thus, Lubbock is served by two rail lines that, along with I-27, enhance its status as a regional freight transportation hub.

4.5.3 *Big Spring*

Despite a favored location on I-20 between Midland/Odessa and Abilene, Big Spring has not yet reached what local economic development stakeholders believe is its potential in terms of manufacturing and distribution. The city's business community and politicians believe that I-27 will enhance the micropolitan area's allure for investment in a distribution center and/or additional manufacturing plants to enhance its current inventory of employers (J. Little, personal communication, October 7, 2020).

The Big Spring Micropolitan Area enjoys direct access to I-20. Thus, I-27 will mean the small city will have two interstate highways. Freight traffic was already heavy at the junction of US 87 and I-20, which prompted the city and other stakeholders in 2020 to obtain funding for construction of a bypass of US 87, to keep trucks out of downtown. Big Spring is developing its transload facility at the airport, a re-purposed military base discussed in Chap. 5 that was transferred to the city as a municipal airport and industrial park in 1977. Because of its location at the eastern fringes of the Permian Basin, it is regarded as an increasingly important locale for the oil and gas industries, as well as agriculture (Big Spring 2020). However, given the intersection of Ports-to-Plains with I-20, stakeholders are focusing their attention on attracting a distribution center, but that could take two decades or more to accomplish (M. Willis, personal communication, November 6, 2020). The bypass constructed in Big Spring to route traffic more efficiently around the city and to the industrial Air Park is an example of the kinds of alterations to the existing highway infrastructure that an expanded I-27 will bring to communities along the corridor that currently endure truck traffic in city centers.

4.5.4 San Angelo

San Angelo is currently the largest city in population in the USA without interstate highway access. Therefore, the city is keen to see the completion of I-27, as well as the more recently designated I-14. Like Big Spring, San Angelo is located at the eastern periphery of the Permian Basin, and its highways support the movement of services and raw materials, such as sand, related to hydrocarbon production. The Permian Basin is a major region of US oil and gas production such that by the late 2010s, the region accounted for 32% of national production of crude oil and 13% of US natural gas (Ports-to-Plains Alliance 2020a). Oil production in the Permian Basin diminished sharply as the pandemic's effects on the economy worsened in 2020. However, by April 2021, demand for oil had increased somewhat, though not enough to boost prices, and hence production, by much (Slav 2021). However, in 2022, oil prices spiked, partly in response to economic recovery after the Covid-related slowdown of 2020, and in part because of the Russian invasion of Ukraine. Oil production began to increase in the first quarter of 2022, though it is a slow process. The Permian Basin to the west of San Angelo represents one of the most likely places in the country for new drilling. San Angelo is home to several gas- and oilfield service companies that work throughout the Permian Basin, including those counties abutting New Mexico, where drilling is most active (G. Andrews, personal communication, March 14, 2022).

The $1.2 trillion bipartisan infrastructure bill signed into law in November 2021 not only designates Ports-to-Plains as an interstate highway, but specifically includes funding for the emerging I-14 corridor, which will span five states as it stretches from Midland-Odessa, Texas to Augusta, Georgia. The I-14 corridor currently has a short stretch completed in 2017 from I-35 just south of Temple, Texas westward to Killeen and Fort Hood; like Ports-to-Plains, the rest of it will comprise existing US highways redesignated as I-14. The Gulf Coast Strategic Highway Coalition, the I-14 Corridor's equivalent of the Ports-to-Plains Alliance, has for the past decade been the force behind the project. The I-14 project was specifically included in the Infrastructure Bill via an amendment by Senators Cruz (R-TX) and Warnock (D-GA) and Congressman Brian Babin (R-TX), who wrote the original legislation for the bill in the House in 2015. Among its selling points is that it will be inland from flood-prone I-10, it will come in close proximity to several military installations, including Goodfellow AFB in San Angelo, Fort Hood in Killeen, Fort Polk in Leesville, LA, Maxwell AFB in Montgomery, Fort Benning, Robins AFB in Macon, and Fort Gordon in Augusta. The route will offer an additional east-west trending freight route to stimulate economic development. The final appropriations for funding will come from Congress, from the legislatures of the five states involved, and the US DOT (Hyde 2021; San Angelo Standard-Times 2021). It is not yet clear if the I-14 project will slow the necessary appropriations for the expansion of I-27.

4.5.5 Del Rio and Ciudad Acuña; Eagle Pass and Piedras Negras

The State of Coahuila is taking the lead among Mexican states in the promotion of the Ports-to-Plains corridor as an important element of economic development in northern Mexico. Local stakeholders in Torreón and Ciudad Acuña have been the most vocal in expressing the impacts of highway improvements from Mazatlán to Monterrey. Ciudad Acuña in particular seems well poised to benefit, given that a high percentage of USA–Mexico traffic through the Acuña-Del Rio binational twin ports is related to *maquiladoras* (assembly plants defined in Chap. 3) on the Mexican side and supportive warehousing and other logistics services on the US side. Stakeholders in the twin cities have long sought to boost traffic over the bridge connecting them. However, such traffic is more heavily dependent on local manufacturing in Ciudad Acuña than on freight shipments to or from the interior of Mexico, given the relative remoteness of the bridge. It is the most westerly freight border crossing of the Mid-Rio Grande Region, well upstream of Laredo and downstream of El Paso. Ports-to-Plains represents a future interstate highway connection for Del Rio, and, therefore, greater freight truck traffic than what currently passes through Ciudad Acuña. The idea for stakeholders of these sister cities is to attract new investment to them and additional bridge traffic (and bridge tolls) which would justify an enlargement of the international bridge. The two cities' leadership teams are working together to promote the idea (MexicoNow 2019; Rovira 2020). Officials of the State of Coahuila and Ciudad Acuña have been participating in meetings and marketing presentations associated with Ports-to-Plains in the USA and Mexico since 2000, with automotive-related manufacturing and wind energy as primary sources of expected growth (Gómez 2010).

The transporting of wind energy blades still lags somewhat behind expectations because of bottlenecks along US Highway 277, which would be alleviated upon improvement of the highway to interstate status. The same applies to transporting of steel I-beams and large tanks. An example of such a bottleneck that would be streamlined by the highway improvements is in Sonora, discussed in Chap. 8 (S. Smith, personal communication, February 20, 2020).

Between 1996 and 2021, northbound freight exceeded southbound freight through Acuña and Del Rio. Total northbound truck crossings increased from 40,000 to 75,000 in the 1996–2017 period. In 2017, the top five exports from the USA to Mexico through the Port of Del Rio were: (1) electrical machinery, equipment, and parts; (2) parts related to the aerospace industry; (3) electronics and computer parts; (4) plastics and related finished goods; and (5) furniture and prefabricated buildings. The top five imports from Mexico through the port that year were: (1) furniture and prefabricated buildings; (2) electronics and computer parts; (3) vehicles (not related to railroads); (4) electrical machinery, equipment, and parts; and (5) plastics and related finished goods (TxDOT 2018).

Much of the northbound traffic out of Del Rio is already using the two, three, and four-lane portions of Ports-to-Plains to avoid the I-35 congestion. Trucks commonly use the corridor to reach I-10 in Sonora for westbound freight movement, and sometimes they go as far north as Big Spring and Abilene to reach I-20 and Dallas-Fort Worth. However, by extending interstate-grade highway to Del Rio, the community is estimated to see a 25% increase in truck traffic shortly after completion (B. Larson, personal communication, October 7, 2020). On the Mexican side, an improved Federal Highway 29 connecting Highway 57 to Ciudad Acuña will surely increase its capacity to handle cargo to and from Monclova, Torreón, Monterrey, and other points in the interior of Mexico (see Fig. 1.2). While exact data do not exist on the amount of truck traffic using Highway 29 south of Acuña, it is estimated that only about 20% of southbound commercial truck traffic crossing the Del Rio–Acuña International Bridge goes beyond Acuña's *maquiladoras* and into the interior of Mexico (J. Castillo, personal communication, March 30, 2022). The Del Rio–Acuña bridge represents the closest truck crossing to the midpoint between Laredo and El Paso, making it attractive to shippers and carriers desiring to connect locations such as Denver, Lubbock, or Amarillo with interior Mexican manufacturing centers of Monclova, Torreón, Monterrey, and Saltillo.

Piedras Negras and its twin city Eagle Pass which currently enjoy two international vehicle bridges and a rail bridge, are likewise expecting greater truck traffic as a result of the arrival of I-27 and a corresponding invigorated highway system on the Mexican side linking Piedras Negras to Monclova, and ultimately to Monterrey and Mazatlán (Castro 2021). International trade through the twin ports as of 2020 include such goods as rail cars, automotive parts, and steel products, which indicates that Monclova and other interior Mexican cities account for a good deal of cross-border shipments there using Mexican Federal Highway 57 (Texas Center 2022).

Table 4.1 provides data on north- and southbound trade through Del Rio and Eagle Pass. Eagle Pass is a good deal more important than Del Rio for cross-border freight, in part because of the more direct highway linkage to Monclova and to San Antonio, and in part because of the Union Pacific and Ferromex rail service to Eagle Pass and Piedras Negras, linking the twin cities to Monclova and points south with San Antonio and points north, east and west. Del Rio relies more than Eagle Pass on local *maquiladora* traffic, though economic development stakeholders in Del Rio, Ciudad Acuña and the State of Coahuila are hoping that Ports-to-Plains will provide

Table 4.1 Total Trade 2019–2021 Eagle Pass and Del Rio (in $ Millions)

	2019	2020	2021
Del Rio exports	2068.7	1632.2	1904.9
Del Rio imports	3113.6	2569.7	2702.2
Eagle Pass exports	7455.0	7570.7	10,477.5
Eagle Pass imports	22,220.2	20,559.9	23,351.1

Source: Texas Center for Border Economic and Enterprise Development. A. R. Sanchez, Jr. School of Business, Texas A&M International University, 2022

the basis for greater amounts of trade through Del Rio's and Ciudad Acuña's ports of entry by capitalizing on its more northwestern location, and therefore, better access to the Permian Basin and the Great Plains. It would require the use of Federal Highway 29, which intersects with Highway 57 some 90 kilometers south of Ciudad Acuña, 55 kilometers southwest of Piedras Negras, and 185 kms north of Monclova. The data reflect that 2020 was impacted the greatest by COVID-19 lockdowns and related economic disruptions, and that pre-pandemic trade levels were reached by 2021 in Eagle Pass, and nearly rebounded in Del Rio.

4.5.6 *Laredo*

Typical of the perspective of Laredo stakeholders is that, as the largest inland port along the USA–Mexico border, and a congested one at that, the Ports-to-Plains Corridor would offer Laredo a shortcut for freight to and from the Mountain States, such that trucking utilizing I-10 west of San Antonio can avoid much of the traffic of I-35. In other words, traffic going to San Antonio and then West on I-10 could go more directly west to connect with I-10 at Sonora. Likewise, it would offer an alternative to I-35 north of San Antonio, a route afflicted by horrendous traffic bottlenecks between that city and Dallas, and I-27 would allow some freight to bypass that crowded segment at more favorable highway speeds. In addition, Ports-to-Plains would strengthen Laredo as a port in that it would be the third interstate highway to serve the city, and the city would be the only USA–Mexico border city with three interstate highways (G. Lindgren, personal communication, December 1, 2021) (Fig. 4.3).

In addition to the confluence of interstates at Laredo, the city is the only site in Texas along the Ports-to-Plains route with actual intermodal capabilities. Both Union Pacific and Kansas City Southern operate container-handling facilities with cranes in Laredo. Shippers routing freight through one or both of Laredo's container facilities would be better able to move containers between northeastern Mexico and the larger urban centers of the Great Plains or Rocky Mountains that have container handling capabilities. In short, economic developers and other stakeholders in USA–Mexico trade view positively the addition of I-27 to Laredo's mix of interstate highway connectivity.

Fig. 4.3 Image of the Port Laredo Industrial Park. (Photo by the author)

4.5.7 Torreón, Monclova, and Mazatlán

Economic development stakeholders of Torreón and the other cities of La Laguna are keenly interested in the development of freight transportation corridors to connect with the USA to amplify the ability of the region to rely on export-oriented manufacturing. The attention on such corridors related to enhancing connectivity with the border underlies the creation of La Zona de Conectividad, an emerging logistics, manufacturing, and freight transfer center (an industrial park) on the north side of Gómez Palacio directly located on the highway linking that city to Ciudad Chihuahua. The marketing of the facility emphasizes not only the connection to Chihuahua (and by extension El Paso-Juárez), but also the Pacific port city of Mazatlán, the westernmost point of Mexico's branch of Ports-to-Plains (Yoder 2009; L. Garza, personal communication, June 22, 2007; L. Cervantes, personal communication, June 19, 2007). Not only are the investors in La Zona de Conectividad interested in capturing some of the multimodal freight passing through La Laguna, but so too are economic developers in Monclova, Piedras Negras, and Ciudad Acuña.

Governor Miguel Angel Riquelme of the State of Coahuila proposed in the fall of 2020 an investment of 2.8 trillion pesos (US$134 billion) on Ports-to-Plains, comprising state and municipal funds, supplemented by private funds (thereby forming a unique public–private partnership by Mexican standards), and a payroll tax known as ISN, or "*Impuesto Sobre la Nómina*." Governor Riquelme emphasized the municipalities of Torreón, Monclova, Piedras Negras, and Ciudad Acuña as the main beneficiaries of, and partners in, the project (Rodríguez 2020). Monclova is crucial to this partnership arrangement to promote the central region of Coahuila for foreign direct investment, because it is a location that is well positioned to utilize Ports-to-Plains. Furthermore, there is urgency to stimulate the manufacturing economy further in light of layoffs in 2020 owing to the Coronavirus pandemic (Vanguardia MX 2021). By late 2021, most such manufacturing in northern Mexico had rebounded to pre-pandemic levels, though the Monclova and Ciudad Frontera urban region could benefit from more assembly plant jobs to accommodate its growing population.

A new industrial park, Parque Industrial Monclova, is a multiphase development under construction on the city's north side and financed by local and regional investors with the objective of attracting manufacturing for export to the USA, particularly automotive parts. The park's investors claim that Monclova's physical manufacturing capacity, specifically industrial parks and plants, is inadequate to meet the region's diversified manufacturing workforce capacity, and therefore, to reduce unemployment. Furthermore, local economic development stakeholders, the developers of the industrial park, and economic development officials of the State of Coahuila view the Monclova region as appropriate for nearshoring of manufacturing activities from East Asia (Vázquez 2020). Inbound parts and components, and northbound output from manufacturing plants in Monclova can utilize Federal Highway 57 to connect to Piedras Negras, San Antonio, and points east and north, and to Highway 29 to Ciudad Acuña and points to the northwest by way of the future I-27. Another likely economic development opportunity presented by such enhanced transportation infrastructure between Monclova and Ciudad Acuña will be the more efficient transporting of steel products from Monclova's AHMSA complex and nearby steel processing plants, discussed in Chap. 2, through Eagle Pass and Del Rio to Lubbock, Denver, and points in the Great Plains.

Mazatlán has become a focus of interest in transportation of freight from Northern Mexico's Pacific Coast to interior areas. For example, Caxxor Group, a private company that develops infrastructure projects, announced in late 2020 its plans to invest in the expansion of the port, including a significant enhancement of its ability to handle containers, as well as liquid, agricultural, and other bulk cargoes. The company's plans include US$3.3 billion for such port expansion, to include more space than currently exists for industrial park development, and to enhance its planned rail connection of Mazatlán by Ferromex to interior areas of northern Mexico, the USA (focused on Chicago), and ultimately to Winnipeg (Mexico News Daily 2020). Caxxor's planned rail corridor somewhat mirrors Ports-to-Plains, and connects directly with it in Mazatlán, Durango, Torreón, Monterrey, and Laredo. It is reasonable to expect that an enhanced Mazatlán highway and rail connectivity would boost the appeal of the city's maritime port, especially in light of efforts by shippers to seek alternatives to Southern California.

4.6 The Permian Basin Petroleum Economy

The Permian Basin continues to produce natural gas exports to Mexico, thanks to two major pipelines completed on the Texas side of the border since October 2020, and two existing pipelines in Mexico. The binational pipeline improvements have enabled gas exports to Mexico from West Texas to increase by 10% year-on-year from March 2020 to March 2021. Additionally, gas pipeline capacity linking the Permian Basin to the Texas Gulf Coast enables exports of liquified natural gas (LNG) through Texas ports (Paraskova 2021). However, because of lingering concerns over the Coronavirus and its impacts on hydrocarbon demand and supply, uncertainty remains among producers, and it spreads far and wide. Producers in the Permian Basin and elsewhere in the USA (and indeed globally) reiterate that the costs of adding new production capacity are not inconsequential, and that they are better served by a slow, cautious approach to bringing production back to pre-pandemic levels. Among those affected negatively by such uncertainty are pipeline operators, and by extension, providers of oilfield pipes and other services. To illustrate, by the spring of 2021, oil pipeline capacity was becoming notably underutilized. At that time, oil production in the Permian Basin was not expected to peak to levels in line with pipeline capacity until at least late 2022 (Slav 2021).

These oil-related trends raise questions about the demand for pipes, steel for pipes, scrap for steelmaking, and frac sand, the key shipped materials used in justifying the need for the interstate-quality highway that the Ports-to-Plains corridor will bring to the region. The rising interest in renewable energy sources nationally and globally will certainly provide the Permian Basin with new activities (Slav 2021). Lingering hopes for new opportunities for shipping natural gas to Mexico for that country's industrial and residential use of it, and to the Gulf Coast for expected increases in LNG production for export will keep pipeline use and installation alive. Likewise, promoters of Ports-to-Plains will undoubtedly insert the expected bright future for hardware for wind and solar energy, a boon to the trucking industry, into their presentations to attract the funding and political interest in the highway project.

4.7 Agriculture and Ports-to-Plains

Ports-to-Plains is an important corridor for transportation of livestock to feed lots in the Texas and Oklahoma Panhandles. The South and West Texas Regions supply much of the cattle for this regional livestock ecosystem. Meanwhile, ranches of northern Mexico increasingly produce yearlings for export to the US Market, a phenomenon explored in greater detail in Chaps. 7 and 8 on economic development of small cities and corresponding counties of South and southwest Texas. The majority of sorghum produced in Texas is exported to Mexico as livestock feed. Corn is also exported for that market (P. Hernandez, personal communication, November 7,

2019; D. Sexton, personal communication, September 4, 2018). Feed lots in the Texas and Oklahoma Panhandles, and producers of yearlings in localities in proximity to Ports-to-Plains will benefit from the more rapid shipment that the corridor will bring about.

A 25-year-old law preventing the importation of potatoes beyond Northern Mexico's 16-mile border zone to control crop diseases and pests will disappear in 2022, as part of a new agreement reached in December 2021 between the two countries. It will enable US potato producers, such as those of Colorado, to export much more of the crop to the Mexican market. Laredo is among seven border crossings that will be allowed to handle it, which has ramifications for the Colorado to Laredo portion of Ports-to-Plains (Mahoney 2021). Agricultural producers in proximity to the Mexican portion of the corridor are expected to benefit substantially, given the location between the current agricultural crossing points of Laredo and the El Paso region. One example is that the State of Chihuahua's apple and pecan producers reportedly experience substantial losses from spoilage because they have to send products to the Port of Laredo and ports in the Lower Rio Grande Valley, which keeps them in trucks and train cars longer than desired. Access to Piedras Negras and Ciudad Acuña will help to reduce such losses (G. Andrews, personal communication, March 14, 2022). Ports-to-Plains is regarded by its proponents as a catalyst for expanding regional and binational agro-industrial supply chains, involving crops, livestock, and feed, for good reason.

4.8 Conclusions

The Ports-to-Plains Corridor represents an economic development initiative designed to bring about enhanced connectivity between several urban areas and rural communities of nine states of the American Heartland and five Mexican states. Its promotion for funding purposes involves a unique intergovernmental arrangement based on an alliance of multiple communities along or close to the route in both countries. It further requires the participation of state-level governments in its planning, financing, and promotion vis-å-vis the Congress, though such efforts differ from state to state. Texas leads the way among American states, while Coahuila stands out as the dominant actor in Mexico, because two of its land ports stand to benefit to the greatest degree. Each community uses the corridor's existing highways, and will use its future enhanced highway infrastructure, in different ways based on varying economic activities and resulting freight loads; meanwhile, stakeholders in the different communities work collectively to bring it about. Furthermore, many communities in proximity to the corridor, though not directly along it, regard it as essential given that multiple highways perpendicular to Ports-to-Plains intersect with it.

Population growth in the Texas, Colorado, and northern Mexican regions that the corridor currently serves is above average for the two countries, which lends justification to more efficient, streamlined highway access to accommodate economic development. To illustrate, despite long-term volatility in petroleum production and the lack (or low rate) of workforce growth in the region's agriculture, West Texas nonetheless is growing faster than the Texas statewide average. The West Texas workforce increased 16% overall between 2010 and 2019, compared to the statewide average of 15.3%, while South Texas, including rural counties, grew 7.4%, still above the national average of 6.3% (Texas Comptroller 2020). This growth suggests that a larger workforce in manufacturing and services in West and South Texas cities is likely and will enable those regions to capitalize on investment by companies in need of shipping of bulk freight, including metals processing and wind and solar energy. Likewise, the border cities of the Mid-Rio Grande Region of South Texas continue to diversify their economies beyond petroleum and cross-border trade activities, like warehousing, and increasingly into the broader service sector. The enhancement of Ports-to-Plains to interstate grade will contribute to more efficient mobility for growing populations, and undoubtedly will become a more substantial asset to assist economic development corporations and local governments to attract the diverse array of employers these regions of Texas and northern Mexico desire.

The corridor represents a suitable case study to illustrate the highly competitive nature of alternative interstate highway routes for freight transportation. The study portrays the "work in progress" nature of all such federally funded and state-directed corridors, especially one on the verge of entering its adolescent stage. The success of marketing the corridor to current users of its existing highways, and to politicians controlling the purse strings has yet to be determined as the latter consider other highway projects in Texas. One facet of Ports-to-Plains is abundantly clear and applicable to other highway corridors: the necessity of different functional economic regions to collaborate enthusiastically to keep the project alive and on the radar screen of the government entities that provide funding.

References

Big Spring (2020) Big Spring Airpark. Retrieved November 6, 2020, from https://www.mybig-spring.com/149/Airpark-industrial-Park

Castro E (2021, February) Coahuila promueve proyecto ports to plains en Canada, Mexico Industry. https://mexicoindustry.com/noticia/coahuila-promueve-proyecto-ports-to-plainsen-canada

Clark D (2020, December 8) Benefits of Ports-to-Plains hailed. Amarillo Globe-News. https://www.amarillo.com/story/news/2020/12/08/ports-plains-benefits-hailed/6498549002/

Dotray M (2021, March 9) Arrington, Cuellar reintroduce Ports-To-Plains act to extend I-27, Lubbock Avalanche-Journal. https://www.lubbockonline.com/story/news/2021/03/09/arrington-and-cuellar-reintroduce-ports-plains-highway-act/6923122002/

Gómez R (2010, September 6) Preparada la participación de Acuña para el encuentro Ports to Plains en Dakota del Sur, Territorio de Coahuila y Texas. http://www.territoriodecoahuilay-texas.com/noticia/preparada-la-participacion-de-acuna-para-el-encuentro-ports-plains-en-dakota-del-sure/4489/

Hyde J (2021, August 5) Senate infrastructure bill includes routing interstate through San Angelo. San Angelo Live. https://sanangelolive.com/news/business/2021-08-05/senate-infrastructure-bill-includes-routing-interstate-through-san-angelo

LEDA (2020) TXDOT impact findings for interstate 27 designation. Lubbock Economic Development Alliance. Https://lubbock.eda.org/wp-content?uploads/2020/06/Ports-to-Plains-Interstate_Extension.pdf

Mahoney N (2021, December 26) Borderlands: US potato farmers preparing for Mexico opening. FreightWaves. https://www.freightwaves.com/news/us-potato-farmers-preparing-for-mexico-opening?utm_source=sfmc&utm_medium=email&utm_campaign=as_daily_12_29_21&utm_term=Borderlands%3a+US+potato+farmers+preparing+for+Mexico+opening&utm_id=93738&sfmc_id=913819

Mexico News Daily (2020, October 14) Rail Corridor would link Mazatlán port with Winnipeg. Mexico News Daily. https://mexiconewsdaily.com/news/rail-corridor-would-link-mazatlan-port-with-winnipeg-canada/

MexicoNow (2019, October 28) Ports To Plains will boost the economic activity of the northern border. MexicoNow. http://border-now.com/ports-to-plains-will-boost-the-economic-activity-of-the-northern-border/

Minor N (2020, September 29) Gardner Bill pushes long-sought eastern plains interstate. But big hurdles remain. Colorado Public Radio News. https://www.cpr.org/2020/09/29/gardner-bill-would-push-long-sought-eastern-plains-interstate-closer-to-reality/

Paraskova T (2021, June 8) The Permian has solved its natural gas pipeline shortage. Oilprice.com. https://oilprice.com/Latest-Energy-News/World-News/The-Permian-Has-Solved-Its-Natural-Gas-Pipeline-Shortage.html

Ports-to-Plains Alliance (2016, May 3) Newsletter (14:9). https://portstoplains.com/index.php/news-events/newsletters/1218-april-2016-vol-14-issue-9

Ports-to-Plains Alliance (2020a) Ports-to-Plains Corridor interstate feasibility study: segment 2 executive summary July 30 2020

Ports-to-Plains Alliance (2020b) Ports-to-Plains Corridor interstate feasibility study: segment 3 executive summary July 30 2020

Ports-to-Plains Alliance (2020c) The History of the Ports-to-plains alliance including early American highway development events. https://portstoplains.com/index-php/our-alliance/ports-to-plains-history

Ports-to-Plains Alliance (2021) Web site. Retrieved December 8, 2021, from https://portstoplains.com

RapaportW(2020,June15)Ports-to-PlainsAlliancerevealsnewdatafrominterstate27expansionstudy. KXAN https://www.kxan.com/news/texas-politics/ports-to-plains-alliance-reveals-new-data-from-interstate-27-expansion-study/

Rodríguez S (2020, October 3) Propone 2 mil 800 mdp para 'Port to Plains', Siglo de Torreón https://theworldnews.net/mx-news/propone-2-mil-800-mdp-para-port-to-plains

Rovira B (2020, March 15) Video: Acuña mayor discusses Ports to Plains project. Rio Grande Guardian. https://riograndeguardian.com/acuna-mayor-discusses-ports-to-plains-project/

San Angelo Standard-Times (2021, November 15) Congress designates interstate 14 across five states with I-14 corridor through San Angelo. San Angelo Standard-Times. https"//www.gosanangelo.com/story/news/2021/11/15/five-state-14-designation-now-final-infrastructure-bill/8630360002/

Slav I (2021, April 14) The permian will never face a pipeline shortage again. Oilpricecom. https://oilprice.com/Energy/Energy-General/The-Permian-Will-Never-Face-A-Pipeline-Shortage-Again.html

Texas Center (2022) Texas Center for border economic and enterprise development. In: Sanchez AR Jr (ed) U.S.-Mexico Trade through South Inland Ports. School of Business/Texas A&M International University, Laredo. Retrieved March 18, 2022, from http://texascenter.tamiu.edu/dt-top-trade.shtml

Texas Comptroller (2020) The West Texas region: 2020 regional report. Texas Comptroller (Web Site) Retrieved March 28, 2022, from https://comptroller.texas.gov/economy/economic-data/regions/2020/west.php

TxDOT (2018) Del Rio, TX: Texas border facts, fall 2018. Texas Department of Transportation. Retrieved October 10, 2020, from http://ftp.dot.state.tx.us/pub/txdot/move-texas-freight/resources/fact-sheets/border/del-rio.pdf

VanguardiaMX(2021,June11)Monclovaestáapuntodetenerunatransformaciónimportante:Fomento Económico, Vanguardia MX. https://vanguardia.com.mx/coahuila/monclova-esta-punto-de-tener-una-transformacion-importante-economico-DUVG3592331

Vázquez G (2020, February) Parque Industrial Monclova, detonará la Región Centro, Mexico Industry. https://mexicoindustry.com/noticia/-parque-industrial,monclova-detonara-la-region-centro%2D%2D

Yoder M (2009) Landscapes of industry and transport: Monclova and Torreón, Mexico. J Big Bend Stud 21:179–200

Yoder M (2021, October 15) Freight transport geography in the era of COVID-19: notes on inter-modal shipping. Paper presentation, Southwest Division American Association of Geographers (Virtual)

Chapter 5
Case Studies in Freight Transport Geography: Four West Texas Industrial Rail Facilities

Abstract US freight tonnage shipped by rail has been sluggish compared to trucking since the Great Recession of 2008–2009. In response, rail companies, and the shippers and communities that rely on them are seeking ways to enhance rail performance, and by extension, economic development. Such stakeholders regard transload and other industrial facilities as essential to the future of US rail, including in West Texas, a region whose economy depends on energy, agriculture, and manufacturing. The region's small- and mid-sized cities are relatively spread out by American standards; therefore, rail development is regarded as essential to their economic development. This chapter examines the evolution of industrial rail facilities in Big Spring, Lubbock, Levelland, and San Angelo, four cities of West Texas located directly along, or in close proximity to the emerging Ports-to-Plains trucking corridor, the focus of Chap. 4. It provides an overview of cargoes handled at each and discusses some of their more important spatial connections. The four facilities are served by distinctly different rail companies, and each has unique infrastructure and switching operations connecting rail and truck service. The four portray somewhat similar, yet somewhat unique, public–private partnership arrangements to finance the expansion and operation of their respective rail ports. The research involved the gathering of data from websites of private and public entities, news articles, and open-ended interviews of stakeholders in freight transport and local economic development.

Keywords Transportation geography · Railroads · West Texas · Economic development · Rail-served industrial facilities

5.1 Freight Infrastructure in West Texas: An Introduction

The Greater West Texas Region is one that is spread out yet is keenly attempting to increase its economic development potential. Rail factors heavily in the settlement history of the region, given that transportation mode's capability to connect distant cities and towns. The benefits of rail-served industrial facilities, an understudied

M. S. Yoder, *Geographical Scale and Economic Development*,
https://doi.org/10.1007/978-3-031-36197-5_5

topic, are capturing the notice of economic developers as they seek greater cost and logistical efficiencies in the movements of bulk freight. Such materials include chemicals, crude oil, fertilizers, crops, agricultural inputs, lumber, aggregates (construction materials such as gravel and asphalt), raw steel, and scrap materials, among others. These facilities enable materials to be moved easily between two or more modes, usually between rail and truck, as is the case with all such facilities of West Texas. Generally, the most advantageous of such industrial facilities, or "rail ports," as many are called, are those with direct access to Class I railroads, meaning the larger carriers like Union Pacific, BNSF, CSX, Kansas City Southern, Canadian Pacific, Canadian National, and Norfolk Southern, all of whose revenues individually exceed $433 million. For heavy loads traveling medium to long distances, the cost savings over truck can be considerable because of the amount of tonnage per transportation employee, lower fuel costs, and therefore greater economies of scale. Furthermore, pollutants are reduced overall when compared with trucking alone. However, the costs of building the necessary facilities, and their land requirements can be considerable, so not all communities would benefit from rail-served industrial facilities (Tanner 2018).

Rail transload and other rail-served facilities in the USA are more often than not participants in public–private partnerships, which makes their study relevant to an understanding of policies for financing infrastructure across the country. As the four facilities included in this chapter illustrate, each is unique in terms of the planning and financing arrangements made with local governments and economic development entities. Some transload facilities are run by railroad companies as stand-alone plots of land where bulk products can be transferred between truck and rail. Other transload facilities involve partnerships between rail companies and local governments and/or economic development corporations. Still other rail-served facilities are industrial parks within which rail lines provide the necessary freight connections to industrial plants and distribution centers. Another type is something in between, with a combination of bulk yards and industrial or distribution buildings. The typical transload facility provides not only rail track but bulk commodity yards for the transfer of heavy loads by cranes or other machinery for lifting them, and subsequent storage. Typically, a train delivers cars with the heavy loads, which then are unloaded for subsequent transfer to trucks that haul materials to its destination through drayage (Tanner 2018).

Rail-served facilities that are successful for economic development generally abide by a few principles. Besides access to a Class I railroad, either directly or by way of a short line railroad, a minimum threshold of the number of cars handled should be met. If not, then a single spur to connect from a rail company's main line to an individual plant would be a more economical choice. There are three types of track arrangements for rail-served facilities. One common solution is a loop track, which offers faster speeds for moving cars, and therefore, allows for a larger number of cars to be handled per week. A loop can connect to the rail company's line in two places. Rail transload facilities are more often than not of this type, given their requirements for handling a large number of rail cars for multiple purposes. A transload facility can be private (for one company) or public, like a small maritime port, for serving more than one company. A second track arrangement type is a basic spur, or "stub-in," which connects to the rail company's line at one end. Rail cars are pushed and pulled, and this arrangement can accommodate a limited number of them. The third type is a siding, parallel to the main track, that can be served by the rail company's locomotive in either direction. No matter which type is built, three topographic (landscape) considerations must be taken into account: the slope of the land, the existence of obstacles such as bridges and tunnels, and the curvature of the existing main rail line. Crossings and switches can be costly, so these features are often subsidized by state-level economic development or transportation agencies (Iowa DOT 2019).

This chapter explores four rail-served facilities in West Texas, three of which are rail-served industrial facilities that are industrial parks, and one of which is a newly created transload facility. They are located in Big Spring, Levelland, Lubbock, and San Angelo (see Fig. 1.1). All four rely to varying degrees on the energy and agricultural production of the region. Each exhibits a unique version of infrastructure financing and public–private partnership, and each is associated with a different rail company. Two involve class I railroads, one is tied to a Class III rail company, and one is operated by a short line railway. The four cases provide lessons for economic development researchers and practitioners, as well as geographers interested in freight transportation infrastructure and logistics. They demonstrate the importance of connectivity between functional economic regions that adjoin each other but are spread out over the relatively sparsely populated West Texas region. Rail and trucking are key to such connectivity in the region, dominated by hydrocarbon energy production and agriculture. Rail provides economic advantages to conquer both bulk and distance, while trucking is necessary for linking to individual energy sites and farming and ranching operations. To carry out the research for this chapter, I relied on official documents from economic development entities and rail companies, news articles, and open-ended interviews.

5.2 A Relevant Feature of Rail Legislative History

In West Texas, the interchange between Class I and short line railroads must be taken into account by economic developers hoping to establish or expand rail-served industrial facilities. This fact of rail geography is regulated by the Staggers Rail Act of 1980. The legislation brought about a deregulation of the freight railroad industry that allowed railroad carriers to enter into more flexible contracts with shippers that many argue was advantageous to both railroad companies and customers in terms of lower prices that would keep rail companies afloat in an environment of competition against increased truck freight haulage. Rail companies could enter into exclusive contracts with shippers and could divest of underutilized tracks that short line companies could then operate. However, it also unleashed notable closing of rail lines that were underutilized. In turn, short line rail companies bought up many such lines. To ensure that the short line companies were not disadvantaged, the act required that track sharing arrangements be less burdensome for the smaller companies, while guaranteeing that the smaller carriers establish desired connections with Class I rail lines (Association of American Railroads 2021; US Government Publishing Office 2015). The facilities at Big Spring, Levelland, and San Angelo are positively impacted by the legislation.

5.3 Case I: Lubbock Rail Port

Lubbock Rail Port is a rail-served industrial park located five miles north of downtown Lubbock along I-27 at FM 1294, roughly equidistant between I-20 and I-40. The Lubbock Economic Development Alliance (LEDA), the developer and owner, makes land available for sale, lease, or for free to companies in need of direct access to a Class I rail line. In 2009, local economic developers saw a need for such a facility, given Lubbock's growing attachment to the Permian Basin energy region, and the growth in potential for agricultural processing. That year, LEDA, a non-profit 501(c)(3), obtained $1.5 million in federal funds to construct three additional rail spurs in the facility to enhance the locality's economic capabilities; that is, to house large manufacturing and distribution companies. That funding was used to begin constructing the rail port on 526 acres (213 ha) of land that the LEDA acquired for such a facility in 2007. Today the facility has a total of five rail spurs, parallel and adjacent to BNSF's north-south line. Partnership with the City of Lubbock was crucial in promoting the idea in the community, given that the LEDA receives sales tax revenues, and to recruiting companies seeking to locate plants in a rail-served facility in West Texas (LEDA 2019). The City's commitment to the development of the industrial park includes tax abatements, while the LEDA makes discounted land available, depending on the integrity of the project. In short, the LEDA does a cost-benefit analysis of each potential tenant to determine the amount of the discount (theoretically up to 100 percent) for land in the facility. The public–private partnership arrangement that the facility enjoys includes locomotive movement agreements with BNSF, the Class I railroad that serves it (J. Osborne, personal communication, November 11, 2020).

The Lubbock Rail Port has a spur-style track layout. Tenants listed on the LEDA website, include: MACSA (Molinos Anáhuac, a flour mill); Hampton Farms (an almond manufacturing and future peanut butter plant, established in 2017); Bayer Crop Science (a plant adjacent to, rather than within the Rail Port, that processes cottonseed); WL Plastics (a manufacturer of "high-density polyethylene pipe"); and Corteva, an agricultural research and development (R&D) facility.

5.4 Case II: Levelland Industrial Rail Park

The Levelland Industrial Rail Park is a rail-served industrial park located in the eastern portion of the Levelland Micropolitan Area. The park, which was planned in 2008 and opened in 2010, is located 25 miles west of downtown Lubbock and is served by the Lubbock and Western Railway (LBWR), owned by WATCO, which intersects with BNSF in Lubbock (Levelland EDC, 2021). The South Plains and Santa Fe Railway built the rail line in 1925 to connect Lubbock and Bledsoe, a town immediately west of Levelland, to provide rail service westward, the one direction from Lubbock where service was lacking. After changing hands two times in the interim, WATCO acquired the line in the early 2000s for hauling agricultural commodities, fertilizers, ethanol, and gas- and oilfield equipment, given the regional economy (Trainweb.org 2020). Land in the 243-acre (98 ha) park is available for sale or lease, much of which is rail-served. The LEDC promotes the site for industrial bulk materials handling, manufacturing plants, and distribution centers. The LBWR (a subsidiary of WATCO) rail line was upgraded in 2002 upon the establishment of an ethanol plant 6 miles east of Levelland, and immediately east of the industrial rail park. Local stakeholders saw an opportunity to attract investment to Levelland by constructing the rail-served facility in 2010. The facility has some 21,000 feet of track, which represents abundant capacity for growth (Levelland EDC 2021).

Like the Lubbock Rail Port, Levelland Industrial Park was established in light of the strong agricultural and energy sectors of the area. The facility's track is laid out in a double-track loop. Tenants include two agricultural processing centers (Penny Newman Grain and Portales Select Peanut Company), four oil and gas service companies, and Titan Transload, a company that provides transload services and rail car storage for the oil and gas business of West Texas (Levelland EDC 2021). In the public–private partnership, the Levelland Economic Development Corporation, an arm of the City of Levelland, which appoints its board members, makes sites available, while the rail company operates most of the switching. Three tenants own their rail spurs and operate "Hercules" type small switching locomotives themselves. The primary track in the facility, referred to as "the loop," is owned and repaired by the LEDC. The latter charges a track use fee of $50 per rail car. Half of the revenues generated from the use fees go to the LEDC's general fund while half is dedicated to repair and maintenance. The remainder of the LEDC's budget comes from a 1/4 cent per dollar of revenues that the city raises from sales taxes (D. Rushing, personal communication, January 13, 2022).

Incentives are provided to companies who wish to locate to the plant, based on employment commitments (at least 20 employees) and on economic benefit to the community, including revenues that will circulate through the county, and tax revenues from the companies' incomes. In short, the LEDC Board determines an expected return on investment (ROI) that each potential tenant will provide to the community. The incentives include discounts for land leases and sales to approved companies, as well as the ensemble of incentives provided by the State of Texas. The expansion of existing tenants' facilities is valued as much by the LEDC as is the attraction of new companies. The latter is illustrated by a manufacturer of polyethylene pipe for water and the oil and gas industry at the industrial park, and the incentives it received. The incentives were offered based on a commitment by the company that it will invest $8 million in its plant and provide 15 full-time new jobs. The LEDC agreed to provide $618,450.00 in incentives that include the provision of nine acres (3.65 ha) of property that enjoys direct rail access. The company is among the first in the facility to utilize the rail service for inputs and finished products (Timian 2018).

The LEDC is attempting to diversify from the unpredictable oil and gas industry by attracting other types of manufacturing, especially in agricultural processing and farm inputs, in order to maintain a healthy local economic base. While the oil and gas industry of the Permian Basin has largely recovered from the COVID-19 economic downturn, exemplified by the rise of oil from $30–40 a barrel back to $70–80 (in early 2022), no significant new drilling is taking place, but existing wells continue to require maintenance, including replacement of steel pipe at the well heads. Therefore, oil and gas are counted among the locality's economic activities that are taken seriously by local economic development stakeholders (D. Rushing, personal communication, January 27, 2022).

The LEDC's director emphasizes that the entity views the community and its economic development as a regional phenomenon. To illustrate, Levelland is often in competition with Lubbock for attracting new companies, but they ultimately cooperate if one or the other is on the company's short list in the site selection process. The thinking is that it is better to have a strong region, regardless of the exact location of a company's plant. Furthermore, the LEDC is a member of the Ports-to-Plains Alliance, because they expect the corridor to enhance their ability to market the industrial rail facility, especially in light of agricultural processing, agro-manufacturing, and supplies for the oil and gas industry. Trade with Mexico in those economic sectors is expected to grow, resulting in an increased need for a divided four-lane highway in the region, some 25 miles from the rail facility (D. Rushing, personal communication, January 13, 2022).

As of January 2022, nine companies were located in the Levelland Industrial Rail Park, and a tenth was in the process of establishing itself in the park. Five of them use rail, and the remainder are primarily oil and gas service companies that do not require rail access. Those that use the rail service, which occurs on average three or four times a week, are a chemical company that produces cleaners (including hand sanitizer and related chemical inputs), and agricultural processing (Levelland EDC 2021; D. Rushing, personal communication, January 27, 2022).

The number of rail cars that have arrived at the facility has varied in recent years, owing to the downturn in oil and gas in the late 2010s, and the Coronavirus-related economic downturn. The downturn in oil and gas activities of West Texas began in 2019 and was accelerated by the pandemic in 2020 before rebounding somewhat in 2021. The impressive number in the first month of 2022 is believed by the community to foreshadow a healthy year (Table 5.1).

Table 5.1 Levelland Industrial Rail Park, Rail Car Traffic 2018–2022

Year	Number of rail cars
2018	6417
2019	3487
2020	1394
2021	2059
2022 (January)	651

Source: D. Rushing, personal communication, January 27, 2022

5.5 Case III: Big Spring Airpark/Industrial Park

Of the four rail-served industrial facilities of this West Texas case study, Big Spring Airpark is the most developed. It consists of an industrial park and rail transload facility for companies in need of bulk freight transfer. Its track is a lengthy spur laid out in a semi-loop fashion. It is clearly at an advantage to many other rail-served industrial facilities of West Texas because of its location on I-20, a major east-west interstate whose western terminus is its intersection with I-10 at a favorable location east of El Paso. It connects Midland-Odessa with important transport hubs such as Dallas-Fort Worth, Shreveport, Jackson, Birmingham, Atlanta, and Columbia, SC before reaching its eastern terminus, where it connects with I-95 in Florence, SC. Even before completion of I-27 southward from Lubbock, Ports-to-Plains has experienced enough growth in truck traffic at its intersection with I-20 to prompt a widening of US Highway 87 at the Big Spring Airpark, in the form of a bypass, discussed in Chap. 4, that provides access to the facility on its south and west sides.

The Big Spring Airpark is a re-purposed military air base. It was originally the Big Spring Army Airfield, a World War II-era training facility for bombardiers. During the Korean War, the airfield became Webb Air Force Base, and was again utilized primarily for pilot training, though in 1967, it was used for training combat troops, specifically Jordanian troops who left that year to fight in the Six Day War in the Middle East. At that point, the base was regarded as non-essential and was turned over in 1977 to the City of Big Spring as the Big Spring Industrial Park and the Big Spring McMahon-Wrinkle Airport, a general aviation facility. Many of the base's original buildings remain and are suitable for commercial use, such as light manufacturing, and they provide lease income to the City of Big Spring (Big Spring 2020). The public–private partnership that developed and enhanced the industrial facility includes tight collaboration between the City of Big Spring, the Big Spring Economic Development Corporation, and Big Spring Rail Systems, Inc. (Worrell 2015).

The public–private partnership arrangement is unique. The City of Big Spring owns the track within the Airpark. Big Spring Rail System (BSR), a line haul railroad headquartered in Glen Mills, PA and established in 2012 to run the switching operations in the Big Spring facility, leases the track from the City. By federal law, Union Pacific is required to provide connection to BSR, which occurs immediately west of UP's rail yard on the west side of Big Spring (J. Little, personal communication, October 7, 2020).

Among the non-industrial tenants at the Big Spring Airpark are four prisons, three of which are federal facilities run by a private corporation, and one of which is run by the federal Bureau of Prisons (Big Spring 2020). The newer development in the Airpark and its immediate vicinity is more industrial- and distribution-oriented, in part because of the addition of 3.3 miles of rail track for direct access to rail-served industrial facilities and for rail car storage. The rail switching service within the facility is operated by Big Spring Rail Service, designated as a short line railroad that connects to the main Union Pacific line that runs through Big Spring, and ultimately connects Dallas-Fort Worth and the West Coast. The original purpose behind the rail service within the Air Park was distribution of frac sand for the booming energy industry of the Permian Basin, though subsequent diversification within the Air Park has occurred. For example, diesel fuel has been transloaded at the facility, primarily for use by oil platforms, and lumber from western Canada for use in telephone poles and railroad ties, and steel pipes used in well heads are transloaded there. A resin pipe company manufactures pipes for use in irrigation of agriculture in the region, and Napa, a major automobile parts retailer, operates a distribution center. Much of the 2.5 miles of track is used for storage and cleaning of rail cars, particularly tank cars (Big Spring 2020; D. Lee, personal communication, October 8, 2020). A future plan for the Airpark, enhanced by the Ports-to-Plains improvements, is the establishment of a mile-long transload facility for bulk cargo to be established on an unused airport tarmac (Big Spring Rail System 2021).

In the future, it is hoped that a distribution center developer will find the location advantageous, given its location along both I-20 and Ports-to-Plains. Given that trucks now transport cotton from Big Spring to Lubbock in fairly large quantities, it is expected that larger quantities could be sent by rail in containers between West Texas and ports of the West Coast for export to Asia, an activity that would, like a large big-box retailer's distribution center, require an intermodal ramp in Big Spring. The activities requiring an intermodal ramp are not immediately on the drawing board, so such infrastructure would be a best-case scenario and a long-term plan. The increased demand in Mexico for Texas sorghum for livestock feed is believed to be a shorter-term goal for transload activities. Given the volatility of the oil and gas industry, such diversification is desired by stakeholders of economic development in Big Spring (D. Lee, personal communication, October 8, 2020).

5.6 Case IV: San Angelo Rail Port

San Angelo's transload facility is the newest of the four rail-served industrial facilities included in this study. Its youth reflects the shorter history of the rail company serving it, a company more recently established than those serving the other three sites. Whereas BNSF and UP established their presence decades ago in Lubbock and Big Spring, respectively, Texas Pacifico Railroad (TPRR), a Class III railroad, is a more recent venture, and one that exhibits an interesting public–private partnership arrangement. Texas Pacifico leases the track from the State of Texas, who invested in rehabilitating the abandoned rail line connecting the USA–Mexico border city of Presidio with San Angelo Junction, a point 65 miles east of the city of San Angelo. Furthermore, the facility itself involves an interesting public–private partnership arrangement. South Plains Lamesa Railroad (SPLRR) owns the facility and operates the switching and other functions within it since its completion in 2022. South Plains Lamesa Railroad purchased the property from the City of San Angelo in late 2019 for $600,000 specifically for the purposes of building a rail transload facility to link to the Texas Pacifico line. South Plains Lamesa, will invest $1 million to develop the facility, and will operate the rail service and develop industrial sites within it (Pesquera 2020; Mahoney2020; G. Andrews, personal communication, March 14, 2022).

Key to the foundation of the rail port is the South Orient Rail Line, which runs from San Angelo Junction westward 371 miles to Presidio, on the USA–Mexico border. The rail line was originally built in the early 1900s as a venture to provide service from central-west Texas to the Mexican Pacific port of Topolobampo, Sinaloa, which represented the geographically shortest route from Kansas City to the Pacific Ocean. The South Orient line was largely inoperative in recent decades until its rehabilitation commenced in 2001. That year, the State of Texas Department of Transportation (TxDOT) bought the rail line, which represents a rare example of public–private partnership in rail service. TxDOT opened up a bidding process for a potential operator of the track in 2001. Grupo México, a company with investments in mining and rail, including Mexico's largest rail company, Ferromex, made a successful bid for use of the track. The public–private partnership is an anomaly, given that railroad companies typically own the track they operate on. In this case, however, the State of Texas owns the track, and the Grupo Mexico-owned subsidiary Texas Pacífico Railroad leases the track from the state. Ferromex owns the track on the Mexican side, from Ojinaga to Chihuahua to the Pacific port of Topolobampo (Cartner 2018; Hyde 2018; Riley 2018).

At the time the arrangement between TxDOT and Texas Pacífico was made in 2001, the track was in dire need of repair in many spots. The State of Texas began repairs, first in the easternmost portion of the line. Subsequent repairs west of San Angelo have been financed by a FASTLANE federal grant (Hyde 2018), a rare example of public sector involvement in rail. The rail line offered only slow service (less than 20 miles per hour) from 2001 to the early 2010s, prior to the most recent boom in oil and gas in the Permian Basin, which was based on hydraulic fracturing. Then, the rail line was largely dependent on shipments of grains and other agricultural products. Once the hydrocarbon boom was in place, the mix of cargos shifted in favor of sand for hydraulic fracturing ("frac sand"), crude and refined oil in tank cars, and steel for the pipes used in oil and gas wells (Riley 2018). Despite increased traffic on the South Orient line, it has largely been limited to points east of Fort Stockton, because of the burning of the border rail bridge in 2008 and 2009 (Hyde 2018). The track between Fort Stockton and Presidio has been completed to a capacity of 40 miles per hour since December 2020, and the rail bridge has been completed as of late 2020. But track rehabilitation on the Mexican side still needs to be completed by Ferromex, and the US Customs and Border Enforcement facility required for inspection and clearance of cargo still needs completion. The approximately $14 million required for funding of the latter had not yet been found by 2020 (Texas Rail News 2020; R. Horton, personal communication, November 13, 2020). This latter federal government facility is the biggest holdup to cross-border rail traffic through Presidio and Ojinaga (G. Andrews, personal communication, March 14, 2022).

Economic development and freight transportation stakeholders in San Angelo imagine that exports to Mexico will become viable over the Presidio-Ojinaga rail bridge based on tank cars loaded with refined petroleum products; it could very well include movements of shipping containers once the rail improvements are completed in Mexico, container-handling facilities are enhanced in Topolobampo, and freight capacities are expanded between the capital city of Chihuahua and the maritime port. The Chihuahua–Topolobampo stretch of the route currently has many curves and tunnels that prohibit some freight movements such as double-stacked containers (R. Horton, personal communication, November 13, 2020; S. Meador, personal communication, October 6, 2020; M. Looney, personal communication, November 13, 2020). The Sinaloa port has a container dock and storage area, and it can accept containers now with manual crane (reach stacker) service (DIGAOHM 2021). Furthermore, the boom in Mexico's automotive industry, largely based on parts, may provide the basis for container shipments from Chihuahua to Dallas-Fort Worth. Imports of many agricultural products from Chihuahua, including apples and pecans, are expected to provide reliable business for Texas Pacífico, which could very well be capitalized upon by distributors and other businesses in San Angelo. In that case, the rail line and Rail Port would be among the factors of site and situation to boost economic development in the city. In the meantime, oil and gas activities in West Texas require replacement pipes at the wells, which is reliable business for Texas Pacifico and the rail transload facility (G. Andrews, personal communication, October 14, 2020; R. Horton, personal communication, November 13, 2020; M. Looney, personal communication, November 13, 2020). Ports-to-Plains provides the basis for local economic development stakeholders to seek out investment in a distribution center that ultimately could use the rail port (G. Andrews, personal communication, October 14, 2020).

With this backdrop of anticipated increases in the already-growing number of railcar shipments by Texas Pacífico and the future expansion of Ports-to-Plains, the rail company and various stakeholders in economic development in San Angelo began planning for a rail transload facility in the city. However, Texas Pacífico was not interested in running the switching operations within such a facility, so a line-haul rail company was needed to round out the partnership by providing switching services. South Plains Lamesa entered into the agreement to develop and manage the property and provide the service of moving around rail cars within it. The company has experience operating a similar facility in Slaton, Texas, 19 miles southeast of Lubbock and 14 miles from the Ports-to-Plains Corridor (San Angelo Economic Development 2020).

The San Angelo facility involves a unique public–private partnership. The City of San Angelo Economic Development Corporation purchased the 180 acres (73 ha) and entered into an agreement with the future operator of the facility, South Plains Lamesa Railroad, whereby the latter purchased the property for $600,000 from the San Angelo Economic Development Corporation. South Plains Lamesa agreed to invest a total of $1 million to develop the property, and as long as investments are made as agreed upon, the city will forgive each of the six annual payments of $100,000 and effectively hand the property over to the operator after 6 years (G. Andrews, personal communication, March 14, 2022). South Plains Lamesa originally planned to lay out multiple spurs ("stub-ins") within the facility, and to plat it so that land can be available to individual companies seeking to establish rail-served industrial facilities, including manufacturing plants, distribution warehouses, and transload sites for bulk cargo (San Angelo Economic Development 2020). In addition to individual parcels for companies to acquire, a transload platform will be open to any clients in need of such service. However, the original plan of installing a series of spurs in a "stair-step pattern" had been altered in favor of a loop, which could handle more rail cars at a time, and more quickly than pushing and pulling small numbers of cars. While the short line rail company will conduct the switching and land sales, the San Angelo Economic Development Corporation will be heavily involved in marketing and promotion of the rail port (G. Andrews, personal communication, March 14, 2022).

As of mid-March of 2022, the facility was on the verge of completion, with some 18,000 feet of track installed, and one company desiring to immediately transload aggregates is ready to use it. South Plains Lamesa had acquired a locomotive, and much of the track had been installed (G. Andrews, personal communication, March 14, 2022). Four additional companies have expressed strong interest in using the rail port upon completion. A local agricultural products distribution company receives dry fertilizers by truck and looks forward to the cost savings of rail shipments. A second distributor of agricultural products will use the facility for moving product by hopper-type rail cars for efficiency and cost savings. A cotton producer currently has to dray product by truck to Fort Worth for BNSF to ship to the West Coast for export; the reinvigorated rail line can streamline that shipping process. A metals fabrication company that purchases steel plate from Mexico expresses that rail would better serve its needs than trucking currently does. A chemical company wants to use the facility for transloading, and for temporary storage of the chemicals in rail cars (San Angelo Chamber of Commerce 2020).

An impact study carried out by the San Angelo Chamber of Commerce (2020) identified the most likely products to be handled in the rail facility in the future. These include agricultural products, fertilizers and other agricultural inputs, wind turbine blades, petrochemicals, wood products (lumber and plywood), scrap metal, steel pipes, and compressed natural gas in tank containers, and refrigerated containers for processed foods. The San Angelo Rail Port and the pending highway improvements as part of the Ports-to-Plains Corridor clearly are having a positive impact on San Angelo's efforts at economic development.

5.7 Conclusions

The four rail-served industrial facilities examined in this chapter exhibit noteworthy differences that will likely pique the curiosity of economic development practitioners and academic geographers alike. The working relationships between the respective economic development entities of each city and the rail companies serving those important freight transportation connection points are quite striking when considering that the basic economic geography of the region of West Texas exhibits quite a bit of commonality throughout. Energy and agriculture abound in all communities of the region. The local business and governing cultures are favorable to public–private partnership in general in West Texas. All of them are within the suburban fringes of their respective cities, owing to the land-extensive nature of such facilities, and each one ties into the emerging Ports-to-Plains Corridor. And yet, the four rail companies have crafted quite different relationships with the localities and their rail-served facilities. The facility in Lubbock does not offer transloading, and one of its tenants is an agricultural processing company whose customer base and its logistics requirements are unique among the four places. The Big Spring facility is unique as a former military base that offers buildings and lengthy rail track loop to attract a broader array of tenants than the other three facilities. The Levelland facility enjoys a favorable partnership with the short line rail company that serves it, and good working relationships with tenants in terms of land acquisition arrangements, such that tenant companies find the facility's slightly remote location advantageous. San Angelo's transload facility exhibits perhaps the most unique set of relationships of the four with the main rail company leading in and out of San Angelo, and with the rail company operating within the facility.

While all rail-served industrial facilities of West Texas examined in this chapter are built on a public–private partnership to some degree, each is unique in the way such relationships play out. In part, the differences are due to the fact that different rail companies have different ways that they relate to local government and to other railroad companies with which they share track or interconnect. Differences also result in the provision of land, buildings, and incentives to investors in industrial space. Such differences contrast with the rather unified approach that stakeholders in each location share in their promotion of Ports-to-Plains. This complex side of economic development based on transportation and related infrastructure exemplifies the unique site characteristics and situation of each place. Oddly, the offerings of rail-served industrial facilities do not figure prominently in the promotion of the Ports-to-Plains Corridor. Conversely, the expansion of I-27, while mentioned, is not the most central feature highlighted in the marketing of each of the four rail- (and truck-) served facilities discussed in this chapter.

Economic developers taking into account freight transportation solutions to attract new investment find that products sitting in trucks or rail cars do not create revenue for companies, and transloading can partly alleviate such inefficiency by freeing up rail cars or truck trailers. Freight that lends itself to transloading tends to include basic products with steady market conditions that exhibit neither dramatic surges nor dips in demand. Agricultural products and inputs stand out, and they represent half or more of Class I rail carriers' business to or from such facilities (Niepow 2017). Furthermore, as the four rail-served facilities included in this study illustrate, long-haul rail shipment reduces costs when compared to shipping by truck, though the latter offers greater flexibility for reaching destinations, and more speed than rail. The shortage of truck drivers enters into the equation by making rail, and transloading to interface between the two modes, more attractive. In short, transloading, by including both transport modes, offers a combination of cost reduction and speed. West Texas is a particularly relevant region for transloading in light of the sustained levels of oil and gas production in the region and the need for sand for use in hydraulic fracturing. Several carriers, including rail and trucking companies, are eyeing the Mexican petroleum market, especially gas, and the ability of West Texas companies to tap into it, which will boost the need for shipment and transloading of frac sand and steel pipe used in hydrocarbon extraction for the domestic and the growing Mexican export market for refined petroleum and LNG (Niepow 2017). Furthermore, the highly productive grain and cotton production of West Texas means that the movement of crops and agricultural inputs like fertilizer need steady, reliable transportation modes to cover the long distances and connect the relatively sparsely distributed population centers of the region (G. Andrews, personal communication, March 14, 2022; J. Osborne, personal communication, November 11, 2020).

In short, the unique geography of West Texas lends itself to the creation of industrial rail-served facilities. The bulk cargoes related to oil, gas, and agriculture spread out over a large collection of functional economic regions, which convinces economic developers of the public and private sectors of the merits of such facilities to service the bulk cargo that the region handles. Despite population growth overall in West Texas, however, not every community of the region can sustain a transload facility. They are worth considering if the local economy demands cost-effective, efficient movement of bulk commodities, and if it can support it. The case studies included in this chapter illustrate that no one size fits all. Class I railroads vary in terms of their relationships with shippers and receivers along their routes, and with adjoining short line and line-haul railroads. A community that may consider establishing a rail-served industrial facility or transload facility must include in its decision its relationship with the dominant rail company serving it. Arrangements for incentives to new and existing occupants of industrial parks differ from county to county, reflecting the piecemeal approaches to building economic development policy at the local level, within the framework of state-level laws and incentives. Likewise, land procurement by companies in need of direct access to rail-served facilities exhibit different arrangements from city to city, as the local economic development entities overseeing recruitment of such business differ in their relationships to local governments and taxpayers.

Several contemporary trends favor the expanded use of rail-served industrial facilities, which may lead to establishment of new ones, not only in Texas but throughout the USA and in parts of Mexico. The signing by President Joe Biden of the Bipartisan Infrastructure Bill in late 2021 means that new road construction and repairs of roads and bridges will be common for several years to come, which translates to the movement of aggregates, lumber, rebar, and other construction materials. Grain supplies at the global scale, due in part to the Russian invasion of Ukraine, will lead to changes in agricultural supply chains, and possibly expanded rail shipments of grains and inputs. Europe's increased demand for liquified natural gas (LNG) in light of disruptions to Russian gas shipments presents an opportunity for expanded gas production in the major shale plays (natural gas accumulations) of the USA, and, therefore, increased shipment of frac sand and steel pipes for well heads.

The struggle to adapt to climate change will result in more rail shipments of wind blades. Facilities to handle the transloading and processing of these goods will likely result in the need for new or expanded rail-served facilities that enhance the economic development potential for many communities.

References

Association of American Railroads (2021) Freight railroads and the Staggers Rail Act of 1980. Association of American Railroads. Retrieved January 12, 2022, from https://www.aar.org/article/freight-railroads-the-staggers-act-of-1980/

Big Spring (2020) Big Spring Airpark. City of Big Spring, Retrieved November 6, 2020, from https://www.mybigspring.com/149/Airpark-industrial-Park

Big Spring Rail System (2021) Big spring rail systems, Inc. Retrieved November 30, 2020, from http://www.bigspringrailsystem.com/about-us.html

Cartner R (2018) On track for success: Texas Pacifico Grupo Mexico. Retrieved December 22, 2021, from http://texaspacifico.com/docs/On_Track_For_Success_BusinessInFocus_May_2018.pdf

DIGAOHM (2021) Dirección General Adjunta de Oceanografía, Hidrografía y Meteorología, Government of Mexico. Retrieved December 25, 2021, from https://digaohm.semar.gob.mx/cuestionarios/cnarioTopo.pdf

Hyde J (2018, October 23). Storied rail line will soon reconnect West Texas with Mexico. San Angelo Live! https://sanangelolive.com/news/business/2018-10-23/storied-rail-line-will-soon-reconnect-west-texas-mexico

Iowa DOT (2019) Developing a rail-served facility. Iowa Rail Toolkit, pp 31–35. https://iowadot.gov/iowarail/railroads/industry/iowatoolkit/Toolkit_Developing.pdf

LEDA (2019) Lubbock rail port infrastructure expansion, Lubbock Economic Development Alliance (LEDA), April 11. Retrieved September 12, 2021, from https://lubbockeda.org/tail-port-expansion/

Levelland EDC (2021) Levelland economic development corporation. Retrieved December 19, 2021, from https://www.golevelland.com/industrial-rail-park

Mahoney N (2020, November 17). New rail port to connect Texas and Mexico. FreightWaves. https://www.freightwaves.com/news/rail-port-connect-texas-and-mexico/

Niepow D (2017, August). Transloading provides railroads with another way to attract business. Progressive Railroading. https://www.progressiverailroading.com/rail_industruy_trends/article/Transloading-provides-railroads-with-another-way-to-attract-business-52369

Pesquera A (2020, September 8) San Angelo City council cuts deal for rail port with private developer. Virtual Builders Exchange. https://www.virtualbx.com/construction-preview/san-angelo-city-council-cuts-deal-for-rail-port-with-private-developer/

Riley C (2018) Crews rebuild 90 miles of South Orient rail line. Construction Equipment Guide, (West Edition #7). https://www.constructionequipmentguide.com/crews-rebuild-90-miles-of-south-orient-rail-line/39694

San Angelo Chamber of Commerce (2020) San Angelo rail port: a proposed rail facility designed to service multi-community users in the concho valley. San Angelo Chamber of Commerce Economic Development, San Angelo

San Angelo Economic Development (2020) San Angelo rail freight facility: multi-commodity regional rail port overview. https://economicdevelopmentsanangelo.com/wp-content/uploads/2021/03/SPLRR-San-Angelo-Rail-Port-Marketing-Brochure-Spring-2021.pdf

Tanner C (2018) Get on track with a rail-served site. Area Dev Q1: 2018. https://www.areadevelopment.com/logisticsinfrastructure/Q1-2018/get-on-track-with-rail-served-site.shtml

Texas Rail News (2020, December 29) 1st train in over 15 years uses South Orient RR tracks to Presidio—but no Rio crossing… yet, Texas Rail News. https://texasrailadvocates.

org/2020/12/23/1st-train-in-over-15-years-uses-south-orient-rr-tracks-to-presidio-but-no-rio-crossing-yet/
Timian E (2018) Levelland Economic Development Corporation Agrees to Terms with Pipeline Plastics, LLC in the Levelland Industrial Rail Park. Levelland Economic Development Corporation, June 7. https://www.golevelland.com/news/ledc-agrees-terms-pipeline-plastics-llc-expansion-levelland-industrial-rail-park
Trainweb.org (2020) West texas & Lubbock railway history. Trainweb.org. http://www.tainweb.org/chris/wth.html
US Government Publishing Office (2015, May 13) Hearing before the subcommittee on railroads, pipelines, and hazardous materials of the committee on transportation and infrastructure, House of representatives, One hundred fourteenth congress, First session, Washington, U.S. Government Publishing Office, pp 114–16. Printed for the use of the Committee on Transportation and Infrastructure. Retrieved January 20, 2022, from http://www.gpo.gov/fdsys/browse/committee.action?chamber=house&committee=transportation
Worrell C (2015, May 11) Big spring to expand its facilities. Railway Age. https://www.railwayage.com/news/big-spring-rail-to-expand-ots-facilities/

Chapter 6
Victoria and Brownsville: Regional Transportation and the Development of Two South Texas Maritime Ports

Abstract Maritime ports and the places with which they connect represent classic examples of functional economic regions. Ports serve as nodes that focus economic activity for their respective regions and are important features of local and regional economic development. They illuminate key geographic concepts of region, connectivity, and the built environment. This chapter explores two Texas Gulf Coast ports, Victoria and Brownsville, as engines of local and regional economic development. Victoria's shallow barge port on the Intracoastal Waterway is an engine for growth of industries relying on bulk cargo, such as petrochemicals. Brownsville is a deep-water port located on the USA–Mexico border, whose hinterland, or functional economic region, includes parts of both countries. Although both ports involve environmental concerns, such as wildlife habitat disruption, the chapter nevertheless concludes that public–private partnerships for these large-scale infrastructure projects are popular with taxpayers, given their impulse to regional economic development.

Keywords Maritime ports · Intracoastal waterway · Victoria, Texas · Brownsville · Navigation districts · Freight transportation infrastructure

6.1 Introduction

Maritime ports and the places with which they connect represent classic examples of functional economic regions. Ports serve as nodes that focus economic activity for their respective regions, and as such, they are regarded as important features of economic development that propel such activity beyond their immediate locations. They require significant alteration to natural configurations of land and water. Thus, the geographic concepts of regions (especially functional economic regions), location, scale, connectivity, and the built environment are central to case studies of ports. This chapter addresses the shallow barge port of Victoria, a small

M. S. Yoder, *Geographical Scale and Economic Development*,
https://doi.org/10.1007/978-3-031-36197-5_6

metropolitan area of South Texas, and the deep-water port of Brownsville, a mid-sized metropolitan area along the USA–Mexico border. The study illustrates the importance of maritime ports to regional economic development.

6.2 The Port of Victoria: An Overview

Small metropolitan areas, those with populations between 100,000 and 249,999, are excellent laboratories for studying processes of local governments working with state governments and the private sector to bring about economic development. A small metropolitan area is defined by the Office of Management and Budget as having a core, or center, with a population of at least 50,000 and an area strongly connected to that core with a population between 100,000 and 249,000 (Bureau of the Census 2010). According to the Census Bureau, there are eight small metropolitan areas in Texas. Each has its own unique histories of how economic development processes play out, so a case study can reveal such particularities exhibited by a given city and its hinterland, while highlighting some general processes for urban regions of that scale. Successful development initiatives in a small metropolitan area require that stakeholders largely be on the same page, and political partisanship becomes muted (Yoder 2016). Such consensus is particularly crucial for a small metropolitan area with a growing barge port that it relies upon, which requires a united community when lobbying for federal funding for infrastructure.

The Victoria Metropolitan Area is a small metropolitan area whose core city is located 50 miles inland from the Gulf of Mexico. It is the largest urban area in the Coastal Bend, a region of Texas that lies between the large metropolitan area of Houston and the mid-sized metropolitan area of Corpus Christi. Victoria's contemporary transportation development follows a strategy of enhancing connectivity with those larger metropolitan areas while capitalizing on the region's more inland location that places it within a large inland portion of South Texas rich in agriculture and the production of petroleum products. Furthermore, the highway and rail portions of its transportation system link with Austin and San Antonio. Thus, the locality possesses some advantages in terms of site and situation, two important themes in the field of geography. The metropolitan area comprises three counties: Victoria, Calhoun, and Guadalupe. Its 2019 estimated population by the Bureau of the Census is 121,032. From the standpoint of transportation amenities, the urban region is well endowed for a metropolitan area of this modest size. Furthermore, the barge port represents a suitable case study of a transport-oriented economic development initiative involving collaboration and interaction of governance at multiple levels and scales, from municipal to county, state, and federal (Fig. 6.1).

Key features of the Victoria Metropolitan Area's transportation system are the future Interstate I-69 (presently US Highway 59), three Class I rail lines that share track rights (UP, BNSF, and KCS), and the Port of Victoria. The latter is a shallow

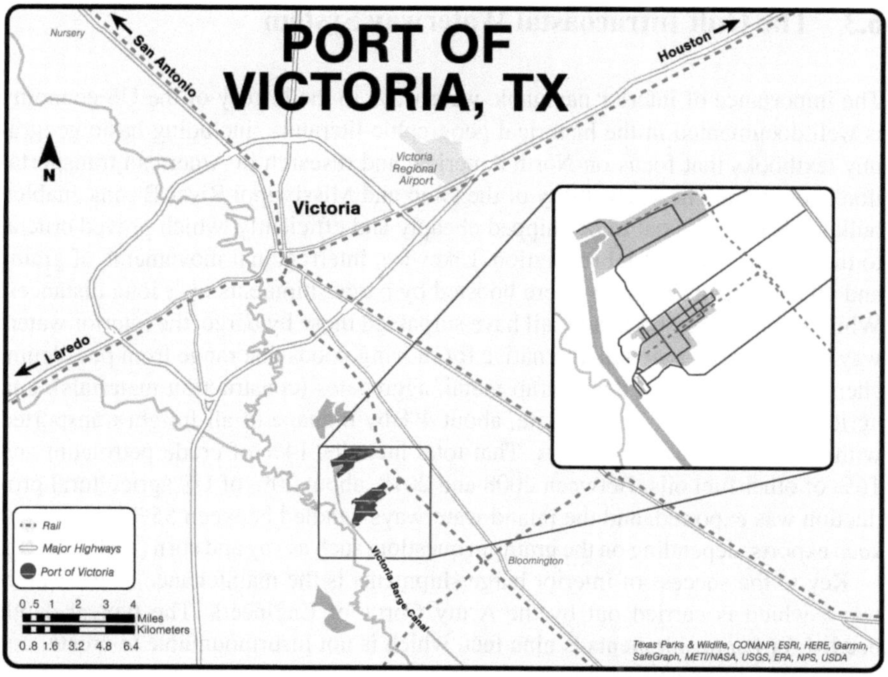

Fig. 6.1 Map of the Port of Victoria. (By Noah Walker)

barge port and rail-served industrial park connected to the country's 3000-mile Intracoastal Waterway System. BNSF and UP share track rights and connect directly to the barge port. The port is within a free trade zone (FTZ) and is designated as a Texas Enterprise Zone. A rail loop within the port, operated by TNW Corporation since the summer of 2021, provides enhanced rail access to tenants. This rail service makes the Port of Victoria an industrial facility that provides service beyond its barge access, including a rail transload facility that interfaces with trucking and barge (S. Stibich, personal communication, October 15, 2021).

The Port received a $3 million federal grant in early 2021 for expansion of the rail loop within the port facility; the grant is matched equally by funds derived from the port's revenues. The source of the federal portion is the Economic Development Administration (EDA) of the US Department of Commerce (DOC) and is part of the CARES (Coronavirus Aid Relief and Economic Security) Act. The EDA granted the funds with the assumption that greater rail capacity at the port will attract more business that requires such infrastructure and connectivity, especially petrochemicals, steel, and agribusiness (Texas Rail Advocates 2021). In 2016, the port handled seven million tons of freight. The main commodities handled at the port include crude oil, petrochemicals, agricultural commodities, and sand for hydraulic fracturing (TxDOT 2016).

6.3 The Gulf Intracoastal Waterway System

The importance of interior navigable waterways to the history of the US economy is well documented in the historical geographic literature, including basic geography textbooks that focus on North America, and research in American transportation geography. The navigability of the Ohio and Mississippi River Basins enabled bulk loads such as coal to be shipped cheaply and efficiently, which proved crucial to the country's industrial revolution. Likewise, interregional movements of grains and other agricultural goods were boosted by barge shipments over long distances. While shipments by truck and rail have surpassed those by barge, the interior waterway system remains a vital alternative for moving goods that range from petroleum, chemicals, and coal to steel, scrap metal, aggregates (construction materials), and agricultural products. To illustrate, about 4% by tonnage of all freight transported within the USA involves barges. That total includes 14% of crude petroleum and 16% of other fuel oils. Between 2008 and 2018, about 20% of US agricultural production was exported, and the inland waterways handled between 55% and 60% of such exports, depending on the grains in question, such as soy and corn (ASCE 2021).

Key to the success of interior barge shipments is the maintenance of the waterways, which is carried out by the Army Corps of Engineers. The typical depth needed for barge shipments is nine feet, which is not insurmountable to create, nor is it too terribly costly to maintain. However, funding in recent decades has been less than desirable, which inhibits the rate of growth of barge traffic, especially as a percentage of all freight by volume. The American Society of Civil Engineers (ASCE) estimates that a $24.8 billion funding gap existed in maintenance of, and capital improvements to, inland waterways between 2020 and 2029, adjusted for inflation, based on recent (2021) levels of spending, and recent levels of freight hauled via inland waterways (ASCE 2021).

Although barge traffic overall in the Gulf Intracoastal Waterway (GIWW) was quite steady from 2007 to 2016, due primarily to a lack of capital investment in improvements to infrastructure and the slow pace of dredging, the infrastructure is nonetheless an important feature of industrial shipping for the Gulf Coast region. The GIWW, 1100 miles in length, links Brownsville, TX to St. Marks, a locality in the Florida Panhandle 30 miles south of Tallahassee. The GIWW specializes in petroleum products and chemical products (ASCE 2021). The waterway ranks third in the USA for inland transportation of freight, behind only the Mississippi River and the Ohio River (Mahoney 2021b). The importance of the GIWW despite lack of investment remains paramount because of its proximity to petrochemical plants and to sources of crude oil, including the Eagle Ford Shale Play and offshore Gulf production, as well as the pipeline network of the Permian Basin of West Texas. The cost savings from shipping by barge compared to truck and rail are considerable. To illustrate, one barge that carries 1500 tons is the equivalent of 58 truck trailers (26 tons each) or 14 large rail hopper cars (100 tons each). The typical load consists of pulling four barges, though larger waterways can accommodate 15 barges together. In total, the GIWW carries an average of 110 million tons of load each year (Kruse et al. 2018). A 1750-ton barge load carries the same dry load as 70 trucks (Mahoney 2021b). For these reasons of bulk efficiency, stakeholders in the Victoria Metropolitan Area are interested in the continued development of barge transport infrastructure and attraction of businesses to use it.

In the Texas portion of the GIWW, petroleum products rank first among the different barge loads by value, including gasoline, kerosene, and other refined petroleum products. In second place is crude oil, and in third place are non-fuel products that include aggregates (road construction materials), minerals, scrap metal, steel, and agricultural products. In 2016, "receipts" (inbound products) at the barge ports of the Texas portion of the GIWW were 4.2 million tons. Of that total, 67% of the bulk was petroleum and coal products; 12% was iron, steel, and scrap metal, and 10% was aggregates, sand, and gravel. That year, "shipments" (outbound products) at the barge ports of the Texas portion of the GIWW were 3.7 million tons. Of that total, 77% were petroleum products, 16% were natural gas and crude oil, and 7% were iron, steel, and scrap metal (Kruse et al. 2018).

6.4 A Brief History of the Port of Victoria and the Victoria County Navigation District

Historically, the mouth and lowest reaches of the Guadalupe River, upon which Victoria is situated, were viewed as a strategically important locale for accessing interior towns and cities such as Gonzales, Cuero, and San Antonio, which stand out in the early settlement history of present-day Texas. Attempts to make the river navigable for interior connection date back to the late 1830s, and the first steamboat reached Victoria, about 45 miles inland, in 1841. The Civil War disrupted such commerce, which quickly bounced back once the war was over, though expanded rail lines in Texas competed with steamboats for the shipment of bulk cargo, such as lumber, coal, and cotton. Moreover, continued needs to clear the channel of sandbars, logs, and overhanging tree limbs diminished the appeal of the river for commerce, and the penetration of the interior Coastal Bend by rail hindered the push to make the Guadalupe River navigable. However, the federal government regarded portions of the region closest to the coast as viable for freight movement in existing bays and by canal such that by 1900, a few sections of Texas bays had been dredged to accommodate barge traffic (Spurlin 2010).

The idea for coastal canals picked up significant momentum in 1905, thus paving the way for the eventual establishment of the Port of Victoria. That year, Congress funded research on the viability of a waterway extending from Donaldsonville, Louisiana to the mouth of the Rio Grande near Brownsville, as well as improvements to the mouth of the Guadalupe River for potential river navigability. Victoria's business and farming communities, in conjunction with the Army Corps of Engineers, sponsored a convention in Victoria to promote an interstate coastal waterway as a draw for new industry and expansion of agriculture in the Coastal

Bend. The idea was generally well received, though some skepticism came from business interests in San Antonio and Freeport, who thought such a canal system would steer traffic to Galveston and Houston. The committee favoring the project became the Gulf Intracoastal Canal Association, whose initial mission was to work with the Army Corps of Engineers to lobby Congress for funding. In 1907, Congress passed legislation to appropriate funds for two short canal segments in Texas and one in Louisiana, and President Theodore Roosevelt signed it into law. Dredging of the Guadalupe River from its mouth to Victoria began in 1908, but the project ultimately lost its luster because of the continual need for dredging, and the resulting inability of barges to travel far enough inland to reach the city (Spurlin 2010).

Because of the problems of dredging, by the late 1930s, the Army Corps and business interests in the Coastal Bend pushed instead for "canalization" of the Guadalupe River, which effectively meant an extension of the intracoastal waterway further inland. The growth of the petroleum industry along the Texas Coast, as well as a recognition of the usefulness of dredged materials (gravel and sand) for the construction industry led to support for a canal of 100 feet in width and nine feet depth, linking San Antonio Bay to Victoria via a canal within the Guadalupe River floodplain. The Army Corps assisted in lobbying for federal funding of the physical work, though the local governments would be required to fund land acquisitions for right of ways. To accomplish the latter, two counties in the region had to form navigation districts (Spurlin 2010).

The Texas Constitution allows counties to go into the business of establishing navigation districts that can issue general revenue bonds for the development and maintenance of navigable waterways, including flood control and conservation. Such districts are political regions, or "political subdivisions," that have governing bodies to administer their work. The members of the governing boards are either elected locally or appointed to the boards by local elected officials, such as a county judge or a commissioners court (Kruse 2016). Bonds are issued to finance construction and improvements that enable navigation in a waterway in a given district to conserve such a waterway and/or to control its drainage. Use fees and other assessments can be charged to pay off the construction debts. Taxes can be levied under strict circumstances, and the revenues generated must be deposited specifically to pay off the construction costs. Furthermore, navigation districts have the power of eminent domain. Navigation districts can collaborate with the US federal government for engineering, for necessary permits, for surveys needed prior to proposed improvements, and for maintenance of the waterways (Kruse 2016). The Army Corps of Engineers maintains the navigable waterways (Miles 2018). Texas has 23 navigation districts, of which five are designated as shallow ports to accommodate barges. The remainder are either deep water ports or are designated for recreation or professional fishing. Of the five barge-oriented navigation districts, two have board members elected by the public, and three (including Victoria) have members appointed by the counties' commissioners courts (Kruse 2016). Victoria's has five appointed commissioners (Miles 2018; Port of Victoria 2021c).

Both Victoria and Calhoun Counties established their navigation districts in 1946, though support in Victoria was stronger than in Calhoun County, as reflected in the required petitions to the respective county governments. In Calhoun County, only the westernmost district of the commissioners court, the only district through which the canal would go, favored it; therefore, the court set up the West Side Calhoun County Navigation District (WSCCND). All districts of Victoria County had majorities of citizens in favor, so the Victoria County Navigation District (VCND) is countywide. In both counties, bond issuances were required to raise the funds for right of ways, and for improvements not covered by federal appropriations. By 1952, the Army Corps determined the path for the canal (100-feet wide, 9-feet deep) and its turning basin terminus, such that no locks and dams would be required. The site is 7.5 miles south of the downtown core of Victoria (Fig. 6.1). VCND had a bond election in 1957, which won by a narrow margin; opposition came from farm and ranch operators concerned about potential flooding, and from skeptics of the claims that the canal would attract enough industry to justify the cost to taxpayers. The WSCCND did not need such an election because the large Union Carbide chemical plant generated enough product to pay for most of the county's portion through its property taxes and canal use fees. Dredging for the canal began in 1958 and its was completed in 1962. The second stage, including the turning basin and a public wharf, was completed in 1969. Interestingly, no eminent domain was needed; rather, some farmland in the flood plain was acquired through condemnation (Spurlin 2010).

In the mid-1970s, ideas to widen and deepen the channel to the same specifications as the Intracoastal Waterway gained strength, as did opposition to them by environmentalists concerned about the disposal of the dredged materials, and what those would do to oyster beds, shrimp, and other wildlife. These problems delayed progress on further channel expansion, but in the meantime, the VCND established the Port of Victoria Development Corporation to enhance the process of attracting industry once channel expansion could be completed. In 1986, the Army Corps identified a suitable, protected site for the waste disposal. That same year, the idea for a rail loop within the industrial park to attract more industry gained momentum. Although some land acquisition was required for the rail right-of-way, the idea came to fruition quickly and the 8000-foot rail was completed in early 1989. Delays of the final channel expansion, due to environmental concerns, the need to raise funds through a bond election, and obtaining land through condemnation for additional dredge disposal sites, were finally overcome in 1999. Economic analysis of the port by an outside impact study in 2005, and local reactions to it generally concluded that early in the twenty-first century, the port had become a successful investment in economic development. The Union Carbide plant (subsequently acquired by Dow Chemical Company) had expanded because of the canal, and two tenants in the industrial park, one that ships gravel and another that ships agricultural products and inputs, flourished because of the canal (Spurlin 2010).

The County of Victoria with encouragement by the Victoria Economic Development Corporation (VEDC) and the City of Victoria have worked closely with the Navigation District to stimulate industrial development in the metropolitan area. The City bought an 1800-acre (728 hectares) portion of the present port facility in 2007 at a favorable price when a planned petrochemical plant at the site failed to materialize. That same year, the VCND bought the land from the City and sold the facility's water rights to the City so that the latter could supply it and gain revenues from its sale (VEDC 2012). In 2008, the District recognized the need for making capital improvements at the site to attract industry. To acquire funds for such improvements, the District floated general revenue bonds, given that revenues would be generated from port activities and from tenants to (among other things) pay off the bonds. A portion of the first issuance of $6 million was used for the $3.5 million repair of a railroad bridge, and the remaining $2.5 million was dedicated to the construction of an 800-foot dock for moving liquid cargo. Although there were no specific clients lined up at the time, the business community of Victoria knew that the locality would gain business, in light of the emerging Eagle Ford Shale Play. A year later, an initiative got underway to extend rail connection from the VCND property to the Intracoastal Waterway turning basin. This led Caterpillar, a manufacturer of heavy earth-moving machinery, to express interest in using the facility for moving containers on barges to their Victoria area assembly plant (VEDC 2012). The Port of Victoria has not yet developed the infrastructure to handle containers; however, the District obtained the ability to issue permits for heavy truck loads (those over 8000 pounds) that normally require issuance by the Texas Department of Transportation (TX-DOT) in Austin (VEDC 2012).

The port receives a small portion of Victoria County property tax revenues, or $.03 per $1000.00 valuation, that comprises about 30% of the port's budget. The remainder of the revenue stream derives from use fees (barge and freight storage, and $.11 per barrel of oil transferred at the port), and leasing of facilities to users and occupants of the port. The port operates its own dock, which is available to companies that do not possess their own facility at the port for loading and unloading non-liquid bulk freight hauled by barges (S. Stibich, personal communication, March 24, 2022).

6.5 Recent Activities and Current Occupants of the Port of Victoria

Crude Oil was the top commodity that passed through the port in 2016, followed by petrochemicals, agricultural products, and sand for hydraulic fracturing ("frac sand"). In 2015, the port handled 6.99 million tons of freight, which enabled the port to generate $6.6 billion in economic impact. A total of 5711 vessels called on the port that year, including barges and tugboats. The port ranked 70th among US ports in tonnage in 2016. The rise in handling of crude oil and frac sand are indicative that the Port of Victoria is integrated into the Eagle Ford Shale Play's economic activity (TxDOT 2016).

An example of the workings of the Port of Victoria as a public–private partnership involves Zinc Resources, LLC. In the summer of 2021, the company reached an agreement with the VCND to obtain access to a land parcel located directly on the "rail loop" in the northern site of the port. The company will recycle dust byproduct of electric arc furnace steel production and turn that otherwise hazardous dust into two useful products: Waelz zinc oxide, and Waelz iron, the former of which is recycled as zinc, and the latter of which is used as a material in road construction (Global Steel Dust 2021). By early August 2021, Zinc Resources had broken ground on the Victoria plant. The partnership includes the leasing of 25 acres (10 hectares) of land in the port's northern sector, and the investment of $60 million by the company to build the kiln. The VCND will ensure ample utility (gas and electric) infrastructure. TNW will provide the rail service, funded in part by a grant from the Economic Development Administration. The VEDC assisted the port in landing the project by providing assistance in recruiting Zinc Resources, LLC. The venture will surely benefit Victoria County by increasing the local tax base (Port of Victoria 2021b).

The port facility also serves as a "fleeting area" for parking or storage of containers (VEDC 2012). Fordyce Sand and Gravel is the only producer of sand and gravel in Texas to offer barge service in addition to mining. Similarly, Equalizer, Inc. provides transloading and storage of bulk commodities for the petroleum industry (frac sand) and for agriculture (fertilizers and feeds) that serve nearby customers (Port of Victoria 2021a). In addition, the TNW-served 3000-acre (1214 hectares) facility will provide storage, cleaning, and repair of rail tank cars, and rail transload services for bulk cargo (Texas Rail News 2021; VEDC 2021).

6.6 Future Plans for the Port of Victoria

The Navigation District and the Port of Victoria foresee the facility becoming a "satellite yard" for the Port of Houston, meaning a place to ship and store overflow containers as a means to alleviate storage pileups at the deepwater port, decentralize the crowdedness, and, therefore, reduce truck traffic in Houston and lower current air emissions. According to the plan, outlined in a memorandum of understanding signed in 2005, the containers would be sent by barge between Houston's port and the Port of Victoria. Among the selling points of this proposed activity is the reduction of truck traffic on the increasingly crowded I-69 corridor, given that sending containers by barge between the ports is intended to be an alternative to moving them by truck (Port of Houston 2005; S. Stibich, personal communication, October 15, 2021). This container-on-barge idea makes sense when considering the increased levels of Houston-Asia container traffic in light of the immense Covid-related bottlenecks at the Ports of Los Angeles and Long Beach, and the resulting desire on the part of companies to find alternative container ports to California. Houston is a logical alternative in part given the growing markets for consumer and industrial goods in Texas metropolitan areas like Dallas, San Antonio, and Austin (Mahoney 2021a). Given the expense required to produce the necessary facilities, the Texas Department of Public Safety would likely need to bless the project and get more involved in its planning (S. Stibich, personal communication, March 24, 2022). Furthermore, there is a company investigating the use of the Port of Victoria for sending finished diesel fuel to Mexico by rail, as part of the port's efforts to plan a larger role than it currently plays in USA–Mexico trade. Furthermore, the "Texas Logistics Center at the Port of Victoria," the emerging name of the facility in light of the expansion of track and rail service by TNW Corporation, will reflect new activities by TNW to market the transload facilities in the southern portion of the port (S. Stibich, personal communication, October 15, 2021).

The port and the navigation district desire to reduce its dependence on county property tax revenues by increasing use fees and land leases. This business strategy will most likely be realized by increased flow of oil by pipeline to the port for further transport by barge, rail, and truck. Presently a pipeline transports oil from the Cuero, Texas area, some 25 miles northwest of Victoria, and it is stored in tanks owned by TFT (Texas Flow Tankage) at the port. The port's administration and the navigation district's board are trying to attract small- and medium-sized businesses to the South Site, which will generate property lease and sale revenues for the port. These officials believe that an expansion of the rail loop, operated by TNW, to the South Site will make the desired arrival of the anticipated new business much more likely. They are planning to install an additional 42,000 feet of track and other infrastructure to expand transload capabilities, at a cost of some $27 million (S. Stibich, personal communication, March 24, 2022).

Property tax abatements have been successful tools thus far for attracting companies to the port and are expected to lead to the development of the South Site. Such abatements typically are tapered and last over a period of 8 years, starting with 90% the first year, and ending after the eighth year. They are justified by port and county officials on the basis of the jobs created by port tenants. It is anticipated that the rail- and barge-served facility will continue to benefit from its traditional activities: oil, aggregates, agriculture, fertilizers, and project cargoes. Upon installation of the additional track, the facility will likewise be able to serve as storage for rail cars (S. Stibich, personal communication, March 24, 2022). The Port of Victoria is evolving into a comprehensive rail-served industrial park with a unique and fairly diverse set of industrial operations and the political backing at multiple scales necessary to sustain its funding for future growth (Fig. 6.2).

6.7 Brownsville: A Deepwater Port of South Texas

Brownsville, a rapidly growing city with a population 186,738 in 2020, is part of the mid-sized Brownsville-Harlingen Metropolitan Area (422,000 in 2020) and is simultaneously considered part of a binational metropolitan area with its Mexican sister city of Matamoros, Tamaulipas, a city of 520,000 as of 2016. The two border cities have enjoyed a strong binational relationship in trade, culture, and family histories for generations, and an increasingly interrelated manufacturing economy dating back to the 1960s, before NAFTA's implementation. Both cities are part of the Lower Rio Grande Valley (LRGV), a large and growing conurbation with a

Fig. 6.2 Aerial image of the Port of Victoria. (Photo by Sean Stibich)

combined binational estimated population of 2.95 million (1.54 million in Mexico, 2020, and 1.4 million in Texas, 2022).

The Port of Brownsville is the only maritime port directly located on the USA–Mexico border. It is a unique case study of port planning and binational trade infrastructure. At nearly 40,000 acres (16,187 hectares), it is territorially the largest port authority holding in the USA (Muñoz 2021). It is a significant economic development initiative in the rapidly growing and vibrant four-county LRGV. The city's population in 2019 was estimated at 182,781 and the metropolitan area's population was estimated that year at 420,392. Cameron County operates three international vehicular bridges that link the county to Matamoros, Tamaulipas. The Cameron County Regional Mobility Authority (CCRMA) operates a rail bridge linking the west side of the city to Matamoros that enhances the locality's International trade linkages. In 2019, the Bridge System handled $18 billion of goods in international trade (Muñoz 2020). The deep-water Port of Brownsville is well positioned to not only tap into, but to enhance USA–Mexico trade at the eastern end of the LRGV and beyond.

Among the most visible industrial features of the 85-year-old port facility are a plant that produces gasoline for export to Mexico, two liquid natural gas plants (and a third on the drawing board) for exports to several markets globally, and a recycling plant that breaks down surplus ships for scrap metal (López 2022; Muñoz 2021). Economic developers of the port and the community at large are hoping to expand upon current steel exports to Mexico through the port. That is in addition to the steel slab brought into the port by an Argentinian company for re-export to a steel mill in Monterrey, Mexico that smelts it into finished product. Keppel AmFELS, a ship-building firm located at the port, finished the first vessel that complies with the Jones Act (that restricts foreign-flagged ships from carrying cargo within US territory) for carrying wind turbine hardware for offshore wind energy production. Wind turbine blades are among the bulk cargoes counted on the import side of the port's ledger. To illustrate, the largest blades imported into the US, destined for 21 wind energy projects, came through Brownsville in 2020 via 131 vessel calls. The port is also unique among maritime ports for its handling of 53-foot domestic-type containers on barges, which carry kitchen appliances manufactured in Monterrey and destined for the Port of Tampa Bay in Florida. During the first half of 2021, more than 24,000 TEUs (twenty-foot equivalent units) were handled at the port (Avery 2021). Finally, a steel mill in Brownsville is expected to transform an increasing amount of imported scrap metal into finished product (Muñoz 2021).

Given that South Texas is among the major American regions for the production of sorghum for export as livestock feed, particularly to China, the Port of Brownsville handles that commodity, and is expected to see increases in grain exports in general. That expectation is based on future expansion of the bulk cargo facilities (dock and grain elevator) at the port. The port receives abundant attention for its growth (both physical and in quantity of cargo handled) in recent years, such that some $200 million of federal funds have been recently approved by Congress for widening the channel, and deepening it ten additional feet from its current 42 feet (López 2022; Muñoz 2021).

The Port of Brownsville and the other elements of the county's transportation system that tie into the port's functional reach represent fascinating examples of inter- and intra-governmental agreement and coordination. The binational planning process is the most complex, and perhaps most fascinating, of the relationships, given that two federal systems are involved. Cameron County and its associated agency, the CCRMA (Cameron County Regional Mobility Authority), carry out most of the planning on the US side while the City of Brownsville Planning and Redevelopment Department likewise provides input. The State of Texas, through TxDOT, allocates funding, conducts planning, and organizes construction and repair of highways, while federal dollars ultimately rubber stamp and finance much of that work. Furthermore, the federal government, through the Army Corps of Engineers, finances and carries out dredging work in the ship channel (Muñoz 2021).

The new two-mile, $25.6 million South Port Connector Road, which opened in March of 2022, illustrates the nature of partnership in the building of infrastructure to access the port. Planning, financing, and marketing of the road, which opens the southern portion of the port to more direct roadway access, involved a partnership between Cameron County, the CCRMA, the Brownsville Navigation District (the governing entity of the Port of Brownsville), the Rio Grande Valley Metropolitan Planning Organization, and Texas Department of Transportation. These entities collaborated to ease traffic congestion through the built-up zone of Brownsville, to streamline cargo movements, and enhance safety, all of which are believed to expand business in the port. Port activity has already been healthy during the Coronavirus pandemic, and is expected to grow in its aftermath, thus justifying the construction of the connector road (Taylor 2022).

The planning of the port's infrastructure, and the functioning of the port itself are made more complex because of the binational nature of the port, specifically the routes approaching it. Tasks on the Mexican side, such as planning, are much more centralized, with the federal government taking on the biggest roles, though increasingly, the State of Tamaulipas and the municipality of Matamoros are assuming larger roles and enjoying a larger share of bridge tolls since the 1990s, when political decentralization of decision making and management to the states gained steam. Furthermore, the port has a unique arrangement, whereby permits can be issued for the trucking of heavier cargo loads than Texas law normally allows, such that the Mexican maximum weight limits apply. The arrangement is limited to traffic over the Veterans International Bridge, that which is closest to the port, and along the highway leading from the bridge to the port. The heavier allowable loads per truck means shippers can save money by using fewer vehicles. The latter could very well have relevance to shippers desiring to import freight from Mexico but use the Port of Brownsville instead of the Port of Houston and, therefore, reduce drayage distances and costs (Muñoz 2021).

6.8 Conclusions

The two cases included in this chapter exhibit the complexities of maritime ports as features of economic development that involve private–public partnerships to create and expand. They illustrate key differences between a barge port and a deep-water port in terms of identifying local and regional economic impacts and defining forelands and hinterlands. For example, the Port of Victoria, like other barge ports, is best suited to efficient handling of project and bulk cargoes, while the deep-water Port of Brownsville has the capability to handle goods shipped more quickly overseas, either as imports or exports. That said, both ports illustrate some commonalities in terms of the geographic scale of economic development. The hinterlands of each overlap with those of other ports. Brownsville's hinterland shares many localities in common with the Port of Corpus Christi, a larger port but one with somewhat less favorable access to Mexico. Given its shallow draft, the Port of Victoria can only handle loads that travel by canal and the Intracoastal Waterway and must rely on nearby ports for transshipment of loads ultimately handled in deep-water ports, such as Corpus Christi and Houston. Both are engines of local economic development in that each serves as a significant rail-served industrial facility, such that heavy industry is attracted to each, which generates necessary employment and related multiplier effects, such as truck and rail transport and logistics.

As the country and the Coastal Bend Region continue their post-pandemic recoveries, the Port of Victoria has definite potential for growth, both in the tonnage of products currently handled at the facility and in diversifying into new activities, thanks to the expansion of rail within the port. It ultimately has the capability to handle more agricultural products, and such project cargoes as wind blades that are bulky and best handled by barge and rail (BNSF 2021). The confluence of different transportation modes in the Coastal Bend Region, whose core is Victoria, enhances the location for temporary storage and transshipment of containers from nearby deep ports, so long as a paved platform is constructed, and reach stackers are brought in to lift containers and move them between barge, rail, and truck trailers. The port has a successful history of receiving majority support from the local business community and voters, as evidenced by the passing of bond elections through the years dedicated to expansions and improvements to the port and its channel.

A shift since the Coronavirus-related freight transportation disruptions is underway toward the use of Gulf of Mexico ports at the expense of the West Coast, and it is likely to continue. Although Victoria cannot handle container ships in the way that deep water ports can, the port will nonetheless benefit from a healthy demand for shipping by promoting its transload capabilities that give the port a comparative advantage over other Gulf Coast barge ports. The anticipated increases in LNG exports from Texas, owing in part to the Russian invasion of Ukraine and Europe's need for alternative fuels to Russian natural gas, can be enhanced by the location and the room for growth that the Port of Victoria offers. The port is a work in progress, and one that economic developers ought to gauge in terms of the potential for large commercial infrastructure brought about by public-sector stakeholders of different levels (federal, state, county, and municipal) in partnership with the private sector, favoring a transport-driven multiplier. However, the port's and the region's fortunes rely as well on the flexibility of the region to shift toward involvement in renewable energy as fossil fuels become slowly replaced.

Like the Port of Victoria, the Port of Brownsville is a regional and local asset that is already leveraging economic development and connectivity well beyond the immediate area. The LRGV region will experience enhanced connections to the rest of the country as Interstate I-69 is completed. Investments to date have made the facility one that local stakeholders are willing to devote additional resources and attention to, given its potential to recapitulate the growth it has brought to the city, the county, and the LRGV Region. The Coronavirus pandemic produced only temporary slowdowns in port activity early on, and by mid-2021, port activity had already rebounded to pre-pandemic levels. In fact, other trends occurring nationally, regionally, and globally are far more important, including the growing interest in wind energy at all scales.

The cases of the ports of Victoria and Brownsville reveal much about the interworking of multiple scales of government to bring about and develop large infrastructure projects that involve significant alterations to the physical landscape. Local governments at the municipal and county levels must coordinate with actors of the private sector who utilize the facilities, to ensure that the commercial activity at each port is economically and environmentally sustainable, and capable of maintaining business at a level that generates revenues for the investments made. The working relationships between local and state governments, on one hand, and the federal government, on the other, are crucial for funding by the US Congress of expansions and improvements carried out by the Army Corps of Engineers. A given port's connections must expand territorially to ensure that freight moving them increases. Ports are among the most visible features of the local landscape that reflect the multiple scales at which local and regional economic development occurs.

References

ASCE (2021) Failure to act: ports and inland waterways–anchoring the U.S. Economy. American Society of Civil Engineers (ASCE) and Ernst Basler + Partner (EBP), January 2021. https://infrastructurereportcard.org/wp-content/uploads/2020/12/failure-to-act-2021-ports-inland-waterways.pdf

Avery P (2021) Brownsville eyeing intra-American trade. World Cargo News, July 14. https://www.worldcargonews.com/news/news/brownsville-eyeing-intra-american-trade-66636

BNSF (Burlington Northern Santa Fe Railway Website) (2021) Port of Victoria. Retrieved July 31, 2021, from http://www.bnsf.com/ship-with-bnsf/rail-development/pdf/port-of-victoria.pdf

Bureau of the Census (2010) Chapter 13 metropolitan areas: classification of metropolitan areas. In: 2010 standards for delineating metropolitan and micropolitan statistical areas; notice. https://www2.census.gov/geo/pdfs/reference/GARM/Ch13GARM.pdf. Retrieved 31 Oct 2021

Global Steel Dust (2021) Proven Waelz Kiln Technology. (Global Steel Dust website). Retrieved October 31, 2021, from http://www.globalsteeldust.com/waelz_kiln_technology

Kruse J (2016) Overview: Texas ports and navigation districts. Transportation Policy Research Center, Texas A&M Transportation Institute. https://static.tti.tamu.edu/tti.tamu.edu/documents/PRC-2016-5.pdf

Kruse J et al (2018) Economic impact of the Gulf Intracoastal Waterway on the states it serves September 2017 to September 2018. Maritime Transportation Research & Education Center (MarTREC), University of Arkansas, Fayetteville. https://martrec.uark.edu/research/tti_giww_final.pdf

López ST (2022) Lopez: 2021 Port of Brownsville year in review. Rio Grande Guardian, January 5. https://riograndeguardian.com/lopez-2021-port-of-brownsville-year-in-review/

Mahoney N (2021a) Port congestion? Maybe Houston is the alternative. American Shipper, March 16. https://www.freightwaves.com/news/port-houston-aims-for-more-asia-imports-amid-congestion

Mahoney N (2021b) Untapped potential: far too little freight on US waterways, experts say. FreightWaves, October 12. https://www.freightwaves.com/news/far-too-little-freight-on-us-waterways-experts-say?j=66668&sfmc_sub=913819&l=349_HTML&u=1347111&mid=514011755&jb=17006&utm_source=sfmc&utm_medium=email&utm_campaign=FW_Daily_10_12_21&utm_term=Read+More%26nbsp%3b&utm_id=66668&sfmc_id=913819

Miles A (2018) Victoria Barge Canal has long history. Victoria Advocate, March 8. https://www.victoriaadvocate.com/news/local/victoria-barge-canal-has-long-history/article_55ce9a54-a803-58a1-a4bb-b25a85e83e91.html

Muñoz M (2020) Podcast: Roberts: trade will bounce back on Cameron county international bridges. Rio Grande Guardian, August 26. https://riograndeguardian.com/podcast-roberts-trade-will-bounce-back-on-cameron-county-international-bridges/

Muñoz M (2021) Podcast: Muñoz: time to celebrate Port of Brownsville's 85th anniversary. Rio Grande Guardian, October 22. https://riograndeguardian.com/podcast-munoz-time-to-celebrate-port-of-brownsvilles-85th-anniversary/

Port of Houston (2005) PHA, Port of Victoria sign intramodal agreement aimed at reducing air emissions, highway congestion. Port of Houston. Retrieved September 15, 2021, from https://www.globenewswire.com/news-release/2005/03/01/323717/73605/en/Photo-Release-PHA-Port-of-Victoria-Sign-Intramodal-Agreement-Aimed-at-Reducing-Air-Emissions-Highway-Congestion.html

Port of Victoria (2021a) Why Port of Victoria. Port of Victoria. Retrieved September 10, 2021, from https://www.portofvictoria.com/why-port-of-victoria/current-tenants/. Retrieved 10 Sept 2021

Port of Victoria (2021b) Port of Victoria welcomes partnership with Zinc resources, LLC. Port of Victoria. https://www.portofvictoria.com/news-and-media/p/item/36839/port-of-victoria-welcomes-partnership-with-zinc-resources-llc

Port of Victoria (2021c) Port of Victoria welcomes new commissioner. Port of Victoria. https://www.portofvictoria.com/news-and-media/p/item/35657/port-of-victoria-welcomes-new-commissioner

Spurlin CD (2010) Port of Victoria. University Press of Victoria

Taylor S (2022) Video: campirano: south port connector is significant asset for RGV's freight mobility. Rio Grande Guardian, March 7. https://riograndeguardian.com/video-campirano-south-port-connector-is-significant-asset-for-rgvs-freight-mobility/

Texas Rail Advocates (2021) Port of Victoria gets $3 million fed grant for rail loop. Texas Rail Advocates, Texas Rail News. https://texasrailadvocates.org/2021/02/13/port-of-victoria-gets-fed-grant-for-rail-loop/

Texas Rail News (2021) Rail operator TNW to co-develop Texas Inland Port at Victoria. Texas Rail News, July 28. https://texasrailadvocates.org/2021/07/28/rail-operator-tnw-to-co-develop-texas-inland-port-at-victoria/

TxDOT (2016) Overview of Texas ports and waterways. Texas Department of Transportation, Senate Select Committee on Texas Ports, May 4 (E.1012)

Victoria Economic Development Corporation (VEDC) (2012) VEDC Presents Port of Victoria Story. [Video] Youtube. https://www.youtube.com/watch?v=lv1H9tkAVjI

Victoria Economic Development Corporation (VEDC) (2021) The TNW Corporation has been selected by the Victoria County Navigation District to help co-develop a 3,000 acre multimodal logistics center. Victoria Economic Development Corporation. https://www.victoriaedc.com/news/tnw-corporation-has-been-selected-victoria-county-navigation-district-help-co-develop-3000-acre

Yoder MS (2016) Cargo transportation infrastructure and urban regional development: the Fort Smith metropolitan area. Urbana 17:14–31. https://urbanauapp.org/wp-content/uploads/Yoder16.pdf

Chapter 7
Economic Development, Land Use, and Commercial Transportation in Two Small Cities of South Texas: Beeville and Gonzales

Abstract Studies of economic development of cities overwhelmingly emphasize the largest of the world's urban areas. Such studies address ways that economic development is deeply intertwined with each city's spatial layout and its transport and supply-chain connections. However, little is written about the economic development of small cities and their regional, national, and global connections. This chapter is the summary of research conducted since the summer of 2018 on two small cities of South Texas, Beeville and Gonzales, that pursue economic development but face challenges related to transportation and to small and inadequately developed workforces. Yet, to varying degrees, each has been impacted by national, regional, and local economic activities and to a lesser extent by international trade. Hydrocarbon energy production had been important to both, but they diverge in terms of manufacturing. Main Street development is a major focus of community leaders in both cities. The two case studies are based largely on qualitative research methods that include interviews and triangulation with data obtained from news articles and from web sites of local governments, non-profit economic development entities, and companies. Thus, the chapter presents not only profiles of Beeville and Gonzales but insights into qualitative ways of studying economic development policies of small cities.

Keywords Small cities · South Texas, economic development · Transportation infrastructure · Beeville, Texas · Gonzales, Texas

7.1 Introduction

Studies of the geography of economic development that focus on American small cities and rural localities are relatively scarce. Yet small cities and rural areas remain important to the country economically, politically, and culturally. Such places are numerous and widespread. Urban economic development is an area of inquiry with a rich literature, despite the shortage of case studies of mid-sized and small cities. Generally, such studies of urban economic dynamism, or its opposite, tend to

M. S. Yoder, *Geographical Scale and Economic Development*, https://doi.org/10.1007/978-3-031-36197-5_7

emphasize the largest of cities. Shanghai, New York's Financial District, London's Canary Wharf, Tokyo, Silicon Valley, and Detroit are among the well-studied urban places whose morphologies and social geographies are intimately tied to their connections with the global economy. The economic and financial news media constantly remind us that dynamic urban regions are witnessing greater shares of economic output, especially because of the concentration they enjoy of technological innovation, specialized manufacturing, engineering, design, and high-value financial and legal services that trade globally. Such studies emphasize that the entrepreneurial state is crucial to the attraction of private-sector investment through fiscal incentives and public–private economic and urban planning (Yoder 2012).

Small and mid-sized cities on average exhibit scaled-back consequences of the interrelationship between flows of money and land use patterns. Small cities experience globalization to varying degrees, ranging from enhanced to diminished investment. Some are overlooked or rejected for investment emanating from beyond their immediate area, such as micropolitan areas of the Mississippi Delta or Appalachia, while others are blessed with amenities that enable them to gain national and potentially international attention, such as Ashland, OR and Burlington, VT. Generally, however, larger urban regions, especially metropolitan areas, possess the assets to enhance global connections, including trained workforces, innovation clusters, and experts in high-value producer services. Many small cities in rural areas certainly have important employers, though their limited abilities to drive the global economy, tied to a lack of agglomeration, more often than not render them dependent on the more advantaged metropolitan areas (Kalafsky and Graves 2018; Yoder 2012).

To illustrate their relevance to geographic studies, metropolitan areas, defined as urbanized areas with populations greater than 50,000, represented 80.7% of the national population at the 2010 Census. This means that micropolitan areas, rural areas with populations spread out or lightly clustered in villages, and the smallest of urban places collectively make up 19.3% (Berg 2012). A micropolitan area contains a stand-alone urban cluster of 10,000–50,000 in population which dominates at least one county. There are 543 such small urban areas in the USA, according to the 2020 Census. Smaller urban areas, those between 2500 and 10,000, are, like micropolitan areas, referred to by the Census Bureau, and by Berg (2012) as urban clusters, of which there are a total of 3087 in the country. Due to the sheer numbers and not-insignificant proportion of the country's population, sub-metropolitan areas are ripe for geographic study.

Small urban clusters less than 10,000 in population make up 9.5% of the total national population, while micropolitan areas comprise 9.8%. Together, however, they account for 86% of all urban places. Not surprisingly then, urban geographers, planners, and economists/economic developers are not exposed to a sufficient array of case studies of places smaller than metropolitan areas to understand the intricacies of each of these kinds of places. Rather than regarding them as incomplete versions of larger cities, small cities should be studied as what they are (Bell and Jayne 2009). Furthermore, few studies of communities and economic centers of this size utilize qualitative research techniques that reveal empirical, descriptive insights into their varied natures (Yoder 2012). Interviews and/or surveys are necessary to understand the full impacts of transportation and other facets of economic developments in small cities located outside metropolitan areas (Goetz and Bandyopadhyay 2013). Such case studies based on interviews enable research on economics and economic development to reveal more than quantitative data (NPR 2019).

This chapter examines two small cities of South Texas as windows into economic development strategies and the impacts of extra-regional trade upon this category of cities. They include Beeville (pop. 12,912 in 2019) and Gonzales (population 7517 in 2019). The two cities, only 93 miles apart, exhibit some significant differences in their strategies to attract and retain employers, and to market their communities to attract investment. Thus, public–private entrepreneurial governance is an important component of the study. Another is the nature of transportation linkages with places throughout Texas, other states of the USA, and Mexico's border states. Neither community is located on an interstate highway. Beeville and Gonzales enjoy direct two-lane US highway connections to San Antonio, Houston, Corpus Christi, and the important border crossings at Laredo and the Lower Rio Grande Valley. Gonzales is closer to an interstate highway than Beeville and enjoys rail connection that Beeville no longer does.

The balance of the chapter includes a brief discussion of research methods appropriate for the study of small-city economic development, and a short review of the literature on economic development and small cities. The next two sections discuss the economic development strategies of each of the two case study communities, the organization and funding of the economic development agencies of each city, and their respective uses of fiscal incentives and land offerings to employers. The chapter then highlights primary similarities and differences in economic development between Beeville and Gonzales, including observations of the pros and cons of current economic development initiatives in both cities. Following that comparative analysis are speculations about the extent to which they might expand economic connections with Mexico. The conclusion provides insights into future challenges of economic development and urban planning in the two communities and others of South Texas and proposes topics for further research.

Case studies of small cities allow for more in-depth examinations of planning, land-use change, and community and economic development than would be the case with more generalized studies of larger numbers of places. Furthermore, case studies facilitate more detailed comparisons (Ruddin 2006). Case studies of individual cities are useful, given that the agglomeration necessary to organize a locality's connections to the global economy are concentrated in cities (Kalafsky and Graves 2018). That said, the experience is different between cities of different sizes, as well as differences between cities within given size categories. This study relies primarily on qualitative research that employs content from news articles, municipal websites, open-ended interviews, and triangulation of the data gathered. The latter involves verification of information between different sources, including interviews, news articles, and data presented on governmental and company web sites. Qualitative research in the form of semi-structured, partly open-ended interviews permits a flexibility in the data gathering process that produces greater detail than standardized surveys, thereby reflecting the unique character of each site (Longhurst 2010).

7.2 A Brief Literature Review of Economic Development and Small Cities

An important theme in urban economic development is the impact on individual urban areas of regional, national, and global transportation and communication connectivity (Kalafsky and Graves 2018). Without attention to small cities, the body of research on urban economic development is incomplete. Small cities should be studied not in terms of how they are incomplete versions of larger ones, but on their own terms. The multiple ways that neoliberal capitalism affects small cities is worthy of study. As such, small cities ought to be examined in terms of the ways that they position themselves to be competitive (Bell and Jayne 2009). The latter include economic development strategies on the part of the public sector (local government), as well as partnerships between the public and private sectors (economic development corporations), collaborations that constitute "entrepreneurial governance." Furthermore, a small city's success at experiencing economic development generally depends on a healthy downtown, especially one that is registered with the Main Street USA Program. Traditional downtown areas serve as a central place that encapsulates the community's history. They are walkable and serve as a core area for communication and commerce. They serve to distinguish small cities from each other in light of standardized suburban style that dominates the category of American cities today. Successful downtowns enhance connectivity throughout a small city through walking, cycling, and other non-automobile transportation modes. Furthermore, healthy downtown areas are considered important for attracting and/or retaining creative individuals with a propensity toward entrepreneurial activities (Smith 2007; Yoder 2015a, b).

Increasingly, researchers of community and economic development conclude that there are multiple advantages of attracting and retaining entrepreneurs compared to attracting existing manufacturing, distribution, and similar companies that demand fiscal incentives and other resources that can strain small-city budgets. Those who start up small businesses, ranging from retail shops to information technology services to small-scale manufacturing, generally prefer the location and its amenities in which they commit to launch. Such amenities include viable downtown areas that foster face-to face interaction and a sense of place (Florida 2014; Yoder 2015b).

Texas is one of the more active states in offering incentives to attract new industry. Incentives that include direct cash payments (grants) to companies, tax abatements, and provision of infrastructure desired by companies are controversial, and disagreements about their effectiveness can be fierce. Critics such as Richard Florida (2018) and Jensen and Malesky (2018) argue that politicians are often eager to offer incentives for political purposes, to claim credit for and demonstrate their competence in attracting business, despite the lack of evidence of the economic success of such incentives. Foremost among the tools used by the State of Texas is the Texas Enterprise Fund (TEF), administered by Texas Economic Development, an arm of the Office of the Governor. The TEF is often referred to as a "closing fund" to seal a deal for a given project. The TEF can only be used in cases where a given project might go to a site in a competing state. The fund is intended for companies that would make large capital investments in a given location in Texas, and would create at least 75 full-time jobs in an urban area, or 25 in a rural area. The proposed location has to approve the project, and the company involved has to have a sound financial track record. The amount of TEF funding for each project depends on the promised number of full-time employees, the wages or salaries, and the timeline of the project. Furthermore, Industrial Revenue Bonds (IRBs) are available to local (city or county) industrial development corporations (IDCs) that are set up to issue bonds to companies for industrial development. The most common is the Tax-Exempt Industrial Revenue Bonds for Manufacturing Projects (Texas Economic Development 2018). Both Beeville and Gonzales look to such state funding for economic development.

Most of the more than 400 communities of Texas identifiable as rural, many of which are micropolitan areas or contain a small city that is the core of its county, have experienced a decrease in population since the early 1990s. However, on average, within both the growing and non-growing categories of such rural areas, immigrants affect demographics significantly. In the growing rural areas, immigrants overall account for a clear majority of the growth. In the shrinking areas, foreign-born immigrants have reduced the rate of decrease. The native-born population has decreased by 19% and the foreign-born population by 96% since 1990. Immigrants are important in agriculture, food processing, and culturally based small businesses that create their own economic multipliers (Trovall 2018; Mathema et al. 2018). Both cases in this chapter are majority Hispanic and have experienced an influx of recent non-native immigrants as evidenced by family-run businesses observable in the retail landscapes of each and reinforced in this study's interviews.

7.3 Beeville: Transportation Challenges and a Military Base Closure

Current economic development initiatives in Beeville, a city located at the juncture of US 59 Highway and US Highway 181, both two-lane routes, are largely instigated by two amenities (see Fig. 1.1). The first is Chase Field, a repurposed naval air station that had been shuttered in the 1990s. The second is the city's historic downtown, whose vitality is fed by its longstanding status within the Main Street Texas and Main Street USA programs. Its courthouse, the focal point of downtown, adjoins US Highway 59, which replicates a typical circumstance for small cities of

Fig. 7.1 Photo of Bee County Courthouse, Beeville. (Photo by the author)

the region: automobile traffic passing through the city that is not bypassed beyond the historic downtown zone (Fig. 7.1). Unfortunately, local fiscal policy emphasizes that infrastructure repairs be done only when necessary, to the detriment of plans for downtown revitalization. Furthermore, interviewees consistently stated that city and county governments bend to the wishes of fiscally conservative voters who prefer lower taxes to downtown redevelopment.

Manufacturing is an economic priority for elected officials and the economic development community, especially in the Chase Field Industrial Airport, a 1600-acre (650 ha) facility with an 8000-foot runway located five miles east-southeast of downtown Beeville. Chase Field had been established by the US Navy, upon purchase from the City of Beeville, as an auxiliary air station for jet pilot training during the Korean War. The facility became a naval air station in 1968, but it was phased out in 1993 at the end of the Cold War (Bee Development Authority, 2022; Bauer, 2017; Leatherwood n.d.). From that point forward, it has been marketed by the City of Beeville and more recently the Bee Development Authority, as an industrial park, though much of the occupancy has been prison-related, run by the Texas Department of Criminal Justice.

The Bee Development Authority was established by the State of Texas in 2001 under its Defense Closure Act to receive federal and state funds, participate with federal and state economic development initiatives, and more easily apply for grants (Bee Development Authority 2022). At present, the BDA is in the process of being folded into a larger economic development entity that includes the BDA, the City, the County, and the Chamber of Commerce, tentatively called the Bee Area Partnership, in the hopes of aligning the interests of all entities to attract manufacturing employment, especially to Chase Field. The economic development corporation will receive public funding from the city and county, private donations, and hopefully assistance from the economic development branch of the Governor's Office (J. Arrisola, personal communication, August 16, 2018; T. Florence, personal communication, August 16, 2018). At present, a company that manufactures polyethylene pipes for petroleum and other large-scale use has begun to set up an operation at Chase Field. Meanwhile, FEMA pays the BDA $70,000 a month for storage of travel trailers and small mobile homes for hurricane disaster relief, on 42 acres of Chase Field's territory, including an unused apron and two unused runways. The income is welcomed by the BDA, as are the nearly 1400 employees at three prisons located at Chase Field (Emsi, 2018; J. Arrisola, personal communication, August 16, 2018).

The city's original industrial park, the Beeville Industrial Park, developed in the 1970s, has seen its manufacturing activities and employment wax and wane. Among its most successful enterprises is Wastequip, a company that manufactures garbage dumpsters and recycling equipment and employs around 125. Bee County Development Corporation (BCDC), which formed in tandem with the development of the 56-acre (23-ha) park, no longer exists and has been effectively replaced by the BDA, which is oriented toward promotion of Chase Field as the locus of the city's future economic growth. BCDC consisted of private investors who received a modest amount of public money through federal funds forwarded to the city for economic development (J. Montez, personal interview, August 30, 2018). The Beeville Industrial Park still has land available, which, combined with Chase Field, indicates that Beeville has a healthy supply of land available for manufacturing and distribution.

Agriculture, including both crops and livestock, are regarded by multiple interviewees of Beeville as stable pillars of the county's and city's economies. However, despite its clear presence in the landscape, production between 2007 and 2012 declined in market value, from $39 million annually to $26 million. Pasture accounted for 70% of land in farms in 2012, while 13% of agricultural land area was in cropland (USDA, 2012a). In 2017, farmers produced $15.5 million in cattle feed (grains and hay), and $20.5 million in cattle. Farm operators produce calves and yearlings for fattening in large cattle operations of East Texas, the Texas Panhandle, and to a lesser extent a nearby slaughterhouse in north Corpus Christi with fairly favorable access to that city's port (R. Butler, personal communication, August 29, 2018; R. Reininger, personal communication, August 29,2018). Thus, while total agricultural output overall has continued to decline at a slow pace, the sector still remains important to the county's identity and economy and has potential for amplifying the county's connections with the global economy.

A key challenge that Beeville faces as it attempts to expand its agricultural, manufacturing, and distribution sectors is its transportation geography. The functioning 8000-foot runway at Chase Field holds promise, especially for attracting manufacturing, aviation repair, and aircraft maintenance companies. However, highway access is not optimal, and rail access is nonexistent in the county. At present, the proposed NAFTA/USMCA highway, Interstate 69, is slated to bypass Beeville by some 33 miles to the east. Originally, TXDOT and the USDOT had planned to expand US Highway 59, which runs through Beeville, into a western branch of I-69, but for at least a decade, no work has been done to accomplish this expansion (J. Montez, personal communication, August 30, 2018). At present, commercial truck through-traffic must exit US 59 for rerouting around the city via Texas FM 351 and US 181. The closest maritime port of significance, Corpus Christi, is 56 miles to the southeast, via US 181, a two-lane highway for most of the route. But the most disadvantageous feature of Beeville's transportation system is the removal of the Southern Pacific (SP) rail line that linked the city to Houston, San Antonio, and Corpus Christi between 1979 and 1994 (TTI & CTR 2011). To serve Beeville was no longer profitable for the rail company, which had been ramping up usage of a parallel line through neighboring Live Oak County that parallels I-37 (J. Montez, personal communication, August 30, 2018; S. Moreno, personal communication, August 30, 2018).

Despite its transportation weaknesses, Beeville exhibits many similarities to other micropolitan areas that have avoided reliance on a single industry producing booms and busts. To illustrate, the city's experience with Covid-19 was not unlike that of other micropolitan areas of Texas. The pandemic led to some temporary closures of retail and restaurant businesses, but they have rebounded, and some new ones are in the process of being established. Many of the city's restaurants adopted shorter hours of operation, while some embraced takeout and curbside service as a way of surviving, especially early in the pandemic. The biggest problem now for such businesses is the shortage of labor. A new Starbucks coffee shop and a yogurt shop were slated to open in 2022 on the suburban north side, and downtown is anticipating a wine bar and a western wear shop. In the manufacturing sector, NAFFCO, a Dubai-based company that assembles fire truck components, committed in 2021 to establish a plant at the Chase Field Industrial Airport that would occupy two of the converted military hangars, and employ some 400 workers (T. Florence, personal communication, March 23, 2022). This boost to Beeville's manufacturing base indicates that COVID-19 has not hampered the city's efforts to attract new employment, and its laborshed contains a sizable population.

7.4 Gonzales: Manufacturing, Historical Identity, and Downtown Revitalization

Manufacturing is quite robust in Gonzales County and the City of Gonzales. That sector produces over $250 million annually, nearly double the more than $140 million generated by retail sales. For a rural county with its modest population (20,731 in 2019), Gonzales enjoys a rather healthy manufacturing economy comparable to some micropolitan areas of the south-central USA (Yoder 2012). The industrial economy rests largely on two major features: agroindustry, and the sizable logistics center of the Texas Gonzales and Northern Railway, a short line rail company. Nearly all industrial activities are immediately north of the city of Gonzales, which provides them access to Interstate I-10 and the east-west Union Pacific (UP) rail line that links San Antonio and Houston and roughly parallels I-10 (see Fig. 1.1). Agroindustry dominates the economy. In 2012, 36% of the county's jobs were in animal (largely poultry) production, 17% were in crop production, and 15% were in spice production. Thus, agroindustry and food processing accounted for more than two thirds of employment, at a time when the Eagle Ford Shale formation was still booming (GCCA 2018). That year, Gonzales County ranked second among Texas counties in poultry (layer and broiler) production, a value of more than $402 million, while cattle production generated $92 million. Thus, agriculture and livestock generated half a billion Dollars (USDA 2012b). Presently, according to the city's website, agroindustry remains important in total employment, though the school district and the Guadalupe Valley Electric Coop are the top two single employers.

The promotion of manufacturing is a priority of the Gonzales Economic Development Corporation (GEDC), an independent 501 (c)(4) entity physically housed in City Hall. It is funded by a State of Texas 4B sales tax levied at the rate of 1/2 cent. The GEDC was founded in 1997 upon passage by the citizens of the 4B sales tax (G. Young, personal communication, August 1, 2018). One impulse behind the creation of the GEDC was the success, by the standards of a county with a rural character, of its original industrial park. Located on the north side of the city along FM Highway 794, the now non-existent Gonzales Area Development Corporation (GADC) developed in the early 1960s the Gonzales Industrial Park, which has no available land remaining. The founders of GADC, a group of local businessmen, formed the association to develop the industrial park by purchasing farmland immediately north of the city, for sale to manufacturing operators. In recent decades, some of these manufacturing landowners have offered their sites for resale to new manufacturing companies (G. Young, personal communication, August 1, 2018; G. Lawing, personal communication, August 22, 2018). The only parcels of land available for manufacturing and related activities lie along US Highway 90-Alt (Sarah Dewitt Drive), and the Eagle Ford Logistics Center, a facility six miles north of Gonzales on FM 794 operated by the Texas Gonzales and Northern Railway (TXGN).

Typical of many counties of South Texas, the extraction of oil and gas has fared heavily in Gonzales County's economic development since around 2008. Activities in the Eagle Ford Shale resulted in a bump in the population of Gonzales; the construction of new lodging to accommodate drillers, truck drivers, and other fracking workers; and wear-and-tear on the city's and county's roads (Bright and Cutala 2013). This extraction of hydrocarbons exists in the present day, which is evident by the continued activity of sand shipments in the TXGN logistics facility (P. Treangen, personal communication, September 14, 2018) and the continued existence of a few oil- and gas-field service companies. Despite the tendency for the Eagle Ford Shale

Play to rise and fall in activity, the oil and gas sector should rightly be considered in community discussions of economic development planning (G. Lawing, personal communication, August 22, 2018).

The TXGN short line railroad has been crucial to the recent growth of the manufacturing sector of Gonzales County's economy. The original rail line dates back to 1882 and has connected with the long-standing (UP) rail line linking San Antonio and Houston, roughly parallel to Interstate I-10. It was acquired in 1992 from Southern Pacific by the TNW Corporation, a developer and operator of short line railroads. The CEO of TNW explains that for a short line railroad like TXGN to be successful in a largely rural region such as Gonzales County, the company must cultivate new business and improve infrastructure. That was the impetus behind the company's development of the private 480-acre (194-ha) Eagle Ford Logistics Center in 2010 (Fig. 7.2). First, the company had to improve the existing track acquired in 1992, which was unusable, and then develop the switching and transshipment center that interfaces with Union Pacific some 12.3 miles north of the city of Gonzales. The entire venture is viewed by TXGN and its holding company, TNW Corporation, as privately-led economic development, though the company does enjoy the federal 45G Short Line Tax Credit (C. Kendall, personal communication, September 26, 2018; P. Treangen, personal communication, September 14, 2018). As stated on Union Pacific's website, "(t)raffic consists of crude oil, grain and animal feed meals, clay, and metal products" (UP 2018). Indeed, a visual inspection of

Fig. 7.2 Photo of the Eagle Ford Logistics Center, Gonzales. (Photo by the author)

the 12.3-mile line, including the Eagle Ford Logistics Center, reveals that companies that rely on the rail service include manufacturers of food products, metal products, and fluids, among others, as well as oil- and gas-field services, four distributors of sand for hydraulic fracturing, and a distributor of livestock feeds (C. Kendall, personal communication, September 26, 2018). In its logistics center are Jim H. Wilson LLC, a company that dismantles surplus rail cars for scrap metal, Sierra Frac Sand, LLC, and various services provided by TXGN, including rail car and locomotive maintenance and parking and transloading of sand and grain.

Agricultural production and related processing represent a stable, longstanding mainstay of the Gonzales regional economy (Baumgartner and Vollentine 2016). However, the municipal government, economic development officials, and the business community of Gonzales emphasize the importance of downtown revitalization and historic preservation to the community's development. Key features of this strategy are the community's place in the history of the Republic of Texas, and the persistence since 1988 of the city's Main Street USA membership. In the beginning, the city manager assembled a community group to research the feasibility of membership in Main Street USA. The Chamber of Commerce headed up Gonzales Main Street in its earlier years. Subsequently, the Department of Economic Development of the City of Gonzales has overseen the affiliation (B. Friedrich, personal communication, July 26, 2018). The Main Street Program covers largely two parallel and adjacent streets, St. Joseph and St. Paul Streets, for a length of roughly 5 blocks. According to the City's website, the heart of the district comprises some eight antique stores, 17 specialty and miscellaneous stores, two theaters (including a functioning movie theater), and four lodging businesses that include a recently renovated historic hotel, a recently constructed new hotel, and two bed and breakfast (B&B) establishments in historic houses. In addition, offices of the Chamber of Commerce and the public library are located in the district. As recently as 1998, there were no restaurants in downtown; in 2018 there were six (B. Friedrich, personal communication, July 26, 2018).

Funding of Main Street Gonzales is carried out primarily through a State of Texas Part 4B sales tax. Under this tax regime, a sales tax of up to 2% can be levied and used for advertising, promotion, and an assortment of business incentives, including the provision of land. The purpose of the tax, which must be administered by cities through a fund, is to enable cities to produce a steady, reliable stream of revenue for economic development (Alley n.d.). Gonzales presently charges 1/4 cent for its Main Street Program, which enables $75,000 to be budgeted for each property via the Gonzales Main Street Business Improvement Grant. Most of the latter is dedicated to improvements of facades of store fronts and other businesses. Since 2009, some forty businesses have participated in such improvements. Secondarily, there are grants available for relocation of utility meters to the backs of buildings, in order to improve sidewalk access and aesthetics. To enhance the appeal of downtown, the business community and the City favor antique stores and specialty shops, such as apparel, to less glamorous businesses such as pawn shops. While at first glance, several store fronts appear vacant, the Director of Main Street Gonzales indicates that few are available for new businesses, because the existing vacant shops are used for storage by their owners, who refuse to make their properties available through sale or lease. The City and Chamber of Commerce are presently looking into potential ordinances to incentivize making such stores available for downtown development. On the other hand, some property owners are beginning to develop loft apartments above or behind shops, a trend that the City and business community strongly favor. Such apartments are believed to be particularly appealing to younger residents who relocate from larger cities such as Austin and San Antonio in search of a walkable community, downtown setting, and small city lifestyle (B. Friedrich, personal communication, July 26, 2018).

Barriers to development of the historic Main Street district exist, however. First, many of the historically relevant buildings, of which there are about 100, are empty store fronts whose owners continue to keep them for storage rather than investing in restoration. When a historic building is revitalized and brought up to contemporary building codes (electricity, plumbing, and the like), its taxable value increases. Given the fiscal reliance on property taxes in the State of Texas, one of nine states with no state or local income taxes, assessed values of improved properties can lead to very high property taxes that then render such renovations expensive in the eyes of property owners. Thus, the higher property taxes too often serve as a disincentive to renovation. Furthermore, development of the second-floor space above shops in the historic downtown often requires ADA compliance, which adds an additional layer of costs to the creation of loft apartments and office space (D. L. Allen, personal communication, August 2, 2018).

The community has a natural branding advantage, given that the first shots of the revolution leading to independence from Mexico and the establishment of the Republic of Texas in 1836 were fired in Gonzales (Cain Tolson 1966). The community brands its downtown and historic buildings based on the "Come And Take It" flag that the Gonzales settlers made in 1836 to protest Mexico's attempt to take away the town's cannon, used to fight indigenous attacks in the area. The flag, the precursor to the first shots fired in the Texas independence movement, can be seen in many spots in the downtown area and is key to Main Street identity (G. Young, personal communication, August 1, 2018).

The coronavirus pandemic had surprisingly little negative impact on the economic development of Gonzales. Similar to other small cities of South Texas, the Gonzales Economic Development Corporation provided some $500,000.00 in small-business grants, and CARES ACT funding enabled small businesses to retain much of their workforces. Although no retail businesses or restaurants closed permanently, some changed the way they do business. For example, two Mexican restaurants shifted to drive-through and curbside service. An antique store described as "high-end" shifted to online sales, resulting in higher revenues overall. Poultry processing and other manufacturing in the county suffered no permanent closure, and at present (first quarter of 2022), an automotive parts manufacturing firm is seriously considering the locality for the opening of a facility. The movement of trucks hauling frac sand, and others related to oilfield service, are regularly spotted in the county, indicating that petroleum extraction in the Eagle Ford Shale Play has by no means disappeared (G. Lawing, personal communication, April 25, 2022).

7.5 Beeville and Gonzales: Similarities and Differences

Anglos founded both Gonzales and Beeville as settlements during Mexico's early independence phase, when Texas was part of the Mexican State of Coahuila y Tejas, whose capital was Saltillo. Both experienced challenges in a region often neglected by Mexican officials, a region characterized by a low population density of Anglo and Mexican farmers, and the constant threat of attacks carried out by the indigenous natives of the area. Yet, in large part because of the origins of the Texas independence movement from Mexico that began in Gonzales, the city has been better able than Beeville to capitalize in recent years on the settlement history of South Texas. Both cities share similar goals for development of their historically relevant Main Street districts. The commitment of each city to provide funding, and local-level policy related to historic preservation, will determine whether or not they succeed.

Both communities desire to experience the kind of economic and demographic growth that Jack Schultz (2004) refers to as "agurbs," or rural places that receive intraregional migrants from inner cities and suburbs. He argues that the USA has now experienced three great waves of movements of people: from declining rural areas to cities, from cities to suburbs, and now from crowded, traffic-afflicted suburbs to small cities and rural counties with agrarian histories, that offer lower costs of living and of doing business, and higher quality of life based on simplicity and tradition (Schultz 2004). The anecdotes I heard of people who now reside in Gonzales and telecommute (or commute outright by vehicle) to Austin, San Antonio, or Houston suggest that the community has the potential to continue this kind of growth. I was told multiple times that it takes no more time for a small business owner or self-employed professional to drive to Austin's airport by US Highway 183 than to drive to the airport from Austin's suburban north side on I-35, a freeway constantly afflicted with traffic congestion. While not as successfully as Gonzales, Beeville could possibly experience some aspects of "agurban growth" by attracting professionals from Houston, a city with the unfortunate distinction of ranking high nationally in terms of lengthy commutes, owing to traffic jams and poor-quality public transit. Schultz's definition of agurb as including natural amenities and picturesque scenery would also favor Gonzales over Beeville, though both cities could potentially focus on this kind of growth in their own ways. Gonzales has begun to develop its river frontage, despite flooding problems. Both communities would need to continue to prioritize, through greater participation of different public- and private-sector stakeholders, downtown revitalization through much more rigorous codes that discourage using historically-relevant buildings as storage space, and encourage improvements of exterior facades.

While both communities have weathered the pandemic quite well, Gonzales currently has the edge over Beeville (and many other South Texas small cities) in the quest to attract employment, because of the TXGN rail infrastructure, the company's logistics center, and the city's fairly good access to Interstate I-10. It also benefits from close access (33 miles) to Seguin, a city of 27,865 (2015) with a high per-capita existence of manufacturing activity and employment among all places in Texas (G. Lawing, personal communication, August 22, 2018; Seguin, 2018). In the case of Beeville, if TxDOT and USDOT officials once again prioritize development of the branch of I-69 that would follow the existing US Highway 59, Bee County would benefit in terms of its ability to attract employment in manufacturing and/or goods distribution, in spite of the lack of rail. Such development, however, would require the construction of a divided, limited access highway loop around the city (J. Montez, personal communication, August 30, 2018). As long as Laredo continues to remain the leading port along the USA–Mexico border, and USA–Mexico trade remains healthy and unhampered by tariffs or other impediments to trade, then such a western branch of I-69 would increasingly make sense, as a way to link Laredo to Houston more directly rather than through the I-35 and I-10 interchange in San Antonio. In the case of both cities' economic development strategies, assuming trade conditions remain favorable, USA–Mexico trade ought to be prioritized.

7.6 Beeville's and Gonzales's Linkages with Mexico

Small cities of South Texas and the counties that house them have fewer commercial connections than one might imagine, given their relatively short aerial distance to the USA–Mexico border. The quality and relative lack of flexibility of the existing cargo transportation infrastructure are not the only factors limiting the links between Mexico and these communities. That said, their connections are worthy of inclusion in research on the geography of economic development of small cities of South Texas. It is difficult to gather exact data on such connections, though estimations of the relative importance of agriculture and food products, manufacturing and transportation services, and labor can be obtained through broadly based agricultural data and interviews of knowledgeable economic development actors of the public and private sectors. Experts in economic development in the region highlight the trade between the two case-study counties and Mexico in agriculture. There is a likelihood of strengthened binational trade in which the communities of this study participate, because of likely expansion of oil and gas exports to Mexico. The latter would be linked to likely increased extractions in the Eagle Ford Shale Play that underlie portions of each of these two case-study counties, and continued liberalization of the natural gas sector in Mexico as Pemex, the state-run hydrocarbons enterprise, and the federal electricity commission began a slow process of opening up some of its functions to private investors in the mid-2010s.

Data on trade between Texas and Mexico exist, as do specific county-level figures of overall production. However, product-specific county data on such exports do not. I maintain the point of view that it is possible to roughly estimate the importance of such binational agricultural trade. The leading agricultural exports from Texas to Mexico in 2016 were beef ($142 million), cotton ($125 million), corn and corn-based products ($126 million), and poultry products ($62 million). Texas agricultural exports to Mexico reached $834 million, a third of which was livestock-oriented, and two-thirds of which was crop-oriented (Texas Farm Bureau 2017; CNAS 2017). It stands to reason that South Texas participated in a good bit of this trade, given that corn, cotton, cattle, and poultry products are all produced in the case study localities. To illustrate, a large cattle fattening operation in Gonzales County imports young cattle, mostly yearlings, from Mexico for additional fattening and eventual shipment to a large slaughterhouse and export company in Corpus Christi. However, it is more difficult to estimate trade in crops because brokers consolidate sales and do not break down sales data by locality (J. Gray, personal communication, August 9, 2018; D. Sexton, personal communication, September 4, 2018).

In short, grains for livestock feed and, secondarily, for human consumption flow southbound, while young cattle flow northbound for fattening as part of the supply chain that culminates in packaged beef. The pattern, however, is gradually changing as Mexico's capacity to produce cattle to slaughter weight and to slaughter them is enhanced by modernization of large-scale beef operations and improved transportation networks, especially in the Laguna region of western Coahuila and eastern Durango. The trend is suggesting that more beef consumed in Mexico will be produced there, though feed grain imports from the USA will remain in high demand (Peel 2018). Immigrants, primarily from Mexico, constitute an important amount of the work force needed to fatten cattle, grow grains, and process poultry products in South Texas (J. Gray, personal communication, August 9, 2018; R. Butler, personal communication, August 29, 2018). Quite possibly, finished poultry products produced in Gonzales County involve the labor of a not insignificant number of Mexican nationals, and some of the product is shipped to Mexico. Grain brokers and poultry manufacturers would need to be queried about details of the movements to Mexico of such products.

7.7 Conclusions and Future Research

Regional planning that occurs at multiple scales, from "megaregions" that span state lines and link together metro areas of two or more adjoining states to individual metro areas and their sparsely populated hinterlands, ought to include the rural areas between the metro areas in their economic development efforts. That way, small cities such as Beeville, Gonzales, and others of South Texas that carry out activities like manufacturing, food processing, and primary agricultural and livestock production and distribution can see their connections to the global system enhanced. As the two case studies demonstrate, a given small city's fortunes are related to the breadth of its transportation connections, to efforts by economic development promoters to attract and retain employers, and to historic amenities, especially Main Streets. The qualitative research methods employed in the study, especially the open-ended interviews, were invaluable in the identification of the different and varied features of their respective efforts to bring about past, present, and future economic development.

The impact of the Eagle Ford Shale Play on economic development in South Texas in the short- and mid-term remains in question in light of fluctuations in drilling and actual output that began in the late 2010s. As Slav (2018) points out, the oil and gas pipeline infrastructure of the Permian Basin of West Texas is at capacity, which could reignite a new uptick in the Eagle Ford Shale Play. The threat of steel tariffs has clearly played a role in the pessimism for new pipeline capacity of West Texas. This could translate to companies' seeking new production regions that are not suffering the same oil and gas transport bottle necks between the Permian Basin and destinations such as Corpus Christi and Beaumont (which are involved in export) as well as Mexican and US domestic destinations (Mosier 2018). Two questions arise. First, will the Trojan plastic pipeline plant provide Beeville an opportunity to boost manufacturing employment, and contribute to enhanced drilling and associated employment in Bee and Gonzales Counties? Second, will the Mexican Administration of López Obrador continue to pursue an opening of the hydrocarbons sector that began under his predecessor, Peña Nieto, in the realms of oil and gas imports by pipeline and drilling into Mexican soil? Booms and busts in production by hydraulic fracturing will need to be analyzed through time to determine the cyclical impacts of such activities on the economic development fortunes of the small cities of South Texas.

Future research will include a historical analysis of the development of transportation infrastructure relevant to the movement of cargo in South Texas counties and their county seats. This will include an identification of the various coalitions that bring about corridors such as the I-69 NAFTA Highway, and the resulting routes of such corridors. Another topic of inquiry relates to the abilities of South Texas counties to participate in global trade in food products, whether chilled poultry, chilled beef, live animals, and row crops. Agriculture brought about the establishment and growth of those communities in the first place, and agriculture will continue to be relied upon as hopefully stable components of those counties' economic development.

References

Alley R (n.d.) What is a 4B sales tax fund? Small Business-Chron.com. https://smallbusiness.chron.com/4b-sales-tax-fund-66612.html. Retrieved July 30, 2018

Bauer G (2017) Beeville, TX. Handbook of Texas Online. https://tshaonline.org/handbook/online/articles/heb04

Baumgartner DH, Vollentine GB (2016) Gonzales County. Handbook of Texas Online. https://tshaonline.org/handbook/online/articles/hcg07

Bee Development Authority (2022) Chase field industrial airport. Retrieved May 11, 2022 from https://www.beedevelopmentauthority.org/chase-field/

Bell D, Jayne M (2009) Small cities? Towards a research agenda. Int J Urban Reg Res 33(3):683–699

Berg N (2012) Census definitions include a wide spectrum of places that count as cities. CityLab. https://www.citylab.com/equity/2012/03/us-urban-population-what-does-urban-really-mean/1589/

Bright E, Cutala L et al (2013) Gonzales comprehensive plan. Texas A&M University, Department of Landscape Architecture and Urban Planning, College of Architecture

Cain Tolson M (1966) Gonzales, Birthplace of Texas Independence 1925–1965. Unpublished master's thesis, Graduate School, University of Texas, Austin

CNAS (2017) Center for North American Studies. Economic Impacts of U.S. and Texas Agricultural Exports to Canada and Mexico. CNAS Issue Brief 2017–01 16 February, Texas A&M University. Retrieved August 18, 2018 from http://cnas.tamu.edu/Impact%20of%20Ag%20Exports%20to%20Canada%20and%20Mexico%20Final.pdf

Emsi (2018) Bee County, TX economy overview. Workforce Solutions of the Coastal Bend, Beeville

Florida R (2018) Why do politicians waste so much money on corporate incentives? CityLab. https://www.citylab.com/equity/2018/05/why-do-polticians-waste-so-much-money-on-corporate-incentives/561149/

Florida R (2014) What cities really need to attract entrepreneurs, according to entrepreneurs. Atlantic City Lab

GCCA (2018) (Gonzales chamber of commerce and agriculture). Gonzales Community Profile. https://gonzalestexas.com/communiyt-profiles/. Accessed 27 July 2018

Goetz AR, Bandyopadhyay S (2013) Regional impacts of trade corridors: recent experiences from the United States. In: Gillen D, Parsons G, Prentice B (eds) Canada's Asia Pacific gateway and corridor initiative: policy trade and gateway economics (volume 1). Centre for Transportation Studies, University of British Columbia

Leatherwood A (n.d.) Handbook of Texas Online, "NAVAL AIR STATION, BEEVILLE". Retrieved August 11, 2018, from http://www.tshaonline.org/handbook/online/articles/qbn04

Jensen N, Malesky E (2018) Incentives to ponder: how politicians use corporate welfare for political gain. Oxford University Press

Kalafsky RV, Graves W (2018) Exports and growth: learning from the case of southern U.S. metropolitan areas. Prof Geogr 70(3):383–394

Longhurst R (2010) Semi-structured interviews and focus groups. In: Clifford N, French S, Valentine G (eds) Key methods in geography, 2nd edn. Sage Publications, pp 103–115

Mathema S, Prchall Svajlinka N, Hermann A (2018) Revival and opportunity: immigrants in rural America. Center for American Progress, 2 September. Retrieved September 11, 2018, from https://www.americanprogress.org/issues/immigration/reports/2018/09/02/455269/revival-and-opportunity/

Mosier J (2018). Trump's steel tariffs are costing Permian Basin pipeline companies millions, but the building rush continues. Dallas News https://www.dallasnews.com/business/energy/2018/08/02/trumps-steel-tariffs-costing-permian-basin-pipeline-companies-millions-building-rush-continues

NPR (2019) National public radio, marketplace podcast, 21 October. https://www.npr.org/podcasts/381444600/marketplace

Peel DS (2018) Mexican beef exports continue to grow. Beef2Live. Retrieved August 18, 2018, from http://beef2live.com/story-mexican-beef-exports-continue-grow-0-139633

Ruddin LP (2006) You can generalize stupid! Social scientists, bent Flyvbjerg, and case study methodology. Qual Inq 12:797–812

Schultz J (2004) Boomtown USA: the 7–1/2 keys to big success in small towns. NAIOP Commercial Real Estate Development Association

Seguin TX (2018) City of Seguin, TX, Seguin Economic Development Corporation. Retrieved September 22, 2018 from https://www.seguintexas.gov/resources_and_statistics/advanced_manufacturing.php

Slav I (2018) Is the eagle ford about to boom again? Oilprice.com. https://oilprice.com/Energy/Crude-Oil/Is-The-Eagle-Ford-About-To-Boom-Again.html

Smith C (2007) Managing downtown revitalization projects in small cities: lessons from Kentucky's main street program. In: Ofori-Amoah B (ed) Beyond the metropolis. University Press of America, pp 269–292

Texas Economic Development (2018) Office of the Governor, Texas Economic Development. Retrieved August 6, 2018, from https://gov.texas.gov/business

Texas Farm Bureau (2017) New report shows economic impact of Texas ag exports. Texas Agriculture Daily. http://texasfarmbureau.org/new-report-shows-economic-impact-texas-ag-exports/

Trovall E (2018) Report: Immigration Curbs Population Decline in Rural Texas Communities. Houston Public Media. https://www.houstonpublicmedia.org/articles/news/politics/immigration/2018/09/10/303421/report-immigration-curbs-population-decline-in-rural-texas-communities/

TTI & CTR (2011) (Texas Transportation Institute and Center for Transportation Research). Abandoned Rail Corridors in Texas: a policy and infrastructure evaluation. Report 0-6268-1, Texas A&M University.

UP (2018) Union Pacific Railroad Web Site. Retrieved September 13, 2018, from https://www.up.com/customers/shortline/profiles_t-z/tgn/index.htm

USDA (2012a) United States Department of Agriculture, 2012 Census of Agriculture. County Profile: Bee County, Texas. Retrieved September 20, 2018, from https://www.agcensus.usda.gov/Publications/2012/Online_Resources/County_Profiles/Texas/cp48025.pdf

USDA (2012b) United States Department of Agriculture, 2012 Census of Agriculture. County Profile: Gonzales County, Texas. Retrieved July 25, 2018, from https://www.agcensus.usda.gov/Publications/2012/Online_Resources/County_Profiles/Texas/cp48177.pdf

Yoder MS (2015a) The sprawling of small cities of Arkansas: the case for sustainable urban planing. The Arkansas Journal of Social Change and Public Service. http://ualr.edu/socialchange/2015/05/17/the-sprawling-of-small-cities-of-arkansas-the-case-for-sustainable-urban-planning/

Yoder MS (2015b) Appendix I. In: Whitehead A, Peterson M (eds) Community development kick start report: Heber Springs. Community Development Institute, University of Central Arkansas, pp 36–37

Yoder MS (2012) Entrepreneurial governance and economic development in micropoltan cities of Arkansas. Midsouth Polit Sci Rev 13(2):47–80

Chapter 8
Small-City Economic Development in Southwest Texas: Uvalde and Sonora

Abstract Small cities of the USA remain an understudied topic of economic and urban geography, despite intriguing variations among them. Economic development at the local scale can be viewed quite broadly through case studies of such cities. This chapter presents a case study of the city and county of Uvalde, a micropolitan area midway between San Antonio and the USA–Mexico border city of Del Rio, and the small city of Sonora, midway between San Antonio and the Big Bend Region. One emphasis is on Uvalde's economic development, including its transportation linkages and infrastructure, its downtown development, and its evolving suburban retail fringe. The chapter additionally examines contemporary economic development at Uvalde's airport, and the strong role that agricultural development plays in the county's economy. The micropolitan area's economy and population continue to grow modestly because of its proximity to both San Antonio and the USA–Mexico border, and its prominent location along US Highway 90. The impact of the 2022 school shooting on the micropolitan area's economic development remains unclear. Sonora, by contrast, struggles to regain its population and economic vigor of the 1970s oil boom era that has since withered, despite its favorable highway access. The small city of Sonora, located in Sutton County and roughly equidistant from Del Rio and San Angelo, is located at the intersection of I-10 and Ports-to-Plains. The community has struggled to regain the success it enjoyed until the latter part of the twentieth century as an important livestock production locality, especially in wool and mohair. Today its focus is primarily on ranching, tourism based on hunting of exotic animals on local ranches, and services to motorists on I-10. Both cities value development of their historical downtown areas.

Keywords Small cities · Main Street development · Ranching · Transportation infrastructure · Uvalde, Texas · Sonora, Texas

M. S. Yoder, *Geographical Scale and Economic Development*, https://doi.org/10.1007/978-3-031-36197-5_8

8.1 Introduction

In the introduction to Chap. 7, I argue that rural areas and small cities in the USA are numerous but are not sufficiently incorporated as case studies in the urban geography and economic development literature. This chapter provides two such case studies by examining the City and County of Uvalde, Texas, which comprise the Uvalde Micropolitan Area, and the City of Sonora and Sutton County, Texas. It considers the current status of economic development and the priorities of local community leaders at the state, county, and city levels for future growth. The viewpoints of private sector stakeholders are included. The study of each locality begins with a brief overview of their economic histories, including the role of transportation in their initial formation and subsequent development. The chapter then examines three important features of Uvalde's contemporary economic development, including brief overviews of downtown redevelopment, the sprawling of Main Street, and an overview of industries and their locations and usage of the locality's transportation system. It then discusses the uncertainties surrounding impacts of Uvalde's mass shooting in 2022. The chapter follows with a portrait of the changing economic geography of Sutton County, from a livestock center to a successful petroleum-producing county to one that is seeking to recapture its growth of prior decades. The chapter concludes that the Uvalde and Sonora cases, coupled with the literature on small-city economic development, show that each county and small city of Southwest Texas is unique in terms of the outlook of stakeholders in economic development, the nature of the interrelationships between different entities involved in economic development, and the particular assets a community enjoys.

8.2 The Uvalde Micropolitan Study Area: Geographic Overview

The City and County of Uvalde County, Texas comprise a micropolitan area whose urban cluster is located 80 miles west of San Antonio on US Highway 90 (see Fig. 1.1). The Texas border city of Del Rio, located directly across the Rio Grande from Ciudad Acuña, Coahuila, is 70 miles west of the city of Uvalde. Uvalde County is immediately south of the Texas Hill Country and north of the four-county Texas Winter Garden Region. The county's western portion is largely *monte*, or semi-arid brush country, and its east is gently rolling terrain as it approaches Medina County and the western suburban fringe of San Antonio. Three rivers, the Frio, Nueces, and Sabinal, are important tourist amenities. Some 15 miles south of Uvalde County lies the northern edge of the Eagle Ford Shale formation, a source of oil and natural gas, in neighboring Zavala County.

In addition to the direct access of Uvalde to both San Antonio and Del Rio on US 90, the city additionally enjoys proximity to the increasingly busy border port cities of Eagle Pass and Laredo by US Highway 83. Highway 83 links to I-35 20 miles north of Laredo. Carrizo Springs, a small city 50 miles south of Uvalde with a profitable history of agriculture and livestock as part of the Texas Winter Garden region, and a high amount of recent oil and gas activities as part of the Eagle Ford Shale Formation, is roughly equidistant between Uvalde and the USA–Mexico city of Eagle Pass, 65 miles southwest via US Highways 83 and 57. Thus, Uvalde's highway connections, albeit largely two-lane infrastructure (US 83 and US 90 west of Uvalde), would seem favorable for connections to the three border crossing points of Laredo, Eagle Pass, and Del Rio. Furthermore, Uvalde is located on Union Pacific Railroad's main east-west line between San Antonio and Los Angeles. Garner Field, formerly a US military air training center that was given over to the city after WWII, has become Uvalde's primary industrial park. The seemingly favorable transportation linkages present something of a riddle, given the conventional wisdom that transportation infrastructure is an essential ingredient in a locality's economic development prospects (Goetz and Bandyopadhyay 2007). That certainly was the case for most of Uvalde's history. As the intersection point of what are now US Highways 90 and 83, historically important routes, Uvalde experienced steady economic and population growth for more than a century, particularly as an important center for agricultural shipments and processing of agricultural and livestock products.

8.3 A Brief Overview of Uvalde's Early Economy

Prior to the construction of the San Antonio–Del Rio route, the territory that is now Uvalde County experienced sheep and goat production during Spanish colonial times, during the years that the locality was part of Mexico and the Republic of Texas, and well into the mid-twentieth century. The establishment of the San Antonio–Del Rio road, which today is US Highway 90, ignited settlement of ranchers, primarily from San Antonio. Seasonal migration of labor, especially of persons newly relocated from Mexico but also of multigenerational Mexican-Americans based in Uvalde, is a defining feature of the region's economic and social history based on mixing of *Tejano* and Anglo culture (Torres 2006). By the 1870s, Uvalde became a hotbed of smuggling operations of goods across the nearby USA–Mexico border. The establishment in 1881 of the railroad served to expand the local economy, despite the fact that the town's leadership demanded that the rail line be located 2 miles north of downtown, given their desire to maintain a peaceful town center. By the 1890s, an iconic hotel and opera house, and a diverse array of retail stores, mohair processing facilities, and a bank appeared in downtown. A rail spur that carried passengers and freight linked downtown with the rail depot 2 miles north (Lawrence 1998). The spur was subsequently abandoned by the early 1960s (S. Anderson, personal communication, August 29, 2019).

8.4 Contemporary Economic Development in Uvalde

A key to Uvalde's ability to sustain its population and quality of life is its downtown revitalization (Fig. 8.1). Improvements to buildings coupled with relatively low vacancy rates of retail and office space, and a safe distance from larger cities that can drain business away from small cities, are regarded by geographers and urban planners as essential to the fortunes of small cities (Otto 2007). Healthy small-city downtowns also depend largely on controlled sprawl and its segregation of land uses along major arterials that draw eateries, other retail, and offices away from downtown (Yoder 2015). The downtown's relative success is based on its attractive courthouse, the city hall, the opera house and the Kincaid Hotel, all of which are located within a block of the intersection of Main Street (US 90) and Getty Street (US 83). These buildings are helpful for spawning upgrades to other downtown buildings, especially those on Getty north of Main. For example, Rexall Drugs was getting a face lift in 2019 and will have a traditional lunch counter. The City's Main Street Program offers grants for remodeling, especially improvements to store fronts. The Convention and Visitors Bureau, a 501(c)(6) non-profit entity, is able to utilize one-cent of the thirteen-cent hotel–motel tax for such grants, for advertising/promotion, and for maintenance of the Convention Center (S. Rios, personal communication, April 3, 2019).

Fig. 8.1 Image of the Uvalde Grand Opera House. (Photo by the Author)

Despite successes in maintaining a relatively vital downtown, most growth in retail, lodging, and offices has occurred along Main Street, and is characterized by an automobile-oriented architecture. Many urban geographers and urban design critics lament this almost universal type of development throughout the USA. They argue that mandated setbacks ultimately result in less efficient land use, less tax revenue per hectare, and an architectural style designed to catch the gaze of drivers rather than the affection of pedestrians (Yoder 2003, 2015). A review of City Directories over the period 1937–1988 reveals that such auto-centric commercial development was rapid, and it transformed the historically important Main Street (US Highway 90 today). The character of East Main and West Main (Main Street east and west, respectively, of the courthouse and city hall) changed dramatically throughout that period. Lodging, chain restaurants, chain retail, and filling stations overwhelmingly became an East Main phenomenon, while local eateries and small retail stores were more dominant on West Main Street. Today, that pattern not only holds but is even more dramatic, as strip malls and a large Walmart are the springboards for retail and other commercial development. Furthermore, the city's automobile dealers, and most of its construction supply retailers, auto repair shops, agricultural supply dealers, and oil and gas equipment outlets are located on East Main.

In the realm of transportation linkages, including freight, Uvalde's transportation infrastructure represents something of a mystery because of its favorable system that in the twenty-first century has yet to expand the city's economic development beyond a modest level. The main Union Pacific rail line from San Antonio to Los Angeles passes through the county and brushes the north side of the city, yet only one quarry in the western portion of the county, one in the easter portion, and a grain silo on the city's north side directly tie into the line. Uvalde's early growth depended on the rail line for transportation to San Antonio and Del Rio, and for shipment of the historically important agriculture and livestock products that turned the city into an important processing and distribution point for the county. However, that agro-livestock industry no longer relies on rail. The spur that had linked downtown and adjoining wool processing mills to the main rail line no longer is operational. Garner Field, a repurposed military air training facility acquired by the city from the federal government after WWII, has become a small hub for aircraft maintenance and repair, the site of two colleges, and an industrial and distribution park with some potential for growth, given the city's location along US Highways 90 and 83, and its proximity to San Antonio and the border ports of Del Rio, Eagle Pass, and Laredo. Yet Uvalde County has little more than grain production exports and immigration to connect it economically with Mexico. Trucking companies based in Uvalde generally haul three types of products: crops and livestock, quarried aggregate materials for construction, and gas- and oilfield equipment and inputs. The existing highway infrastructure is adequate for the profitability of DKM, a company located on the city's north side that removes, renovates, and resells used pipes in several states (D. McLaughlin, personal communication, October 8, 2019).

In their study of the impacts of freight corridors on regional economic development, Leigh and Blakely (2017) conclude that convenience and time saving often matter more than absolute accessibility or distance. Schultz (2004) found several economically vibrant towns and small cities ("agurbs") that are more than 25 miles from an interstate highway. Gutfreund (2004) illustrates how detailed case studies, such as that which he carried out in Middlebury, VT, are necessary to understand multiple and nuanced ways that transportation systems can shape not only economic development of small cities but also their spatial form. Likewise, a study by Yoder (2015) of Morrilton and Stuttgart, Arkansas highlights the merits of such case studies of cities located, respectively, along and distant from an interstate highway.

Goetz and Bandyopadhyay (2007) conclude that there is no one-size-fits-all formula for transportation and economic development in the case of towns and small cities that are not part of metropolitan areas serving as transportation cores. Their analysis included a review of the master plan for the proposed Ports-to-Plains, a 1400 miles long corridor that would involve improvements to much of the highways that link Laredo and Denver via Lubbock (see Chap. 4). They state that some small cities will not benefit from such transportation infrastructure projects, but that such development is necessary if a given small city is to participate in regional development, to avoid isolation. A small city such as Uvalde needs to have some product that is bulky and valuable enough to justify rail sidings, and associated delays in the movement of trains from stopping to drop off and pick up rail cars (I. Jaime, personal communication, August 30, 2019). In the Uvalde micropolitan area, only three such places exist: two quarries producing aggregate materials for construction a few miles east and west of the city center, respectively, and on a much smaller scale, a grain mill in Uvalde operated by Southern Commodities that sees only occasional rail activity despite its location directly on the UP route (S. Anderson, personal communication, August 29, 2019).

The existing highway system is, in the view of most stakeholders in Uvalde's economic development, favorable for workforce mobility. Among the city's residents are commuters to surrounding counties in all directions. Most likely those employed in San Antonio are few, but certainly a number of ranchers, and agents (and other employees) of CBP (Customs and Border Protection) working in neighboring counties reside in Uvalde (V. Di Piazza, personal communication, March 7, 2019; B. Mitchell, personal communication, March 7, 2019). Such residents contribute to the local retail economy, and factor into the growth in recent years of the sprawl of retail land uses, especially national chain stores, along East Main Street. Thus, much of the discussions I had with local economic development officials emphasized Uvalde's "laborshed" (the functional region corresponding to the commuting work force that resides in Uvalde County). The collective view of stakeholders on commuting of Uvalde's residents for work is confirmed by data by the Bureau of the Census (Table 8.1).

The commuters from surrounding regions to Uvalde represent a key to the city's retail growth, as do fiscal incentives, mostly tax abatements, provided to retailers who establish stores in Uvalde (Table 8.2). This includes one national retail chain store that negotiated with the city, the county, and the Uvalde Area Development Foundation to forego tax abatements, and instead receive cash for remodeling the facility they came to occupy in a commercial strip center on East Main. Retailing

Table 8.1 Commutes to jobs from Uvalde County by distance, 2020

Commute distance	Count	Share of total (%)
Less than 10 miles	4277	40.7
10–24 miles	873	6.4
25–50 miles	793	7.6
Greater than 50 miles	4754	45.3
Total commuters	10,497	100.0

Source: Bureau of the Census (2020). https://onthemap.ces.census.gov/

Table 8.2 Commutes to jobs in Uvalde County by distance, 2020

Commute distance	Commuter count	Share of total (%)
Less than 10 miles	4287	48.5
10–24 miles	802	9.1
25–50 miles	869	9.8
Greater than 50 miles	2889	32.7
Total commuters	8847	100.0

Source: Bureau of the Census (2020). https://onthemap.ces.census.gov/

and lodging are boosted by the micropolitan area's fairly robust tourism industry based on recreation in the county's rivers, and the transformation of a fair amount of the county's farmland into game hunting lands (DeVol and Crews 2019). Uvalde is 55 miles from the proposed Ports-to-Plains corridor, whose early version links Laredo, Carrizo Springs (the closest point along the corridor to Uvalde), Eagle Pass, and Del Rio to the Permian Basin and Colorado Plains via US Highways 277 and 83. The impact of the corridor on Uvalde's transportation system and economic development remains uncertain. Interstate I-10, 100 miles north of Uvalde, accessed by two-lane US 83 is regarded as reasonably close by most trucking companies and shippers (D. McLaughlin, personal communication, October 8, 2019). Trucks are commonly seen on US 83 between Uvalde and Junction, Texas, and contribute to traffic jams downtown, where it intersects with US Highway 90.

Agriculture and livestock remain important linchpins of the Uvalde micropolitan economy. In addition to the continued participation in beef supply chains through cow-calf operations and production of mohair, farmers in the county produce winter wheat, cotton, corn, and forage crops for livestock. A small but not insignificant portion of the fattening of calves involves animals imported from Mexico and traded through the county's livestock exchange. Yearlings are sold regionally and to feed lots in west Texas and the Panhandle. Trucks are key to such participation of Uvalde in geographically expansive supply chain (M. Haynes, personal communication, April 4, 2019; S. Korzekwa, personal communication, August 4, 2019). The county exhibits an interesting agricultural geography, including goat production (for mohair) in the northern part due to rocky soils there, ranches to the west where annual rainfall totals are lower, horticulture in the extreme southern portion of the county connected to the traditional Winter Garden Region, and grains suited to the slightly higher precipitation in the county's eastern portion. The proximity to the Winter Garden Region, a four-county region of irrigated vegetable production south of Uvalde County, enables some of Uvalde County's operators of fragmented farms to diversify their businesses by working land to the south of the county (M. Haynes, personal communication, April 4, 2019).

Uvalde's economy is rather diverse for a micropolitan area compared to those of the region dominated by one or two large generators of income, like agriculture/livestock and petroleum extraction. Companies that provide oil and gas services continue to exist in Uvalde, as does the company that carries out used pipeline extraction and resale. Garner Field, the city's official industrial park, contains a few aeronautical companies. Southstar Aircraft Interiors retrofits business jets, as does Lancair, which also manufactures the parts for four-seat private aircraft kits sold nationally and internationally. Other companies at the facility provide general aircraft services, including maintenance. Federal Express is expanding its current facility at Garner Field, which handles primarily packages sent by ground. In addition to the 23 companies and other entities at the airport are a regional CBP facility and the campuses of Southwest Texas Junior College, and Sul Ross University at Uvalde. In short, despite the limited amount of manufacturing in the micropolitan area, its repurposed military airfield nonetheless houses a fair amount of employment, and factors into the city's continued, albeit modest, population growth (S. Anderson, personal communication, August 29, 2019; V. DiPiazza, personal communication, March 7, 2019; B. Mitchell, personal communication, March 7, 2019; H. Gonzales, personal communication, June 20, 2019).

8.5 The 2022 Mass Shooting in Uvalde and Possible Impacts on Economic Development

On May 24, 2022, the Uvalde community was crushed by a nightmare that no one could have imagined. An 18-year-old resident of the city murdered nineteen children and two teachers at Robb Elementary School, on the city's near west side. As of Spring of 2023, questions remain about placing blame for the woefully inadequate response by different law enforcement entities to the shooting, which has received attention globally. The divisions within the community, as well as between Uvalde and the State of Texas, combined with the lack of trust in different governing entities, including the City of Uvalde, the State of Texas, and the Uvalde Consolidated Independent School District, raise serious questions about the future of the city and its development. There are plans to demolish the school and replace it with one that commemorates the victims, and a public memorial has been promised. A common narrative in media coverage of the tragedy is that the community is close-knit, and home to families spanning multiple generations. While it is challenging to predict the community's resiliency at this point, its longevity may very well translate to a continuation of the stable economic development experienced there over the past few decades.

Clues from other communities that have experienced mass shootings may prove insightful. A study of the economic consequences of mass shootings in the USA between 2000 and 2015 concludes that cities that suffer mass shootings experience slightly lowered property values, reduced business investment, and diminished tourism and local consumer confidence. These traits are believed to be reinforced further by widespread media coverage of the shootings (Brodeur and Yousaf 2019). The small city of Newtown, Connecticut, a suburb of Danbury and New York City, experienced a temporary downturn in its downtown retail economy in the weeks and months after the catastrophic Sandy Hook Elementary School shooting in 2012 (Satija 2013). This appears not to be the case in downtown Uvalde, whose town square has functioned for many months since the shooting as the site of a heavily trafficked makeshift memorial a mile northeast of the school. A mass shooting in 2018 at Santa Fe High School, located in the city of Santa Fe, Texas in an exurban portion of the Greater Houston Metropolitan Area, led to the immediate establishment of a resiliency center, funded by grants, for providing mental health services. Like Uvalde, the Santa Fe community experienced ongoing "pain and outrage" in the aftermath of the shooting, as citizens faced difficulties coping with the event and arriving at a consensus when placing rightful and proper blame. Community leaders of Santa Fe are concerned that it may be difficult to retain young citizens, though no significant exodus has emerged yet. Economic development initiatives are largely directed at retaining as many young citizens as possible, and at promoting a "buy local" campaign to boost Santa Fe's retail economy. The latter has been regarded as successful, based on steady increases in retail sales tax revenues (Zepeda, R., personal communication, April 5, 2023).

Newtown, Santa Fe, and Uvalde are all different types of small cities, which adds another layer of complexity to economic development forecasting in the case of Uvalde. Most likely the ongoing enthusiastic efforts to create a permanent memorial site to the victims of the Robb Elementary shooting, a new elementary school, and an enhanced resiliency center to provide mental health services, may eventually be celebrated as community assets that provide the basis for the community to return to its cohesiveness, especially once the story of the law enforcement response becomes clearer. Compared to Newtown and Santa Fe, Uvalde has developed as a small city with a more diverse economy than is the norm for suburban and exurban communities, and this fact may very well underlie a successful recovery from the tragedy. That would depend, however, on the ability of the local government entities (city, county, school district) and the community college to work cohesively on community and economic development initiatives, and on the ability for such entities to attract new residents, retain current employers, and to retain as many of their own employees as possible.

8.6 Sonora and Sutton County: A Southwest Texas Community Seeks a Path to Economic Development

Sutton County (pop. 3372 in 2020) and the county seat, Sonora (pop. 2502 in 2020), are located on the western edge of the Edwards Plateau some 135 miles northwest of San Antonio and 70 miles south of San Angelo (see Fig. 1.1). Both the county and city have shrunk slightly since 2000. The county has a semi-arid climate of approximately 20 inches of annual precipitation and thin, poorly developed soils that sustain grasslands and dispersed groupings of oak, juniper, and mesquite trees, a landscape suitable for livestock production. The native Americans who populated the area prior to European settlement in the mid-nineteenth century were relatively few in number and highly mobile. The first Anglo settlement of the county relied on the Devils River to facilitate cattle and sheep ranching. Within a decade, in the early 1880s, ranch land was being fenced off, though water was scarce in portions of the area not adjacent to the river. Wells were necessary to sustain the livestock economy, which by 1900 was dominated by a small number of large-scale ranching operations (Hosmer 2021).

The town of Sonora was boosted as a settlement in 1887 after the digging of a well located adjacent to the present-day Sutton County Courthouse, and in 1890, Sonora became the county seat. The county's cattle ranching expanded rapidly in the 1890s, in part because of additional drilling of wells (Hosmer 2021). In part, the ranching industry expanded because Sonora became an important commercial center, owing to its relative isolation, which fueled a successful retail economy. Ranchers, who were relatively well off, knew what retailing looked like in larger cities such as San Antonio, so local retailers modeled their stores to cater to their tastes; moreover, the lack of rail service to Sutton County meant that shopping and other trips to San Antonio could not be done on a regular basis, thus fueling the local retail economy (Wright 2020). While sheep outnumbered cattle in 1900, the latter were growing more rapidly in number. However, between 1900 and 1930, cattle diminished in number in the county while sheep and goat herds expanded, owing to vibrant markets in wool and mohair. Mechanical shearing meant less labor was required for wool and mohair production, so it became a more profitable industry (Hosmer 2021). Mohair involves a supply chain of raising Angora goats, shearing, washing, spinning, and weaving. Sutton County was initially involved in all steps, but today the region participates only in the earliest two (C. Cahill, personal communication, February 19, 2020).

Before World War II, oil and gas began to take off, albeit slowly, while post-Depression downward trends in agriculture and livestock applied the brakes to the county's production of sheep, goats, and cattle. By 1950, oil and gas, rather than ranching, was the faster growing industry in the county. Drought between 1950 and 1956 served to slow sheep and goat ranching, and ranchers began to look to wildlife management and deer hunting for income on ranches. The petroleum boom lasted until the latter 1970s, at which time drilling diminished because of the industry's volatility (Hosmer 2021). The natural gas boom involving extraction through conventional wells (pre-fracking) was a significant part of the Sutton County economy until deposits dried up in the 1990s. Gas production in the county has, therefore, been on the decline for nearly three decades, as hydraulic fracturing did not take off in the county, and only a small number of productive wells remain on county ranches. Oil and gas services are limited in the county, though what does exist tends to supply the eastern Permian Basin. For example, Cahill Company, the largest industrial-type employer in the county, provides oil- and gas-field services such as creating and maintaining earthen roads linking to fracking well sites near Fort Stockton, Midland, and Odessa (C. Cahill, personal communication, February 19, 2020). Four petroleum pipelines are planned for passage through the county, which would result in tax revenues. Two of the four would be directed to the Gulf Coast, most likely for liquified natural gas (LNG) exports (D. Smith, personal communication, November 7, 2019).

Generally, local stakeholders believe that the failure of rail service to permanently take hold served as a roadblock to the county's economic development. Tracks were installed in the 1930s to link Sonora with San Angelo, but no track was laid south of Sonora. The economic growth of Sonora was not sufficient to keep rail service, so it was abandoned by 1960 (Hosmer 2021; D. Smith, personal communication, November 7, 2019). It is believed that Sonora would have become a much more vibrant place economically had rail service extended southward to Del Rio. In that case, I-10 could have provided a bigger impact to the community had a more robust rail line existed, along with a rail transload facility.

The county's agricultural economy has changed somewhat in the twenty-first century. The agricultural base remains oriented primarily toward livestock, such that, according to the 2012 US Agricultural Census, Sutton ranked first among Texas counties in number of goats, 14th in sheep and lambs, but only 188th in cattle. Pasture in 2012 accounted for 94.6% of all farmland (USDA 2012). Modest amounts of wheat and oats, as well as baled hay are produced in the county, and many of the largest ranches have begun to be divided, owing in part to inheritance and to lack of interest in paying taxes on large holdings. As is the case in Uvalde County, hunting leases are now as important economically as livestock, especially under conditions of smaller ranches, wildlife tax exemptions, and often absentee landowners. Goat, sheep, wool and mohair production still occurs in the county, though the raising of goats and sheep for meat instead of wool is on the rise (P. Hernandez, personal communication, November 7, 2019). The Sonora Wool and Mohair Company, established in 1929, is still in business (SEDC 2021). Furthermore, on the more numerous and smaller land holdings, animal stocking rates come into play. Whereas each unit of cattle requires some 30 acres in the county, each unit of sheep requires about 6 acres, and each goat requires five. Some sheep and goats are produced for export to Mexico. The county is not as competitive as others in wetter parts of the state at cattle production, so most is in the form of raising calves up to 6 months old, as opposed to yearlings, for sale elsewhere for additional fattening. Sutton County has little in the way of improved pastures as found in wetter areas of South Texas; rather, rangeland is relied upon, which involves much lower stocking rates (P. Hernandez, personal communication, November 7, 2019).

The Sonora Economic Development Corporation (SEDC), a Type 4B economic development corporation, is funded by a half-cent municipal sales tax. The entity will provide reduced property taxes and Business Grants for businesses that promise a favorable number of employees and potential to expand the local tax base, on a case-by-case basis (SEDC 2021). The city's location at the intersection of I-10 and US Highway 277 (Ports-to-Plains) is a topic of intense discussion for both the municipal and county governments. To illustrate, that intersection is regarded as inadequate to handle the interchange of large loads such as the blades for the rapidly growing wind energy business, so the city and county are working with the Texas Department of Transportation on an expansion of the interchange, which would include a short bypass. The bypass is of concern to some businesses in the central business district that rely on traffic flows in the center of the city; however, one probable bypass route would keep truck and automobile traffic closer to the retail district than the alternative routes. Highway infrastructure is clearly important to the community, as evidenced by the SEDC's funding of the county judge's expenses as a member of the Ports-to-Plains Alliance (D. Smith, personal communication, November 7, 2019).

Despite the importance of highway infrastructure for the development of an energy service sector of the local economy, it is not clear whether an enhanced US Highway 277 would reverse the recent decline in population of Sonora and Sutton County. As one local economic development stakeholder explained, the locality is something like a "donut hole," with an interstate highway, and potentially a second one (I-27), passing through it. The population is too low to rely on a distribution center or other warehouse-oriented facility to generate the employment to attract new residents.

Besides deer hunting leases, the local business community identifies retailing as the best generator of employment for the community; therefore, incentives will likely be targeted toward attracting a sizable hardware store or tractor supply and feed store. The City of Sonora provided $275,000 in incentives for its Love's Travel Stop (a national chain of auto- and truck-oriented gasoline stations and convenience stores) located 4 miles east of Sonora on I-10; however, that business has yet to meet the 40-employee threshold required for the incentives. The city provided water and sewer infrastructure to the site, but underestimated the overall costs. Because few fueling stations exist along that stretch of highly traveled I-10, it is expected that the investment will soon pay for itself (D. Smith, personal communication, November 7, 2019). Adding to the headwinds of developing retail businesses, a recent anthrax outbreak harmed cattle production and deer hunting, both of which saw decreases in the number of head (P. Hernandez, personal communication, November 7, 2019).

Tourism does little for the local economy, but has the potential to do more, especially in the heart of downtown. The courthouse, built in 1893, has recently been renovated through a million-dollar grant from the Texas State Historical Society, and a ranch museum occupies the old jail house close by (Fig. 8.2). A nature center draws a few hundred tourists a year, a mere fraction of the visitors to the Caverns of Sonora, 8 miles west of the city (D. Smith, personal communication, November 7, 2019). The low population produces something of a dilemma in that there is not a

Fig. 8.2 Sutton County Courthouse, Sonora. (Photo by the Author)

sufficient labor force to attract new business, and there is not a sufficient job base to attract new residents. A result of this "catch 22" is that Sutton County is a distant part of the labor shed of Midland-Odessa. However, the eventual completion of Ports-to-Plains through the county is expected to attract new employers and residents. The State of Texas is said to be committed to the timely expansion of the I-10 and US 277 interchange, which itself will make the locale attractive for investment in economic development, and more than merely traffic passing through (S. Smith, personal communication, February 20, 2020).

8.7 Lessons from Southwest Texas: The Future of Ranching, a Transportation Riddle, and the Weathering of the Pandemic

Uvalde and Sonora Counties are both well positioned to take advantage of the regional trend in the diversification of ranching to include game hunting. White tail deer are still popular among hunters, but Southwest Texas is home to exotic game animals such as axis deer (chital), antelope, and exotic species of sheep, because the semi-arid grasslands of the region roughly resemble those creatures' natural habitats. The income ranchers derive from charging guests by the animal they shoot (which typically is $3500 for an axis buck and $600 for a doe) is welcomed, especially when prices and market conditions for the region's traditional livestock are less than desirable. Furthermore, ranches are well equipped for this tourism, not only because of abundant land to raise such game but also because most have at least some pastureland that exotic game animals can utilize for feeding. Critics of such hunting point to the fact that game animals are raised by ranchers using livestock-type feeding practices, thus producing docile animals that are easy to kill. They criticize the practice of guides driving guests to the animals in jeeps as unsportsmanlike. Critics often use the term "canned hunting" and "captive hunting" to depict what they see as the ranching of game animals. They also point to the overgrazing that some species, such as axis deer, a creature native to Asia, cause in the drier parts of the region. Too often, these animals escape from the owners' ranches onto neighboring ones that then find their forage capabilities deteriorated. Supporters of the industry, including many conservationists, point out that some of the species are endangered in the wild, so the managed production of them actually helps maintain their numbers. Finally, many ranchers do not permit hunting of the animals, but charge the guests an admission fee to view them in a non-zoo setting (Ferguson 2021).

A second compelling way to compare the two localities is that both, for different reasons, present suitable examples of what I call "the transportation riddle." The conventional wisdom is that there is a positive correlation between available freight transportation infrastructure and economic development, but the relationship is not always clear (Yoder 2018). Sonora enjoys favorable interstate highway access via I-10 (and Ports-to-Plains in the future) but no rail line; Uvalde enjoys the Union Pacific rail line but lacks interstate-grade highway access. In the case of Sonora, most likely the small size of the county's population and its relative isolation from urban centers at least micropolitan in size is more of a problem than its lack of rail. Uvalde's highway limitations are most likely insignificant anyway because cross-border traffic through Del Rio and Ciudad Acuña would be oriented to San Angelo and points beyond, rather than through Uvalde. Acuña's maquiladora connections to San Antonio and points east certainly use US Highway 90, but San Antonio's freight traffic to and from the interior of Coahuila and points beyond in Mexico continue to use Eagle Pass or Laredo as crossing points. Clearly the connectivity of the two communities historically impact, respectively, upon their economic development, notwithstanding Sonora's location directly on 1–10 and US Highway 277. Prior to the interstate highway system, Uvalde enjoyed a favorable position between Del Rio and San Antonio, connected by rail and early road access that boosted the community's fortunes, while Sonora never escaped its relative isolation. Thus, both counties' locational characteristics, more so than transportation features, hamper their ability to attract new employment. As such, both communities continue to rely on ranching and post-ranching (hunting) activities on their rolling and picturesque rural landscapes, and the potential growth of tourism that may very well result.

A third topic of comparison and contrast between the two cases of small-city economic development is their respective experiences with the coronavirus pandemic. Both had quite similar experiences in terms of the health of small businesses, especially in the retail and hospitality sectors. In Uvalde, most of the hardships that brick-and-mortar retail and restaurants faced occurred in 2020 when lockdowns and social distancing were the norm. Nearly all such businesses survived, in large part because of federal funding through the CARES Act, including the stimulus checks to individuals, and the Paycheck Protection Program (PPP) that provided forgivable loans for payroll, mortgage interest rates, and lease rates. Only one restaurant closed permanently, though many survived by transitioning to take-out and curbside service. Prior to the pandemic, Uvalde had a number of eateries that served only lunch and dinner, and they maintained such schedules through the pandemic and afterward. In fact, that model became popular for a small number of other restaurants that have found it difficult to hire employees. The Main Street Development initiatives of 2019 have rebounded, such that an investor based in San Antonio has purchased several underutilized buildings downtown for eateries and other entertainment-related businesses. Uvalde's city manager attributes the city's success in weathering the pandemic to its relatively diversified economy and its lack of dependence on a single large employer (V. Di Piazza, personal interview, April 25, 2022).

Sonora similarly saw its economic development efforts back on track by latter 2021, despite a severe negative impact from the pandemic in 2020. Only one business shuttered, though its location within a historic building downtown has subsequently become occupied by a coffee house whose owner desires to capitalize on Sonora's downtown setting. Two gift shops transitioned to online sales exclusively during the early months of the pandemic, one of which has remained that way since, while the other has returned to in-store sales and continued online sales, with the result of an increase in total business. As in the case of Uvalde, as well as Beeville and Gonzales, discussed in Chap. 7, the slowdown in retail, restaurant and lodging business negatively impacted tax revenues for the city; by latter 2021, tax revenues have returned to pre-pandemic levels. The pandemic served as a catalyst for downtown merchants and the mayor to apply for grant money for Main Street improvements and marketing. Furthermore, the Texas Legislature held up funding for many non-Covid projects in 2020 and 2021, resulting in a delay of the expansion of the I-10 and US 277 interchange (D. Smith, personal communication, April 26, 2022). Sonora, like Uvalde, proved quite resilient economically in the aftermath of Covid.

8.8 Conclusions and Topics for Further Research in Uvalde and Sonora

There is arguably as much variation in levels of success of economic development within each region of the USA as between regions. Some small cities grow, and others decline in all regions of the USA. Therefore, case studies of successful small urban places such as Uvalde, as well as those that decline or remain stagnant, such as Sonora, are necessary, and potentially applicable nationally. This is especially relevant to the study of transportation linkages of towns and small cities. The cases of the Uvalde Micropolitan Area and Sutton County add to a list, albeit one that is not yet sufficiently large, of such research. The qualitative approaches employed in these case studies are useful for the examination of economic development in other small cities of southern and southwestern Texas, and arguably beyond the region. Likewise, similarities can be identified through such research. The communities' relatively similar experiences navigating the coronavirus pandemic shed light on the topic of urban resiliency at the scale of small cities.

Future research might include more detailed study of the historical evolution of the two cities' landscapes in tandem with the mohair, cattle, cotton, and wool industries, and the relatively high amount of movement of agricultural workers who resided in each community and contributed heavily to each locality's culture in the twentieth century. This would include additional work with historical documents such as City Directories and interviews of long-time residents to further portray the underlying economic activities that led to Uvalde's initial commercial landscape development downtown and along the rail spur connecting downtown to the main east-west rail line north of town, and Sonora's once vibrant downtown. The transportation systems of each could benefit from further study. For example, owners of several trucking firms that serve Uvalde, including a large one that presently specializes in shipping farm machinery and forage crops throughout Texas and New Mexico, could offer insights into the locality's connectivity outside the immediate region.

Finally, in light of the high amount of USA–Mexico trade that benefits Texas directly, and especially the state's border zone, the Uvalde Micropolitan Area and Sutton County should investigate ways to expand their connections with Mexico beyond pass-through trucking, crop agriculture, and livestock. The latter two activities could benefit the communities through further growth; therefore, they warrant more detailed study through such means as interviews of crop and livestock brokers and accumulation of crop- and livestock-production data from Texas A&M University. Warehouse development will likely expand in the border cities of Del Rio and Eagle Pass and put pressures on those cities' land markets, which could provide opportunities for relatively close small cities like Uvalde and Sonora to help alleviate some of that pressure, while participating more in the distribution functions related to cross-border trade.

References

Brodeur A, Yousaf H (2019) The economics of mass shootings. IZA Institute of Labor Economics, Discussion Paper Series IZA DP No. 12728. https://repec.iza.org/dp12728.pdf

DeVol R, Crews J (2019) Most dynamic micropolitans. Walton Family Foundation

Ferguson W (2021) How Texas hunting went exotic. Texas Monthly, February. https://www.texasmonthly.com/travel/how-texas-hunting-went-exotic/

Goetz AR, Bandyopadhyay S (2007) Regional impacts of trade corridors: recent experiences from the United States. In: Gillen D, Parsons G, Prentice B (eds) Canada's Asia Pacific gateway and corridor initiative: policy trade and gateway economics (volume 1). Centre for Transportation Studies, University of British Columbia

Gutfreund OD (2004) 20th-century sprawl: highways and the reshaping of the American landscape. Oxford University Press

Hosmer BC (2021) Sutton County, Texas. Handbook of Texas Online. Texas State Historical Association (Updated in 2021 from the original 1952 entry). https://www.tshaonline.org/handbook/entries/sutton-county

Lawrence JS (1998) The development and progress of Uvalde, Texas 1881–1917. Unpublished master's thesis, Angelo State University

Leigh NG, Blakely EJ (2017) Planning local economic development: theory and practice, 6th edn, Sage

Otto A (2007) Downtown retailing and revitalization of small cities: lessons from Chillicothe and Mount Vernon, Ohio. In: Ofori-Amoah B (ed) Beyond the metropolis. University Press of America, pp 245–268

Satija N (2013) Businesses suffer after nearby school shooting. National Public Radio Morning Edition, April 18. https://www.npr.org/2013/04/18/177721487/newtown-ct-businesses-suffer-after-nearby-school-shooting

Schultz J (2004) Boom town USA: the 7 1/2 keys to big success in small towns. National Association of Industrial and Office Properties

Sonora Economic Development Corporation (SEDC) (2021) Retrieved December 30, 2021, from http://www.sonoraedc.org

Torres AM (2006) Historias de Mi Gente: nineteenth and twentieth century Uvalde County Texas. Anita M. Torres

United States Department of Agriculture (USDA) (2012) Census of agriculture

Wright RB (2020) Rebuilding the Mayfield Mercantile Company: architecture and commerce in Sonora, Texas, c. 1900. Southwest Hist Q 124(1):50–67

Yoder M (2003) Evolution of a commercial strip in a Texas-Mexico border city: Laredo's San Antonio highway. Southwestern Geographer 7:49–75

Yoder M (2015) The sprawling of small cities of Arkansas: the case for sustainable urban planning. Arkansas Journal of School Change and Public Service. https://ualr.edu/socialchange/2015/05/17/the-sprawling-of-small-cities-of-arkansas-the-case-for-sustainable-urban-planning/

Yoder M (2018) Economic development, land use, and commercial transportation in two small cities of South Texas. Paper presentation. Southwest Division of the Association of American Geographers Annual Meeting, Baton Rouge, LA, United States, September 27

Chapter 9
Geography and Economic Development: Lessons Learned

Abstract A fundamental purpose of this book is to show that economic development is an area of inquiry that overlaps significantly with the perspectives of the discipline of geography. This concluding chapter provides a summary of the geographic concepts related to economic development that are discussed more thoroughly throughout the book. The geographic concepts emphasized include location, region, scale, distance, connectivity, and the built environment. The chapter additionally includes a brief summary of two additional themes of the book: public–private partnerships and the impact of Covid-19 on the book's case studies of local and regional economic development. It argues that there are common takeaways among the case studies in terms of the juxtaposition of geography and economic development, but also that each locality and region reflect unique economic development initiatives. Likewise, economic geographers can learn from such case studies the importance of understanding the processes inherent in economic development, including public–private partnerships, planning, policy making, and promotion of locales and transportation infrastructure projects. The chapter concludes by introducing future research topics in the geography of economic development in Texas and Mexico.

Keywords Economic development · Geography · Location · Scale · Connectivity · Built environment · Public–private partnership · Covid-19

The cases presented in this book highlight ways that fundamental concepts in the discipline of geography apply broadly to economic development initiatives, though in different ways in each region and locality. The geographic concepts emphasized include location, region, scale, distance, connectivity, and the built environment, all of which overlap. Simultaneously, topics in the fields of policy and planning are central to this collection of studies, and they differ sufficiently from place to place and from industry to industry to warrant a series of case studies The juxtaposition of spatial variability in economic development with the heterogeneous nature of financing of economic activity through public–private cooperation requires the carrying out of a collection of studies to portray ways that policy, planning, and

M. S. Yoder, *Geographical Scale and Economic Development*,
https://doi.org/10.1007/978-3-031-36197-5_9

geography intersect. This concluding chapter, a discussion of the general outcomes of the book, highlights broad similarities between the case studies on the one hand, and, more importantly, the fundamental reality that no two economic development initiatives are completely alike when it comes to their histories, associated financing and planning policies, and their geographic traits. The chapter concludes by introducing future research topics in the geography of economic development in Texas and Mexico.

9.1 Location

The two main facets of location emphasized in this book, site and situation, are key to the geography of economic development. Site characteristics, or the amenities of a location that make it suitable for investment, whether private, public, or both in combination, include such features as the availability of incentives provided by all appropriate levels of government (e.g., local and state) and the politics of public financing of infrastructure at different scales. Other relevant and essential site characteristics are the commitment by local governments and other development stakeholders to plan for economic development, the availability of necessary infrastructure, and an appropriately prepared workforce. The personalities and priorities of the stakeholders determine a lot of these site features, but so too do the histories and norms of local, regional, and state politics, whether in Texas or Mexico, that form the foundation upon which contemporary initiatives are built. The physical terrain of a given location, such as Victoria's ability to create a barge canal and the soils that are ideal for cotton production in the immediate vicinity of Levelland and Lubbock, can be an essential site feature that enhances one or more directions in a community's or region's economic development above others. The culture of public-sector leadership and cooperation with stakeholders of the private sector is a positive site feature of Gonzales, San Angelo, and Big Spring, Texas that brought about not only their rail-served industrial (transload) facilities but the direct transportation linkages underlying their success. Likewise, the importance of history in the local cultures of Beeville, Gonzales, Uvalde, and Sonora, Texas as expressed in their architecture is a site characteristic that translates to the persistence of those communities' central business districts and desires to preserve the Main Street retail experience in each.

At the global scale, China's Belt and Road Initiative (BRI) is a tremendous effort to export Chinese technology, goods, and construction expertise to primarily developing countries in need of improvements in infrastructure of various kinds. The countries in which BRI operates are well disposed to the financing offered by China, which may or may not work well for those countries in the long run. UNESCO's World Heritage Sites are local elaborations of a global process of enhancing the preservation of numerous historical and environmentally sensitive sites, which boosts local community and economic development, primarily through tourism, but also through sustainability. In other words, BRI and UNESCO provide ways to leverage local site characteristics for much larger ends.

Workforce availability and workforce development are important site characteristics. Nearly all of the US and Mexican localities included in this book boast of facilities to train workforces. In many cases, the provision of such training is included under the banner of incentives. A major objective of community colleges in the USA is workforce training, a feature that enhances a locality's ability to attract new investment. Many Mexican industrial park developers highlight the workforce training offered by local technical schools and, in some cases, by individual companies.

Land is a key site feature. Its availability and cost are crucial to investment in a given region, whether a town, small city, metropolitan area, or conurbation of multiple cities. The West Texas rail-served industrial facilities are examples of the public and private sectors working in their own ways, but also in tandem, to alter land use; the public sector provides land that the private sector uses. The rail-served industrial facilities of Gonzales, Levelland, Big Spring, San Angelo, Lubbock, Victoria, and Brownsville all involve partnership between the public and private sectors in land offerings for industry; the same applies to Monterrey, Silao, and San Luís Potosí.

Capital is the third essential site feature that is interrelated with labor and land. This comes in the form of credit, other finance arrangements, and, perhaps most relevant to economic development, fiscal incentives. For example, Texas Pacifico Railroad leases track from the State of Texas, the owner of the track. The Big Spring Rail Company leases the rail loop in the Big Spring Airpark from the City of Big Spring. Some of the industrial sites in Levelland are offered to investors under a lease-to-own arrangement. All cities of Texas promote state-level incentives available to companies choosing a site in Texas over one or more in other state(s).

Situation, or relative location, depends today on transportation infrastructure; therefore, it is a dynamic feature of location that can change fairly rapidly through time. Imagine the impact of the construction of the airport and later I-20 in Big Spring, Texas. Prior to the existence of those transportation features, Big Spring's economy was quite limited to livestock and to crops that were less perishable that could withstand slow shipment to Fort Worth and other processing centers. The improvement of rail lines in Mexico has made possible the ability for recently established ports like Manzanillo and Lázaro Cárdenas to realistically compete with Los Angeles and Long Beach for container handling and, therefore, participation in intermodal shipping, one of the greatest technologies underlying globalization since the 1950s. Rail transload facilities enable locations with both rail and highway to be ever closer to source areas of bulk cargo, such as asphalt and sand quarries of the western and southwestern portions of Texas and the places where the aggregates and frac sand are needed. The rail transload facility at Levelland, Texas enables the agricultural sector of west-central Texas to overcome distance and enjoy economies of scale when shipping and processing crops and agricultural inputs. The transportation infrastructure facilities that permit such rapid, efficient movement of goods do not appear out of thin air; rather, they require public–private partnerships to bring about the investment and planning that go into them. The unique rail geography of West Texas, and the different arrangements between rail companies, land developers (e.g., economic development corporations), and local governments illustrate how situation and site variations work together, such that case studies are crucial to understanding the multiple ways that location underlies economic development.

9.2 Regions

Regionalism is an essential theme in geography that directly applies to economic development. Chapter 1 includes discussion of how the functional economic region is the most appropriate for understanding the spatial or territorial character of economic development. Because the regions are defined more by activities than by legal matters such as official national or state boundaries, their delineation can be quite fluid. The forelands and hinterlands of ports are among the most obvious examples of functional economic regions, and these become altered in tandem with changes in the markets for the goods being shipped. To illustrate, wind energy blades entering the port of Brownsville by ship or barge, and shipped out by truck or rail, most likely will be sourced from different regions and will end up in different places where they will be installed. The port's physical infrastructure for handling such project cargoes will determine how feasible the port itself is for that market, as will the road and rail infrastructure connecting the port to the locations of the end users. The ability of the Port of Houston to handle shipping containers when compared to Los Angeles, Long Beach, and even New Orleans and Savannah will influence shipments to and from that locale. The different ports, working in tandem and in competition with each other, possess their own forelands and hinterlands, and these can change with events such as economic downturns (or upturns), pandemics, and the like.

As in the case of functional economic regions for maritime ports such as Victoria, Brownsville, and Houston, interior ports will see their equivalents of forelands and hinterlands change in conjunction with shifting market conditions. It is much more difficult to determine the territories of a given dry port's foreland and hinterland, because of the lack of clarity in defining imports and exports, but the principle of the regionalization of their connectivity applies. Evolving transportation systems linking to the interior ports will impact upon the functional economic region of each. Thus, Interpuerto Monterrey exhibits changes in its regionalization as Ferromex and Kansas City Southern de México change their rail shipment schedules, and the state and federal governments improve upon the quality of highways to accommodate trucks.

In a similar way, rail transload facilities in West Texas will see their functional economic regions altered by changing markets for oil- and gas-field service equipment, frac sand, cotton, and fertilizers. Such regions will also be modified by improvements to transportation infrastructure, whether highways, rail lines, or both. The Ports-to-Plains Corridor, by improving upon federal two-and four-lane highways to limited access interstate grade, will expand the reach of all of the transload facilities located along it, or in close proximity to it. The enhanced connectivity of Lubbock, Levelland, Big Spring, and San Angelo to communities further away will most likely boost the business of the rail-served industrial facilities located in each. Likewise, the continued renovation of the Texas Pacifico rail route between San Angelo and Presidio, and between Ojinaga, Chihuahua, and the port of Topolobampo, will enlarge the scale of San Angelo's functional economic region. In short, changes in market conditions, coupled with investment in repair and enhancement of freight transportation infrastructure, serve to boost regional economic development; at the same time, they shore up expansions of functional economic regions.

The development of interior ports and rail transload facilities can produce a reinforcing effect, as such facilities boost the capability of a municipality or county at the heart of a functional economic region to attract investment in a factory or distribution center, whose activities enhance the need for expansion of the port or transload facility, and so on. This mutual reinforcement illustrates just how dynamic functional economic regions can be. Various actors of the public and private sectors create those regions' boundaries and internal operations in tandem.

9.3 Scale

The scale of participation and cooperation between different economic stakeholders, and in many cases different localities, is a geographic phenomenon fundamentally underlying economic development. That is why geographical scale figures so prominently in this book. The functioning of economic development at multiple scales is perhaps most obvious in transportation infrastructure initiatives. For example, intermodal dry (interior) ports throughout Mexico rely on planning and facilitating legislation at the federal and state levels, as well as the efforts at the local level to bring them about. The SCT, or Secretariat of Communications and Transport, in Mexico promotes such facilities all over the country, and participates in their planning, as part of its overall objective of enhancing the country's freight transportation capabilities to attract investment, both domestic and (increasingly) foreign. Foreign Direct Investment (FDI) is fundamental to the country's efforts to increase nearshoring of manufacturing from locales in East and Southeast Asia to Mexico, to boost economic development nationally through new employment opportunities, and the transfer of technology (albeit limited) to different cities of Mexico. Thus, the policy of attracting nearshoring through planning, incentives, enhanced freight handling facilities and improved transportation corridors occurs at multiple scales. Nearshoring and foreign investment in globally functioning manufacturing clearly involve the juxtaposition of the global, the regional, and the local scales; supply chains for goods ranging from automotive components and apparel to medical supplies involve global-scale investment and shipments of parts, regional shipping arrangements, and local plants and workforces. Logistics operations must be nimble to bring such activities together.

Maritime ports as engines of economic development likewise illustrate the realities of multiscale activities. The Port of Victoria illustrates ways that different communities in and near the Coastal Bend Region of Texas historically have worked together to enhance transportation infrastructure that can be utilized by producers of crude oil and petrochemical products, and other related energy-intensive manufacturing, in need of long-range connectivity. The Port of Brownsville produces economic impacts in the community itself, and in the Lower Rio Grande Valley Region of which it is a part, through the funneling of freight movements between the binational region and beyond, throughout the port's foreland, and in its binational hinterlands of Texas and northern Mexico. While each of the port cities of sub-Saharan Africa, South Asia, and Southeast Asia that are developments of the Belt and Road Initiative (BRI) are heavily planned by the Communist Party of the Peoples Republic of China, they nonetheless feed off of local, subnational, and national economic activity in the respective participating countries. Unfortunately, little evidence yet exists that BRI is enabling much of an evolution beyond the traditional exports by such countries of primary products (raw materials). Thus, that particular global initiative yields new meanings to port forelands and hinterlands that have yet to fully play out.

9.4 Distance

The geographic concept of distance is crucial to economic development and to the delineation of functional economic regions. For example, the most essential objective of nearshoring is to reduce the distance (and geopolitical friction) of the movement of parts and components in supply chains. Under circumstances of manufacturing, distribution, supply chains, and transportation corridors, one typically finds that distance-decay is a fundamental principle, unless extenuating technological factors come into play, such as air cargo or Internet activity. A good illustration of distance-decay is the diminishing of border-related economic activities in small cities of South Texas, discussed in Chaps. 7 and 8. The large South Texas city of San Antonio, and even larger metropolitan areas of southeast and north Texas (Houston, Dallas-Fort Worth), maintain strong connections with the USA–Mexico border and with economically influential cities of Mexico, whether on the border or in the interior. Thus, urban size and the economies of scale that larger urban centers enjoy can nullify the distance-decay principle. As the concept of relative location (situation) demonstrates, technology can help to overcome the limitations of distance. Likewise, the sizes of cities and the concentration of activity in them come into play by making long-distance connections more feasible when the freight transport infrastructure assets of a given site are favorable. The Port of Manzanillo is further in distance to Fort Worth than is Topolobampo, and yet Manzanillo's well-developed port, blessed with essential intermodal infrastructure, handles much more inbound maritime freight than the smaller port of northern Sinaloa. Thus, distance is important in the spatial arrangement of economic development, including nearshoring, but it is by no means the most important geographic factor when population density and transportation technology come into play.

9.5 Connectivity

Each case study included in this book displays the importance of transportation to bringing about the spatial connections necessary to global, regional, and/or local economic development. Not only are rail lines, highways, and maritime routes essential, but so too are pipelines for the movement of petroleum-based raw materials, and the Internet in the case of logistics and other communication needs. All of these tools of connectivity must be taken into account by economic developers, and public- and private-sector stakeholders in the growth of national, regional, and local economies. Once connectivity is established and enhanced, it is often difficult to alter it, as evidenced by the array of lingering supply chain bottlenecks resulting from the Coronavirus pandemic. For example, the nearshoring to Mexico of parts, components, and complete goods normally manufactured in China can be (and is) done, but it often involves winding down production in a plant that has previously received enormous investment and developed valuable expertise, and then establishing a new plant (or expanding an existing one) in Mexico and modifying shipping and other logistics arrangements. Likewise, port congestion in California could lead to the use of alternative ports such as Houston, requiring different contractual arrangements that can be difficult to make in a timely manner. Thus, connectivity is a geographical element of economic development that cannot necessarily be changed overnight; nonetheless, it is fundamental to the initiatives to maintain or grow the economy of a country, region, or city.

When pondering the important place that connectivity holds in economic development, a question arises about the future of globalization. Economic and political commentators debate the extent to which the rise of nationalism in Europe, Asia, and the United States, and increased calls for protectionism and self-sufficiency, are signs that globalization may be waning. One thought is that regionalism will become stronger, and this would be enhanced by regional preferential trade agreements at the expense of the World Trade Organization's global trade rules. This raises further questions about the future scale and role of functional economic regions.

9.6 The Built Environment

The built environment, another important geographic theme, involves land use planning to mitigate the costs of construction and various environmental and aesthetic externalities. There will be opponents to big projects, such as industrial parks, rail lines (with the threat of chemical spills), and even highways, especially when truck congestion, traffic delays, and noise are irritating to citizens. For example, despite the economic jolt to the Brownsville economy from Elon Musk's SpaceX launch pad, fans of nearby nature preserves express vociferously their dislike of the venture. The Utah Inland Port, a sprawling intermodal facility on the west side of Salt Lake City with rail connections to Oakland and Long Beach, is under the microscope of environmental groups concerned about potential spills and contamination of air and water. Furthermore, many infrastructure projects are regarded as unsightly features of the built environment that must be kept at a distance from residential and retail land uses. Thus, economic developers driving such land uses need to be concerned about these unintended consequences. Land tenure can become an issue, as encapsulated in the histories of land acquisition for some interior ports of Mexico, as discussed in Chap. 3. On the other hand, revitalization of downtown districts, such as Main Streets of small cities, are more often than not celebrated for improving aesthetics, traffic flows, heritage, and tourism development.

9.7 Impacts of Covid-19 on Economic Development in Texas and Mexico

The coronavirus pandemic is widely recognized as the biggest shock since the 2008–2009 recession to national, regional, and local economies around the globe. This was especially the case during the first year of the pandemic (early 2020 to early 2021), while resilience and recovery have marked many economies at different scales late in 2021 and in 2022, especially those of the advanced economies and middle-income emerging markets. The recession-like downturn of the global economy in 2020 led to lockdowns in factory settings that harmed manufacturing output and to social distancing in brick-and-mortar retail establishments, including restaurants, which boosted Internet sales of consumer goods. Many governments, especially in the most advanced economies, provided social spending in the form of relief funding to soften the impact of the pandemic, and many such efforts did in fact enable consumers to spend; however, the lockdowns resulted in (mostly temporary) closures of manufacturing plants, which created lingering shortages of goods and fed inflation. Consumers temporarily shifted away from consuming in-person services such as sports events, cinema, concerts, and dining. Overall, given the ability of so many localities to rebound economically, the pandemic's economic impacts have not been as severe as originally feared in 2020. That said, overall workforce dynamics, expressed most commonly as a shortage of workers, have made it more difficult for many small retail and hospitality businesses in small cities of Texas to operate normally.

Each case study highlighted in this book has been impacted by the pandemic, albeit for various reasons and in different ways. Because a great deal of the economic activities underlying development projects, such as transportation infrastructure development, have proven resilient, most of the case study localities and development initiatives were not derailed. For that reason, the book makes mention of the impacts of the virus and responses to it, but it does not dominate the content. In part, the pandemic's impact on each case has produced a set of largely common outcomes, especially for the small cities of Texas included in the study. Given that expectations by economic development and health policymakers are that normality will return (at least as far as Coronavirus is concerned), I will summarize a few examples of how the pandemic altered the trajectory of economic development initiatives, such as Main Street projects, freight transportation corridors, and interior ports. It is an ongoing problem and one that is not fully resolved, and certainly a topic meritorious of reflection in subsequent studies of economic development at different scales. The appropriate time to study recent history is likely the point at which the pandemic is nearly universally regarded as endemic. Thus, the present book provides brief snapshots of an ongoing global health crisis and its role in altering personal and societal priorities and economic development responses.

The case of USA-Mexico trade in steel, the examples of Mexican interior intermodal ports, and the planning process for the Ports-to-Plains Corridor are marked by temporary pandemic-related downturns in manufacturing activity and energy production, followed by returns to near normalcy. Shipping bottlenecks at maritime ports factor into new predictions of nearshoring of activities from East Asia to Mexico. The West Texas rail-served industrial facilities and the two Texas Gulf ports addressed in Chaps. 4, 5, and 6 likewise saw early pandemic-related disruptions to day-to-day activities as well as future plans for expansion that largely have returned to the drawing board. The rapid fall in prices of oil and gas in 2020 continue to impact the nature of freight that passes through those localities, despite rapid price increases in 2022 related to Russia's invasion of Ukraine. Surprisingly, the small Texas cities have proven quite resilient economically, most likely because none relied on a large-scale economic activity that proved vulnerable to the pandemic; rather they bounced back, albeit with some interesting alterations to the ways they were developing prior to 2020. As of the third quarter of 2022, oil shortages and high gasoline prices have done little to dampen freight movement, though tourism saw a slight downturn, which modestly impacted the abilities of those communities to return fully to future economic development plans conceived in 2019–2020. In short, the impacts of the pandemic have been accelerated by unrelated geopolitical concerns and are difficult to pin down with precision as the threat remains of a return of the virus through new variants. Economic development stakeholders will, out of necessity, incorporate resiliency into their future plans.

9.8 Policy and the Geography of Economic Development: Public–Private Partnership

The changes in land use and the built environment associated with economic development is brought about through partnership between the private sector and the public sector at multiple levels of governance operating at multiple scales. Such collaboration is a theme that runs through every case in this book. It manifests itself quite differently in Texas and Mexico, as well as between each case in Texas and each in Mexico.

Property tax abatements and workforce training are among the more important offerings by the public sector, but not the only ones, to bolster economic development. The State of Coahuila provides such incentives to companies in Monclova in the hopes that they can buy output from the AHMSA steel plant for processing and the manufacture of finished steel products. The three intermodal facilities highlighted in Chap. 3 rely on public-sector fiscal incentives and investment by rail companies in infrastructure to attract and retain the strong manufacturing base of each of the three cities' economies. Likewise, the public sector invests in the roads accessing those facilities. Federal- and state-level investment in the Ports-to-Plains Corridor and in rail-served industrial facilities of West Texas are viewed as essential to building the agriculture and energy industries of that greater functional economic region. These public–private partnerships, discussed in Chap. 5, vary considerably, and can involve municipal, county, and/or state participation. As described in Chaps. 6, 7, and 8, local incentives, ultimately financed by taxpayers, underlie the efforts of small and mid-sized cities of South Texas to bolster manufacturing, distribution, and even tourism. Such public–private partnership tends to function quite well, but can be controversial in the eyes of activists and voters in opposition. Economic developers nationwide (if not worldwide) are advised to become keenly aware of the advantages and disadvantages of relying on such incentives for boosting the fortunes of their communities.

In short, researchers and students of the geography of economic development ought to be mindful of state and local laws in Texas and other states related to fiscal incentives and other public-sector investment in economic and transportation projects. The federal system in the USA is complex and produces varying laws from state to state. Likewise, in Mexico, while the federal government retains greater influence over the planning for economic development, there nonetheless are notable differences between the 32 states in the ways that they participate in and compete for economic development.

9.9 Topics for Further Research

Given that this book has merely scratched the surface of the geographic study of economic development in Texas and Mexico, many pertinent topics remain to be studied. Qualitative research methods, including open-ended interviews and the collection of data from official websites and news articles, would be useful for all of them. This section provides a partial list of topics relevant to the contemporary landscape of economic development as both countries grapple with lingering coronavirus and global issues of supply chain disruptions and inflation. The respective roles of the public and private sectors in maintaining existing engines of economic growth, and bringing about new ones, should be understood by researchers and practitioners of the disciplines of geography and economic development.

Since Texas relies so heavily on international trade with Mexico and vice versa, the inland ports along the border are meritorious of examination and comparison. International bridges are complex pieces of infrastructure that require binational planning and consensus at multiple levels of government: municipal, county, state, and federal in the case of Texas; municipal, state, and federal in the case of Mexico. The prospects for nearshoring of manufacturing from East Asia to Mexico, and enhanced shipment of freight through Mexican maritime ports and across the Mexico land bridge to the US border both involve growth in traffic through the binational border ports. Already, cities such as Pharr, Del Rio, and Laredo are planning for the increased growth, and additional cities are expected to follow with plans for new or expanded vehicular bridges spanning the Rio Grande. Warehousing and industrial parks on both sides of the border will be needed to nurture the growth of USA–Mexico trade. After all, proposed new rail routes and enhancements of highways linking northern Mexico and the USA–Mexico border are discussed with greater frequency by private- and public-sector stakeholders.

The USMCA (T-MEC) is a driver of multinational economic development between the USA, Mexico, and Canada whose impacts on regions at multiple scales (national, regional, local) are in need of ongoing study. The automotive industry continues to evolve throughout and between the three countries, and adheres to the geographic concepts of location, connectivity, regional organization of production, and impacts on the built environment, through factories and transportation infrastructure. A rather understudied feature of USA–Mexico trade lies in the agricultural sector. The crossing points for livestock and crops undertake marketing of their locations with vigor and expand refrigerated warehousing and livestock processing centers. Whether the facilities involved in USMCA trade, or the markets and local multipliers of the goods produced and shipped, academicians and practitioners alike will find these dynamic trends in economic development worthy of study.

Rail activity in both Texas and Mexico, respectively, is expected to increase, and both political entities will require new infrastructure to handle greater quantities of the freight of international trade. Already the overcrowded ports of Los Angeles, Long Beach, Oakland, and Seattle are investigating ways to efficiently move freight by way of shipping containers into the interior of the USA. The facility of Alliance Texas, located immediately north of Fort Worth, is becoming an important rail port (as well as a cargo jet port) and logistics center. A similar facility is in the process of expansion on the west side of Salt Lake City, which already has established improved rail connections with Long Beach and Oakland. There is every reason to believe that rail companies and port authorities will pursue feasibility studies for more such facilities, most likely in one or more localities of Texas where interstate highways connect favorably with rail lines. Expensive intermodal container lift facilities, or intermodal ramps, would be needed there. Cities with such facilities, such as San Antonio, are ripe for economic development and related research.

As the coronavirus pandemic recedes and air traffic reaches its 2019 levels of both cargo and passenger movements, airports will increasingly be seen as engines of growth for many cities of Texas and Mexico. The "aerotropolis" concept is already on the minds of many planners and economic development stakeholders, such as in Monterrey, San Antonio, El Paso, and Harlingen. Such urban sectors, heavily defined by their aviation connections, occur at multiple scales, from Dallas-Fort Worth to Uvalde; they ought to be researched much more by geographers and economic developers. Likewise, the interstate highway corridors of Texas that are still emerging, such as I-27, or already in progress in the case of I-69, will require many years to complete, and it will be prudent to study the impacts on the economic development of cities and counties along those routes. Small and large cities alike are impacted by such highway corridors. The question remains whether small cities of South Texas can participate to a greater extent in USA–Mexico trade than they currently do, given their proximity to the border. The same, of course, applies to small cities of the northernmost zones of the Mexican states of Sonora, Chihuahua, Coahuila, Nuevo León, and Tamaulipas. This requires an understanding of interior port forelands and hinterlands, to better comprehend how such localities connect to the transport nodes that the inland port cities represent. In short, small cities close to the border, but not directly on it, are ripe for economic-development research.

Perhaps most importantly, the impacts of the global threats of climate change, coronavirus, and geopolitical turbulence on local economic development is a collection of topics in greater need of study. The pandemic and the Russia–Ukraine crisis have impacted economic development at multiple scales, from global to local; documentation of their effects in Texas and Mexico are meritorious of continuous updated studies, and a series of inquiries once they are resolved. Human–environment interaction, an important theme in the discipline of geography, should be taken into account by researchers of the geography of economic development. Will new industrial parks in the suburban fringes of cities of Texas and Mexico impact drainage and vegetation that are so important to mitigating the effects of climate change? Will renewable energy be developed in such a way as to efficiently overcome the distance of providing service to citizens and industries?

Former Speaker of the US House of Representatives, Tip O'Neill famously declared that all politics is local, and this book has demonstrated that the principle applies equally to economic development. After all, global initiatives play out at the local level. Geography and economic development go hand in hand; therefore, planning for local and regional development ought to include an understanding of that fundamental relationship and incorporate it ahead of time into the planning process. Economic development is a key activity that underlies place-making. The ways that places are made through the development process are enhanced by the assets, and inhibited by the weaknesses, of the places themselves. A keen awareness of this will help to reduce mistakes, and to unleash economic development success stories with desired outcomes of growth and employment that are sustainable. The needs of citizens and nature must not be left out of the equation.

Index

M. S. Yoder, *Geographical Scale and Economic Development*, https://doi.org/10.1007/978-3-031-36197-5

MIX
Papier aus verantwortungsvollen Quellen
Paper from responsible sources
FSC® C105338

If you have any concerns about our products,
you can contact us on
ProductSafety@springernature.com

In case Publisher is established outside the EU,
the EU authorized representative is:
Springer Nature Customer Service Center GmbH
Europaplatz 3, 69115 Heidelberg, Germany

Printed by Libri Plureos GmbH
in Hamburg, Germany